The Climatic Water Budget in Environmental Analysis

The Climatic Water Budget in Environmental Analysis

John R. Mather
University of Delaware

Lexington Books
D.C. Heath and Company
Lexington, Massachusetts
Toronto

Library of Congress Cataloging in Publication Data

Mather, John Russell, 1923-
   The climatic water budget in environmental analysis.

   Includes index.
   1. Hydrologic cycle. 2. Ecology. 3. Land use. I. Title.
GB848.M37   551.4'8   77-17726
ISBN 0-669-02087-7

Published simultaneously in Canada.

Printed in the United States of America.

International Standard Book Number: 0-669-02087-7

Library of Congress Catalog Card Number: 77-17726

To my colleagues
at C. W. Thornthwaite Associates
Laboratory of Climatology who,
over the years, have so effectively
advanced the concept and usefulness
of the climatic water budget.

Contents

List of Figures

List of Tables

Preface

The water budget is a daily or monthly accounting of moisture inflows, outflows, and storages at a particular place or over a geographic area. The present study seeks to approach the water budget from the viewpoint of climatology because most of the factors that affect the budget—precipitation, evapotranspiration, moisture storage in the soil, surface runoff, and the movement of water through the root zone in the soil—are either basic climatic parameters or are related to them.

The first two chapters introduce the climatic water budget and show how the budget can be evaluated on either a monthly or daily basis from readily available climatic data. Chapter 3 describes how the water budget can be utilized in large-scale studies of climate, soils, vegetation, and ocean levels. Chapter 4 deals with the use of the water budget in hydrologic studies including computation of streamflows, lake levels, and estuarine inflows and outflows. Chapter 5 shows the use of the budget in various agricultural studies, focusing mainly on irrigation scheduling and the relation of water budget factors to agricultural yield. Chapter 6 discusses applications of the water budget to the study of forest ecosystems, emphasizing forest productivity, water use of different covers, the effect of land use changes on basin yield, forest fire danger indexing, organic decomposition, and the relation of tree vigor to insect attack. Chapter 7 shows the use of the budget in land use planning and suggests how a water budget approach can be utilized to predict the influence of urbanization on recharge to the water table. The final chapter deals with the impact society has had on the water budget, describing how our various environmental activities, both willful and inadvertent, have changed areal water budgets.

An appendix provides detailed instructions and tables for the computation of a water budget from data of temperature, precipitation and latitude of a place. Selected graphical representations of water budgets from various parts of the world are included.

Evaluation of a water budget provides quantitative values of various moisture factors that are important in understanding the water resources of a place or an area. It is hoped that the present work will demonstrate how the water budget can be a very practical tool in applied environmental research because it provides quantitative information useful for solving various real problems in many different fields.

Acknowledgments

I would like to express my sincere appreciation to the many individuals and groups who have helped in the preparation of this book and especially to the various reviewers both known and unknown for their many sympathetic and helpful suggestions. Special thanks must go to those who have given permission to use material from other books, journals, or reports. Permission has been graciously given by the McGraw-Hill Book Company to use some artwork originally prepared for inclusion in *Climatology: Fundamentals and Applications* (1974) by the author. Appreciation must also go to the staff of C.W. Thornthwaite Associates Laboratory of Climatology, Centerton, New Jersey, for their great help over the years in assisting in the collection of much basic data used here; to Karen Woods and Pam Donnelly for preparation of the artwork; and to Nancy Mayer for her help in assembling the figures, tables, index, and glossary. To my wife and children must go special appreciation for their patience and understanding through the many months while the book was in preparation. And finally, to my secretaries, Susan Zullitti and Elizabeth Zimmerman, who typed early drafts of the book, and Bernice Williams, who carefully and cheerfully typed the final version, I extend my sincere thanks for their great help.

**The Climatic Water
Budget in
Environmental Analysis**

1

Introduction to the Water Budget

The term "water budget" has several quite different meanings depending on the temporal and spatial scales being considered. On the macroscale, water budget can be used in the same sense as hydrologic cycle, the annual global balance of water in the oceans, atmosphere, and earth in all of its various stages. On the mesoscale, we may consider the water budget of a region or a major drainage basin. On the microscale, we may investigate the water budget of a field of vegetation, a forest stand, or even an individual tree.

The water budget of a place, a region, or of the whole world is an accounting, for some selected time period, of what happens to the precipitation. It is concerned with a quantitative evaluation over time of the various ways that the precipitation can be dispersed, utilized, stored, or changed. Though simple in concept, it is often a most complex undertaking to try to evaluate all the factors of the budget even at a single place. Few factors such as interception of precipitation, evapotranspiration, infiltration, soil moisture storage, underflow, or deep percolation are measured except only under short-period experimental conditions at a very small number of places in the world.

Though much is known about the principal factors that influence the water budget—namely, precipitation and evapotranspiration—our knowledge still has serious gaps. Average precipitation over a drainage basin, for example, may actually be less well understood than evapotranspiration losses from the basin, although the former may be measured at several sites and the latter not measured at all but only estimated on the basis of other measured factors. Though precipitation can be thought of as a true climatic factor, evapotranspiration is under only partial climatic control. It is, in part, influenced by human activities, by soil and vegetation, and by geology and topography.

The water budget can be quantitatively evaluated by various methods. Some are quite complex and involve such detailed observations that they are nearly impossible to evaluate in practice. Others are so simple that they fail to discriminate between different climatic, soil, or vegetation situations. Users need to understand the different methods that exist so that they may select the most useful one based on the nature of results sought as well as on the availability of input data.

Water budgets have been used over the past few decades in many different fields. Problems in hydrology and agriculture come immediately to mind as logical places where knowledge of the water budget can provide quantitative answers to such specific questions as the monthly or annual streamflow in

1

ungaged streams, the available water supplies for reservoir storage or irrigation, or the probabilities of flooding or drought. But the water budget affects many other aspects of human life and livelihood. It is a basic tool in environmental analysis. For example, information on the distribution of soils and vegetation, the effect of a suburban development on local groundwater recharge, the development of realistic forest fire danger rating systems, and the understanding of seasonal changes in sea levels all can be obtained from using the water budget approach.

When the seasonal march of precipitation is compared with the march of water need in a water budget, one obtains information on many aspects of the water relations at a place. First, it is possible to estimate *actual evapotranspiration* or the actual loss of water from plant and soil surfaces, which, in many cases, is different from the climatic water need or potential evapotranspiration defined as the water loss from a homogeneous, closed cover of vegetation that never suffers from a lack of water. It is extremely difficult to measure actual evapotranspiration in practice because of its dependence on such factors as soil type, land use, plant cover, and soil moisture content.

Second, the difference between potential and actual water loss provides a quantitative value of *moisture deficit* at a place, the amount by which available moisture fails to satisfy the climatic demand for water. The deficit is a measure of the agricultural need for water by means of irrigation. Third, when precipitation exceeds water need, excess moisture that infiltrates the soil will first be used to recharge the soil root zone. After this has occurred, any remaining excess water will become *water surplus* and be lost from the soil by subsurface runoff. This water will ultimately find its way back to streams and rivers or be used to recharge the groundwater table. Fourth, during those periods when water need is greater than precipitation the water demand is met in part by using stored soil moisture. Thus, it is possible to calculate the amount of *soil moisture storage* at any time either on a daily or monthly basis. This factor has utility in problems of the tractionability or trafficability of soils or in construction or farming operations where moving or plowing soil is necessary. These four factors—actual evapotranspiration, water deficit, water surplus, and soil moisture storage—derived from computations of the water budget are significant in any effort to understand or use the water or energy resources of an area.

The water budget has been used and, at times, misused in many ways throughout human history in our efforts to modify nature to improve human welfare. A basic examination of the working of the water budget on a worldwide scale emphasizes the great mobility of water in the atmosphere. On the scale of a watershed, the water budget gives us a new insight into the control exercised by human actions over such factors as overland runoff, infiltration, and evapotranspiration. Knowledge of the water budget on various temporal and geographic scales is necessary if we are to place into proper perspective our efforts at modifying both climates and land use.

2 Evaluation of the Climatic Water Budget

A water budget is an account over some period of time of all moisture gains, losses, and storages for a particular place or area. Seldom are all factors of the water budget measured at a place for any length of time. Thus, to evaluate the budget, it may be necessary to revert to other means to estimate those factors that are generally not measured.

Evapotranspiration and Its Determination

Among the factors often not measured is the evapotranspiration loss from the soil and vegetation cover. Evapotranspiration can be evaluated by a great number of methods. In general, the methods can be catalogued (1) mass transport techniques; (2) aerodynamic or profile techniques; (3) eddy correlation techniques; (4) energy-budget techniques; and (5) empirical (generally bookkeeping) techniques.[1]

Mass Transport Techniques

Mass transport expressions have generally been developed from Dalton's early expression $E = C(e_o - e_a)$ where C is a constant empirically determined and usually containing a wind speed term, while e_o and e_a are the saturation vapor pressure at the surface and in the air above.[2] Because measuring the vapor pressure at an evaporating surface is very difficult, many variations of the Dalton expression substitute other vapor pressure measurements (such as the saturation vapor pressure at the temperature of the surface, if that can be determined) with corresponding loss of accuracy. Various methods of expressing the effect of wind speed have been introduced into recent mass transport expressions.

Aerodynamic Techniques

Use of aerodynamic or profile techniques requires making certain assumptions concerning the turbulent diffusion of heat and water vapor in the atmosphere. Vertical diffusion of moisture is assumed to be proportional to the product of the height gradient of moisture content and a turbulent-diffusion coefficient.

3

This latter coefficient is a function of the intensity of air turbulence in the surface layer and is assumed to be dependent on the wind speed profile. When air temperature is not near neutral stability, atmospheric buoyancy influences the diffusion coefficient.

Eddy Correlation Techniques

The more recently introduced eddy correlation technique recognizes that upward diffusion of water vapor can only occur if upward moving turbulent eddies are more moist than downward moving eddies. The magnitude of the flux is determined from simultaneous observations of vertical wind speed and moisture content of the air. The average product of these two terms when multiplied by air density and specific heat gives the moisture flux caused by turbulent transport plus the flux caused by average vertical air movement (the mean flux). The difference between these two fluxes is the flux caused by turbulent eddies. Sensitive and fast-response instruments are required for these measurements so that reliable observations are difficult to obtain.

Energy-Budget Techniques

Energy-budget techniques involve the partitioning of available net radiation, R_n (incoming long- and short-wave radiation minus outgoing reflected and long-wave radiation) into its different categories of use at the earth's surface. Evaporation is determined as a residual of the other measured terms. If the energy used in photosynthesis and other minor exchanges is neglected, the energy budget can be written as

$$R_n = S + H + LE$$

where S is the soil heat flux, H is the atmospheric heat flux, and LE is the energy going into the evaporation of water. When the soil is fully charged with moisture, some investigators feel that S will be quite small.[3] Under this condition $B = H/LE$. It has been suggested that under optimum moisture conditions, R_n would be primarily used for LE so that both S and H could be neglected as a first approximation.[4] The effect of advection of energy was also considered to be negligible in this case.

Combination Techniques

The energy-budget and aerodynamic approaches have been combined into what may be called combination techniques in an effort to eliminate most unmeasured terms. One combination technique expresses the evapotranspiration from a moist, short green cover (E_T) as

$$E_T = \frac{\dfrac{\Delta R_n + f(u)(e_a - e_d)}{\gamma L}}{(\Delta / \gamma) + 1}$$

where Δ is the slope of the saturation vapor pressure curve versus temperature (mb/K), γ is the psychrometric constant (mb/K), R_n is net radiation (erg/cm^2 sec), L is latent heat of vaporization for water (cal/g), $f(u)$ is a wind function equal to $0.35(0.5 + u_o/100)$ (mm/day) over open water, and $e_a - e_d$ is the saturation vapor pressure difference obtained from the air temperature and the dewpoint temperature both taken at screen height.[5] The ratio Δ/γ is dimensionless and is essentially a weighting factor used to assess the relative effects of energy supply and ventilation on evaporation.

Because observations of duration of bright sunshine, mean air temperature, mean vapor pressure, and mean wind speed are required, the expression is more difficult to evaluate than other, possibly more empirical, expressions. The range of possible applications might, however, be wider because the inclusion of more factors active in the evaporation process makes the expression more valid under a wide range of meteorological conditions. The expression has been widely tested with very satisfactory results. Later investigators have suggested ways to simplify the equation with the loss of some degree of validity. The original expression or some of the later modifications have, however, proved to be extremely valuable in many different types of water budget studies.

Empirical Techniques

Various empirical or bookkeeping methods to estimate evapotranspiration from a moist vegetated surface exist. These expressions for potential evapotranspiration, as we might call this water loss from a moist closed cover of vegetation, are generally useful because they are simple to evaluate, requiring only limited climatic data. Thornthwaite,[6] fitting data of evaporation from watersheds and irrigation plots to air temperature, obtained the following expression for unadjusted potential evapotranspiration (in cm/month)

$$e = 1.6 \left(\frac{10t}{I} \right)^a$$

where t is monthly temperature (°C), I is an annual heat index (determined from the sum of the 12 monthly heat index values, $I = \Sigma i$ where $i = (t/5)^{1.514}$ and t is mean monthly temperature; a is a nonlinear function of the heat index equal to

$$a = 6.75 \times 10^{-7}I^3 - 7.71 \times 10^{-5}I^2 + 1.79 \times 10^{-2}I + 0.49$$

These expressions are complicated and mathematically inelegant. They can only be evaluated readily with the use of tables and nomograms.[7] Unadjusted potential evapotranspiration is the water loss for a 30-day month with each day 12 hours long. This value is adjusted by a factor that expresses how the actual day and month length differ from these values.

Many other expressions for potential evapotranspiration exist, ranging from the very simple assumption that it can be approximated (in mm) by the mean monthly temperature (°C) doubled,[8] or even tripled in some months,[9] to the very involved combination method, already described,[10] or one that involves a multiple regression equation of the form

$$Y = a_0 + a_1 x_1 + a_2 x_2 + a_3 x_3 + a_4 x_4 + a_5 x_5 + a_6 x_6$$

where Y is the latent evaporation in cc which can be converted into inches of potential evapotranspiration by multiplying by .0034.[11] Eight possible variations of this latter expression using different combinations of available data have been suggested as can be seen by the list of a coefficients included in table 2-1. Multiple regression coefficients based on 900 test cases ranged from $R = 0.67$ to $R = 0.86$ using different combinations of the six variables (maximum air temperature in °F; temperature range; daily solar energy at the top of the atmosphere, Q_o in ly; daily total sky and solar energy on a horizontal surface estimated from $Q_s = Q_o$ (0.251 + 0.616 n/N) where n is daily bright sunshine and N is duration of daylight, both in hours; daily total wind run in miles; and daily mean vapor pressure deficit in mb). The coefficients in table 2-1 were derived by use of Bellani plate atmometer readings of latent evaporation at six stations across Canada during summers from 1953 to 1957.

In selecting a method for estimating potential evapotranspiration, investigators must decide between ease and simplicity of evaluation on one hand and increased accuracy through the inclusion of more related factors on the other. The combination or multiple regression methods already described appear, for example, to provide reliable values of daily or monthly evapotranspiration under a wide range of environmental conditions but they require considerable data so that they are neither easy to use nor of widespread applicability. Estimates are often used for some of the generally unmeasured terms but when this is done some of the advantages of using the more complex methods are lost. The simple Thornthwaite expression can be readily applied worldwide. It has been found to provide reasonably reliable values of monthly evapotranspiration especially if marked monthly changes in humidity (as in a monsoon climate) do not occur.

The Thornthwaite expression is less effective on a daily basis because daily variations in wind speed and humidity are not included in the expression for potential evapotranspiration. The advantage of its wide usefulness often out-

Table 2-1
Coefficients in the Multiple Regression Equation[a] for Calculating Latent Evaporation (Y) from Meteorological Variables (X)[b]

Method	a_0	Max. Air Temp., °F a_1	Daily Temp. Range, °F a_2	Daily Solar Energy Q, Top of Atmos. 1y a_3	Daily Total Solar Sky Rad. 1y a_4	Daily Total Wind Run, Miles a_5	Daily Mean Vapor Pressure Deficit, mb. a_6	Multiple Regression R^c
I	−87.03	9.28×10^{-1}	9.33×10^{-1}	4.86×10^{-2}	0.00	0.00	0.00	0.67
II	−55.60	6.87×10^{-1}	2.84×10^{-1}	9.13×10^{-3}	6.85×10^{-2}	0.00	0.00	0.74
III	−42.28	-2.28×10^{-2}	1.09	5.06×10^{-2}	0.00	0.00	2.99	0.81
IV	−108.80	1.13	9.20×10^{-1}	3.59×10^{-2}	0.00	1.31×10^{-1}	0.00	0.72
V	−26.69	-2.32×10^{-2}	5.57×10^{-1}	1.96×10^{-2}	5.31×10^{-2}	0.00	2.41	0.83
VI	−78.68	8.97×10^{-1}	3.40×10^{-1}	1.66×10^{-3}	6.13×10^{-2}	1.18×10^{-1}	0.00	0.80
VII	−69.30	3.50×10^{-1}	1.04	4.03×10^{-2}	0.00	1.01×10^{-1}	2.31	0.82
VIII	−53.39	3.37×10^{-1}	5.31×10^{-1}	1.07×10^{-2}	5.12×10^{-2}	9.77×10^{-2}	1.77	0.86

Source: W. Baier, "Recent advancements in the use of standard climatic data for estimating soil moisture," *Annals of Arid Zone*, vol. 6, no. 1 (1967).

[a]Regression equation $Y = a_0 + a_1 x_1 + a_2 x_2 + a_3 x_3 + a_4 x_4 + a_5 x_5 + a_6 x_6$.

[b]Latent evaporation (cc) × .0034 (ins./cc) = PE (ins.); temperatures in degrees F; energy in 1y per day; and vapor pressure deficit $e_w - e_s$ in mbs.

[c]R = Multiple regression coefficient for 900 test cases; R = 0.40 for P = 0.01 and six independent variables.

weighs its inability to reflect short period changes in wind or humidity. Although many studies have sought to demonstrate the advantages of one method over another, there is still no universally agreed on method for estimating the climatic water needs of a place.[12] The use of the Thornthwaite expression in many later examples is dictated, in large measure, by its ease in evaluation and by the availability of many pertinent examples, but it is no more accurate than other estimates. Because Thornthwaite's expression for evapotranspiration is based on only air temperature and length of day, its use with precipitation in a water budget results in what might be called a climatic water budget.

The Climatic Water Budget

The climatic water budget is a monthly, weekly, or daily comparison of water supply (precipitation or P) and climatic demands for water (potential evapotranspiration or PE). Potential evapotranspiration has been defined as the water loss from a large homogeneous, vegetation-covered area (albedo, or percentage of incoming solar radiation reflected from the particular surface, of 22 to 25 percent) that never suffers from a lack of water. Potential evapotranspiration is primarily a function of climatic conditions (energy from the sun) and is not a function of type of vegetation, type of soil, soil moisture content, or land management practices.[13] Actual evapotranspiration does, of course, depend on all these other factors in addition to the climatic factors.

Whenever precipitation exceeds the climatic demand for water, the soil moisture storage will increase, a water surplus may develop, and the groundwater table may rise resulting in increased runoff from the area. When climatic demands for water are greater than precipitation, soil moisture storage will be depleted, the water table may fall and there will be a deficit of water in the soil. By comparing precipitation and potential evapotranspiration for daily or monthly periods it is possible to obtain quantitative values of (1) amounts of water stored in the soil; (2) water surplus or excess water above the climatic demands; (3) water runoff that will ultimately find its way back to the ocean in the surface streams; and (4) water deficit or climatic demands for water not met by available precipitation or stored soil moisture.

Some of the moisture stored in upper soil layers during rains evaporates from the surface of the soil, whereas some is made available to the plants. Most of the water that enters the plant through its roots is later lost by transpiration from leaves and stems. The amount of water in the upper layers of the soil that is available to plants, recharges the groundwater table, or supplies the surface streams depends almost entirely on the balance between the precipitation that adds water and the evaporation that removes it.

Precipitation and evapotranspiration respond to different forces so that they are seldom similar in amount or distribution through the year. In some areas, there is more precipitation than evapotranspiration in every month of the year; in other areas, the evapotranspiration demand is greater than the precipitation in every month of the year. In the former areas, the soil remains full of water and the excess runs off through and over the soil every month to contribute to perennial stream flow. In the latter areas, there are no permanent rivers and the drainage is ephemeral—an arid or semiarid climate exists. In most areas of the world, however, precipitation is deficient in one season of the year and excessive in another season so that periods of both moisture surplus and moisture deficit follow one another.

It must be pointed out that there is not an exact relation between stream types and climate because perennial streams such as the Nile will continue to flow through desert areas. Under such conditions, however, they become influent streams losing large volumes of water to the water table well below the surface stream. Many streams in areas with both surplus and deficit conditions during the year will also continue to flow because of the great lag in subsurface flow reaching the stream and to the possible contribution of groundwater to the stream regime. However, even with such perennial streams in subhumid areas, dry period flows are usually greatly reduced in quantity.

The Monthly Water Budget Bookkeeping Procedure

Precipitation and Potential Evapotranspiration

To illustrate the water budget bookkeeping procedure, consider the average monthly precipitation and potential evapotranspiration at Wilmington, Delaware. The average monthly data are given in table 2-2 along with the remaining steps in the bookkeeping procedure. Detailed descriptions of each of the steps and of the use of the various tables needed to obtain each of the derived values are included in appendix I.

At Wilmington, monthly potential evapotranspiration is found to vary through the year from 0 in January and February to a peak value of 150 mm in July. Total climatic water demand for the year is 728 mm. Monthly precipitation or the climatic water supply is much less variable through the year with the lowest value occurring in October (78 mm depth) and the greatest monthly precipitation in August (128 mm). Average annual precipitation is 1130 mm at Wilmington, some 402 mm greater than the climatic need or demand for water.

Monthly precipitation and potential evapotranspiration never coincide at Wilmington. There is too much precipitation in fall, winter, and spring and not enough during the summer season. Subtracting potential evapotranspiration from precipitation results in a series of positive and negative values clearly identifying periods of potential water recharge to or removal from the soil.

Table 2-2
Average Climatic Water Budget Data for Wilmington, Delaware
(All values are in mm depth)

	J	F	M	A	M	J	J	A	S	O	N	D	Year
PE	0	0	15	43	89	128	150	135	94	52	20	2	728
P	87	80	96	91	92	98	119	128	93	78	82	86	1130
P–PE	87	80	81	48	3	−30	−31	−7	−1	26	62	84	
ST	150	150	150	150	150	122	99	94	93	119	150	150	
ΔST	0	0	0	0	0	−28	−23	−5	−1	+26	+31	0	
AE	0	0	15	43	89	126	142	133	94	52	20	2	716
D	0	0	0	0	0	2	8	2	0	0	0	0	12
S	87	80	81	48	3	0	0	0	0	0	31	84	414
RO	69	74	78	63	33	16	8	4	2	1	16	50	414
DT	218	224	227	212	182	138	107	98	95	120	166	200	

Note: *PE* is potential evapotranspiration, *P* is precipitation; *ST* is soil moisture storage in the root zone; Δ*ST* is the change in storage from one month to the next; *AE* is actual evapotranspiration; *D* is water deficit; *S* is water surplus; *RO* is runoff; and *DT* is total moisture detention within or on the soil.

Plant Root Zone–Water Storage and Removal

Before continuing the monthly water budget, it is necessary to establish the depth of water that can be stored in the root zone of the soil. Soils differ in their water holding capacities—fine sands can hold approximately 100 millimeters depth of water per meter depth of soil (mm/m), sandy loams 150 mm/m, silt loams 200 mm/m, and clays 300 mm/m or more. The depth of rooting of plants varies not only through the season as the plant develops (figure 2-1) but also from one species to another and even within the same species if grown on different soils. Plants tend to be more deeply rooted in sandy soils and less deeply rooted in clays.

In the present computations, assume that we have pasture vegetation on sandy loam soil (available moisture storage in the rooting zone equal to 150 mm). At Wilmington, *P–PE* is positive from October through May. Even if storage in the soil had been 0 in September, a situation that really only occurs in very dry desert areas, the excess precipitation over potential evapotranspiration during the October-April period would have brought storage back to 150 mm by the end of May, the maximum amount of water that can be held in the soil against the force of gravity.

Many investigators have considered the way in which water is removed from soil storage by plants. Different suggestions concerning the relation between actual and potential water loss from the soil (*AE/PE*) and soil moisture content can be represented in a simple diagram (figure 2-2). Curve *A* assumes that

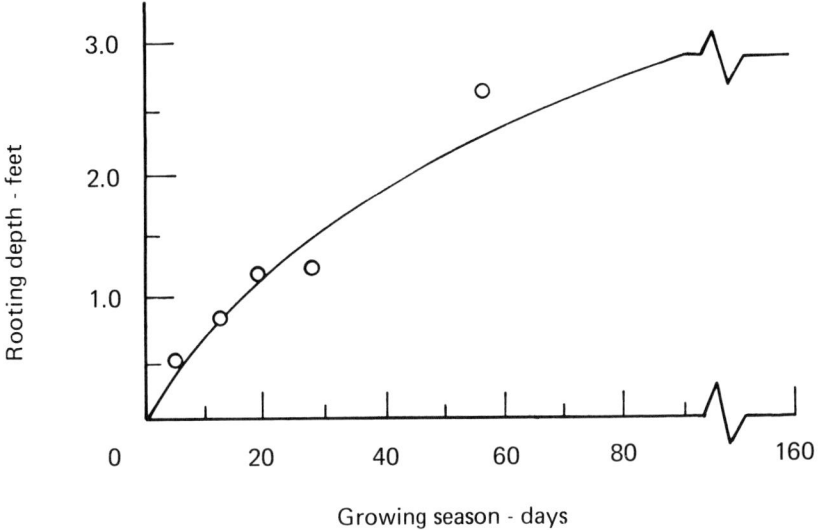

Source: E.W. Rochester and C.D. Busch, "An irrigation scheduling model which incorporates rainfall predictions," *Water Resources Bulletin,* American Water Resources Association, vol. 8, no. 3 (1972).

Figure 2-1. Change in Rooting-Depth for Cotton with Time

evapotranspiration is independent of available soil moisture while curve *C* assumes that rate of water loss varies directly with soil moisture content. The other labeled curves assume equal availability of moisture up to the point at which demand exceeds supply to the plant roots. A sharp decrease in the ratio of *AE* to *PE* follows because the plants will then have increasing difficulty in obtaining all the water they need. The computations shown in table 2-2 assume a relation similar to curve *C* although any other graphed relation could be incorporated into the water budget model if desired.

At Wilmington, soil moisture storage is at field capacity (150 mm) at the end of May. To determine the amount of storage in the soil at the end of June, it is necessary to consider the various inputs and losses of water during that month. Precipitation (*P*) is 98 mm and potential evapotranspiration (*PE*) 128 mm in June. The vegetation needs 30 mm more depth of water than it receives from precipitation. We assume that the vegetation is able to use all of the precipitation as it falls. This assumption may, of course, result in some error if there are very heavy thundershowers on sloping, poorly vegetated ground so that an appreciable amount of overland runoff develops. The plant roots try to obtain the additional 30 mm from water already in storage in the soil. When the soil is at field capacity, the roots are able to remove this water from storage easily but as

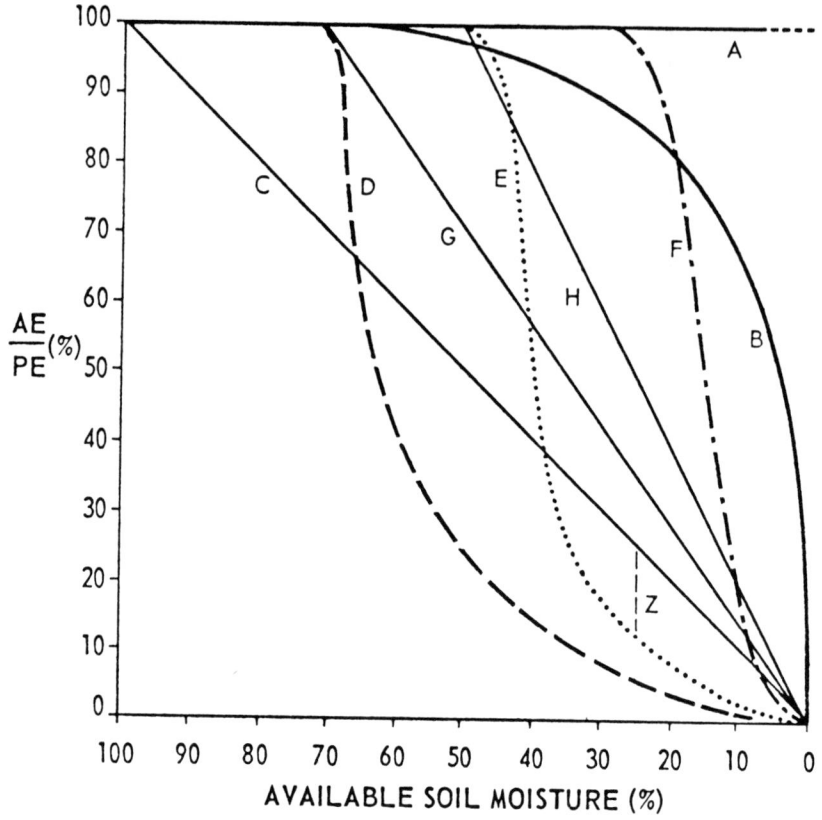

Source: W. Baier, D.Z. Chaput, D.A. Russelo, and W.R. Sharp, "Soil moisture estimator program system," *Technical Bulletin 78,* Agrometeorology Section, Plant Research Institute, Canada Department of Agriculture (1972).

Figure 2-2. Various proposals for the Relationship between the Ratio of the Daily Actual Evapotranspiration to the Potential Evapotranspiration (Expressed as a Percentage) and Available Soil Moisture

the soil begins to dry, water removal from the soil becomes increasingly difficult. The relation shown in curve *C* (figure 2-2) suggests that the ability of plants to satisfy their needs from storage is proportional to the ratio of actual water stored in the soil to the amount that can be stored at field capacity. That is, when soil moisture is at 75 percent of field capacity, plants can obtain 75 percent of their additional needs from the soil.

Actual Evapotranspiration

The remaining rows in the bookkeeping procedure (table 2-2) develop from the foregoing calculations. Storage change is merely the actual change in storage from one month to the next, either positive or negative. Actual evapotranspiration is equal to potential evapotranspiration whenever P is greater than PE. Whenever $P-PE$ is negative, actual evapotranspiration equals precipitation for the month plus the change in storage (disregard the minus sign for storage change). This means, of course, that the actual water used by the soil and plant cover equals all of the precipitation plus whatever additional water plant roots can remove from the soil root zone (storage change). Actual evapotranspiration in July at Wilmington is 142 mm, a total resulting from 119 mm of precipitation plus 23 mm of water removed from storage in the soil.

Water Deficit and Surplus

Deficit is merely the difference between potential and actual evapotranspiration month by month. Surplus is the excess $P-PE$ whenever soil moisture storage is at field capacity. Thus, in months when $P-PE$ is positive there can be no deficit of water; when $P-PE$ is negative there can be no surplus of water. Surplus does not always occur when $P-PE$ is positive, however, for as long as soil moisture storage is below the available water-holding capacity of the soil, no surplus can develop.

Water surplus, as defined in the climatic water budget, represents moisture that is not needed for evapotranspiration or for recharge of the soil root zone. It is the excess moisture after climatic demands are satisfied and upper soil layers are restored to field capacity. Thus, it is available to move through the soil (or overland) to the water courses as runoff. With areal integration of the point values of surplus computed for a year over a watershed, one can achieve a value that is in reasonable agreement with the gaged streamflow from the watershed. The nature of the relationship is discussed in more detail in chapter 4. At Wilmington, assume that 50 percent of the available surplus in any month will run off. The remainder will be held over and added to surplus in the following month and thus made available for runoff in that month (of which only 50 percent will run off). Computations of runoff should start in December after the long period without calculated surplus.

Total Moisture Detention

The last line in the water budget computations, moisture detention, represents the total amount of moisture that is held temporarily on or within the soil at the end of the month in question. Moisture detention is made up of three quantities: (1) moisture in storage in the soil (storage row); (2) any snow that might be stored on top of the soil; and (3) that portion of total water surplus which has not run off in the particular month but which is temporarily held for later runoff. At Wilmington, the January moisture detention is 218 mm. It is obtained by summing 150 mm of soil storage, 0 mm of snow storage, and 68 mm of surplus that has not run off in January but is being held over and added to the February surplus. Moisture detention can be well above field capacity temporarily for it represents, in part, water that is slowly moving downward in the soil under the force of gravity but that has not left the root zone by the last day of the month.

Graphical Representation of the Water Budget

Though the bookkeeping procedure permits quantitative evaluation of each factor of the water budget, graphical representation of *PE, AE,* and *P* provides easy identification of periods of surplus, deficit, soil moisture utilization, and recharge and makes possible direct comparisons between stations. The graphical presentation of the water budget has months on the horizontal scale and depths of evapotranspiration or precipitation on the vertical scale. Monthly totals of precipitation and both potential and actual evapotranspiration are plotted on the graph at the end of each month. Figure 2-3 is a graphical representation of the water budget computations for Wilmington given in table 2-2. Appendix II includes examples of water budgets for a representative selection of stations on all continents. These graphs illustrate the principal differences that occur in potential evapotranspiration, precipitation, and the other factors of the water budget in the major climatic regions of the world.

In plotting the water budget, it must be remembered that moisture removed from the soil by vegetation during periods when *PE* is greater than *P* (soil moisture utilization) must, over time, quantitatively equal the soil moisture recharge. Thus, areas on the diagram representing utilization and recharge must be equal. Actual evapotranspiration equals potential evapotranspiration until precipitation drops below potential evapotranspiration. When precipitation exceeds potential evapotranspiration again, actual and potential evapotranspiration once again are equal. Thus, the line representing the monthly course of actual evapotranspiration will begin to differ from potential evapotranspiration at the point on the diagram where the *P* curve crosses over and becomes less than the *PE* curve. It continues to differ from potential evapotranspiration until *P* once again exceeds *PE.* The areas under or between curves should represent quantitatively the actual values of *PE, AE, P,* deficit, surplus, utilization, and recharge.

Water Budget Computations for Successive Years

It is often desirable to evaluate water budgets at a place year by year for a long period of time. Such computations increase our understanding of monthly and annual variability in factors of the water budget as well as of the likelihood of

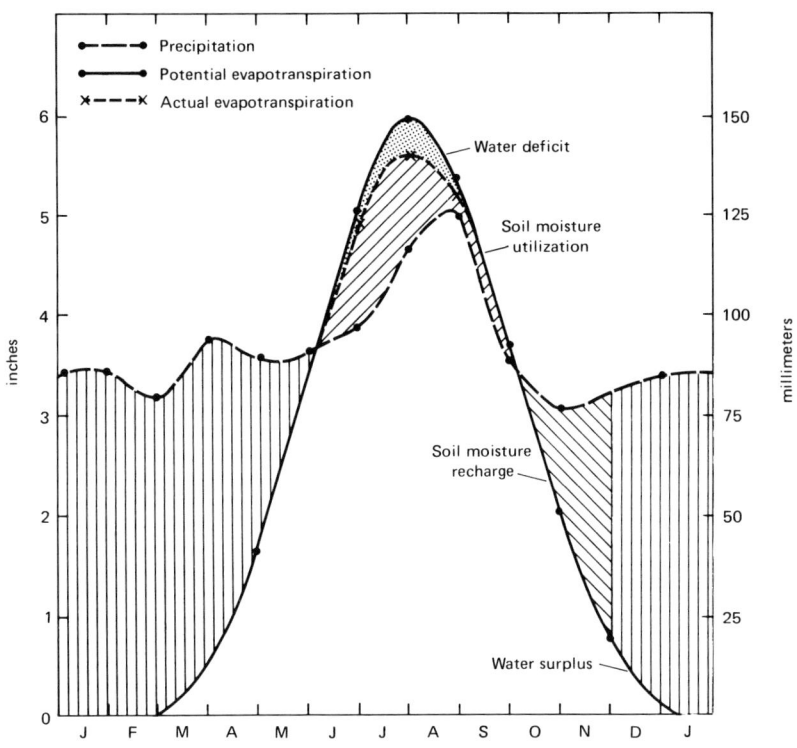

Source: J.R. Mather, "Factors of the climatic water balance over the Delmarva peninsula," *Publications in Climatology,* Laboratory of Climatology, vol. 22, no. 3 (1969).

Figure 2-3. Graphical Representation of Water Budget for Wilmington, Delaware

different critical values that are unavailable from long-term average water budgets. For example, long-term average computations provide only a value of surplus or of deficit in each month because of the way the bookkeeping procedure is arranged. However, in individual years, a particular month might have either a surplus or a deficit depending on the actual precipitation and evapotranspiration for the month in question. Computation of water budgets for individual years will show that June, for example, will have surpluses in some years and deficits in others because of variations from year to year in June precipitation. The long-term mean value may show a deficit in that month; if we used only the long-term mean we might never appreciate the frequency or likelihood of surpluses in that particular month as well.

An example of year-to-year fluctuations in the factors of the water budget for Wilmington, Delaware, is shown in figure 2-4. These individual yearly budgets can be compared with the long-term average budget shown in figure 2-3. The yearly analysis covers the period from 1964 to 1967 and includes periods of both dry and moist conditions.

Though the curves of potential evapotranspiration do not change greatly from year to year, precipitation varies both in annual amount and seasonal distribution. As a result, water surplus and deficit vary more from year to year at a place such as Wilmington than they do at stations hundreds of miles apart within eastern North America using average water budgets. Although average water budgets reveal, in general, the amount and extent of periods of surplus and deficiency of water, they do not indicate possible variations in the magnitude of these factors from year to year.

Evaluation of a Daily Water Budget

Sometimes information on day-to-day changes in factors of the water budget is necessary—for example, in scheduling irrigation applications or in evaluating the possibility of flooding within a month from high precipitation values on a small watershed. Values of precipitation and potential evapotranspiration may be compared daily as well as weekly or monthly, if desired.

The use of daily values in a water budget will produce results that differ from those obtained from monthly computations (just as the results achieved from evaluating individual yearly budgets differ from those obtained from use of long-term mean values of precipitation and evapotranspiration). It is not difficult to understand the reasons for this. When a water budget is evaluated for an individual month, precipitation during that month is compared with potential evapotranspiration and either a water surplus or a water deficit will occur during the month (or both quantities will be zero). However, if daily values of potential evapotranspiration and precipitation are used, it is not unusual for rainfall to be distributed within the month in such a way that both a deficit and a surplus occur in succession. Thus, summation of daily values for the entire month might reveal both water surpluses and deficits at the station that could not, of course, be possible using only monthly climatic values. Three different sets of water surplus and water deficit values are possible, therefore, depending on the method of computation. Smallest values of water surplus and deficit will generally result from the long-term average computational process whereas the largest values of surpluses and deficits will occur using daily data.

Table 2-3 illustrates some of the differences associated with computations based on daily and monthly values. At Wilmington, Delaware, in July 1975, total monthly rainfall was 142 mm while monthly potential evapotranspiration was 151 mm. Precipitation failed to meet water need by 9 mm. In this example,

17

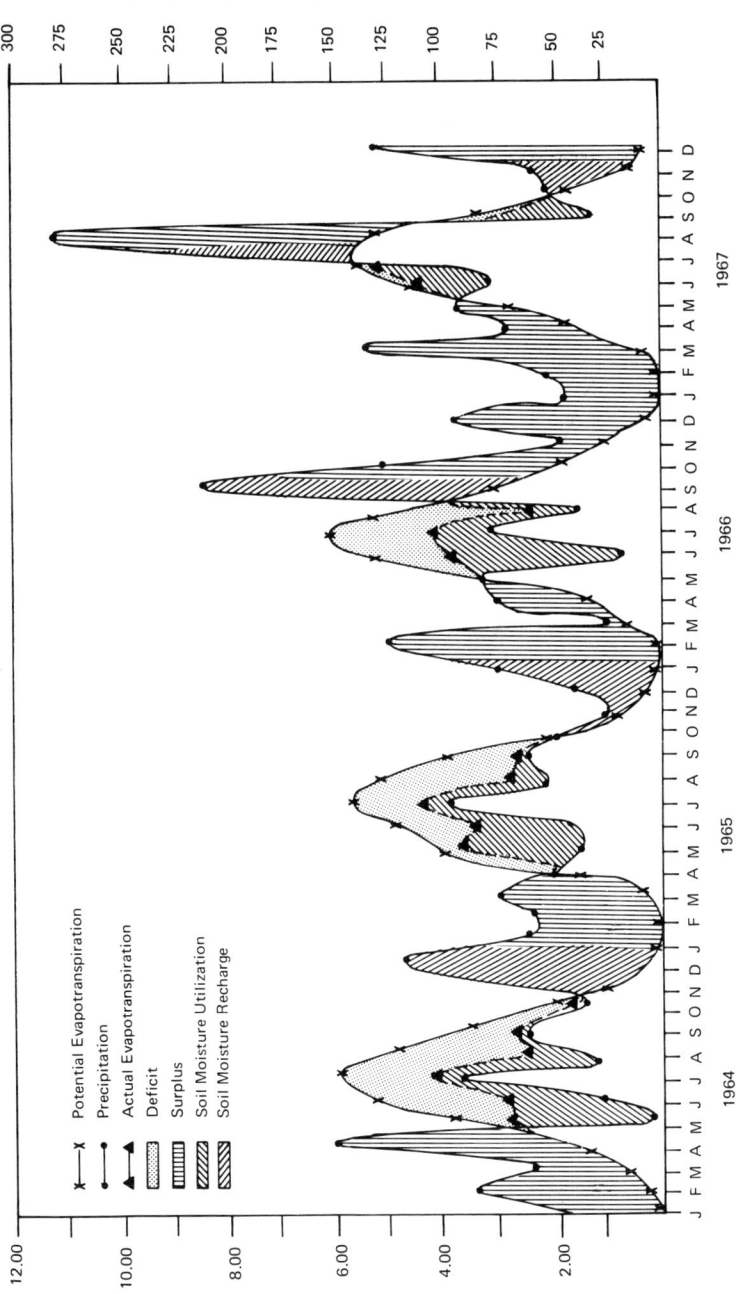

Figure 2-4. Monthly Water Budgets, Wilmington, Delaware, 1964-1967

Table 2-3

Daily and Monthly Computations of the Factors of the Water Budget, Wilmington, Delaware, July 1975

(Values in mm; storage 100 mm at field capacity)

Date	PE	P	P–PE	ST	AE	Def	Surp
				60			
1	4	0	−4	58	2	2	0
2	5	0	−5	54	4	1	0
3	5	10	+5	59	5	0	0
4	4	0	−4	56	3	1	0
5	5	0	−5	53	3	2	0
6	4	2	−2	52	3	1	0
7	5	0	−5	50	2	3	0
8	5	0	−5	47	3	2	0
9	5	9	+4	51	5	0	0
10	5	4	−1	50	5	0	0
11	4	1	−3	49	2	2	0
12	5	7	+2	51	5	0	0
13	4	65	+61	100	4	0	12
14	5	3	−2	98	5	0	0
15	5	5	0	98	5	0	0
16	5	0	−5	93	5	0	0
17	5	4	−1	92	5	0	0
18	6	0	−6	87	5	1	0
19	5	0	−5	82	5	0	0
20	6	28	+22	100	6	0	4
21	6	1	−5	95	6	0	0
22	5	0	−5	90	5	0	0
23	5	0	−5	86	4	1	0
24	5	0	−5	81	5	0	0
25	5	3	−2	80	4	1	0
26	4	0	−4	77	3	1	0
27	4	0	−4	74	3	1	0
28	5	0	−5	70	4	1	0
29	5	0	−5	66	4	1	0
30	5	0	−5	63	3	2	0
31	5	0	−5	60	3	2	0
Total	151	142			126	25	16

Computations based on monthly data						
Begin ST	P–PE	New ST	ΔST	AE	Def	Surp
60	−9	54	−6	148	3	0

assume that 100 mm of water can be held in the soil at field capacity; previous computations reveal that at the beginning of the month the soil was holding 60 mm of water. Because 40 mm of water were required to fill soil storage capacity and because Wilmington experienced more need for water than precipitation, surplus would have been 0 and storage would have dropped from 60 to 54 mm by the end of the month on the basis of monthly data alone. A water deficit of 3 mm would have occurred. Based on daily computations of evapotranspiration and measured daily precipitation, however, water surplus for the month is seen to be 16 mm and deficit is 25 mm. Using monthly data in the computations gives only a value of water deficit. Both surplus and deficit are smaller with monthly computations than with daily computations.

Thornthwaite devised his water budget bookkeeping procedure originally using monthly temperature and precipitation data. Later, however, he recognized the utility of daily evapotranspiration data for irrigation scheduling. He extended the water budget bookkeeping technique to include daily data. However, the Thornthwaite formula for potential evapotranspiration is more a monthly formula than it is a daily formula. Thornthwaite's relation includes no terms expressing the influence of wind speed or humidity of the air. In mid-latitude, where most months do not vary strongly in wind speed or humidity, the Thornthwaite formula gives reasonable monthly values of potential evapotranspiration. In other areas, however, where wind or humidity can vary markedly from month to month, as in a monsoon area, the Thornthwaite formula for evapotranspiration will overestimate or underestimate water loss. This limitation has long been recognized and it is possible to adjust for it on the basis of monthly computations.

The same limitation applies more significantly when daily values of potential evapotranspiration are obtained from the Thornthwaite formula. Within a month there can be marked changes in daily wind speed and humidity, especially in areas experiencing large air mass contrasts. The Thornthwaite formula, which ignores humidity and wind, cannot be responsive to these significant daily changes and so computed daily potential evapotranspiration may deviate markedly from actual conditions.

On the basis of reliability of the basic evapotranspiration formula, monthly computations are probably more realistic than daily computations. If daily values of evapotranspiration are needed for scheduling supplemental irrigation, for example, it would be preferable to use one of the other evapotranspiration expressions that takes into account daily differences in wind speed and humidity of the air and their effect on the daily rate of water loss.

3

Environmental Systems

Descriptions of the processes that shape the world around us emphasize the roles that energy and water budgets play. Nearly all the energy driving the physical systems that comprise our surface environment comes from the sun. Though energy is the forcing function, energy alone is not sufficient to produce the changes that we note. Energy must have water, atmosphere, surface materials, or vegetation on which and through which to operate.

Water, air, and surface materials are all part of a total earth system. They interact with one another and they can be divided into numerous subsystems. Much recent work in physical geography has been concerned with understanding the interactions of the various systems and subsystems that make up our environment. One technique is by means of budgets that express the input, storage, and output of quantities. The present concern is with just one such budget approach—an understanding of the water budget—the input of moisture, its storage in the system, and moisture output in the form of evapotranspiration and runoff. In the following chapters the factors that are derived from the water budget—actual evapotranspiration, soil moisture storage, moisture surplus, and moisture deficit—will all be used to increase our understanding of how the systems in our environment interact. This chapter attempts to utilize factors derived from moisture and energy budgets to achieve a more rational understanding of the distribution of climates, the great vegetation and soil systems, and the seasonal changes in sea levels.

Climatic Classification

The term "climate" has a rather particular meaning as it is used in the concept of a classification.[1] Climate is quite complex when each of its variables is considered in turn; there would be no purpose to base a classification on a complete catalog of all variables at a place, because no two places would have exactly the same climates. Rather, a meaningful classification must be based on only those active factors which are capable of broad generalization or abstraction. But the reason for a classification must also be considered in the selection of the elements utilized. For example, climatic classifications useful for such things as the design of air conditioning systems, flying weather requirements, or television transmission might require only a few selected criteria to define class intervals with large areal extent and usefulness.[2] These would be quite specialized classifications and might not really reflect "climate" to many.

The work during the last decade on climatic classification for human comfort utilizing a combination of several weather variables to express the effect of the atmospheric environment at a place on human well-being represents a broader but still specialized type of classification.[3] Of more general usefulness are those classifications which have attempted to define and describe those active elements of climate which divide the earth into a small number of climatic regions on the basis of easily defensible criteria and which are related to the large-scale soils and vegetation zones.

A common mistake in this type of classification work is to consider that climates only identify the areas between various climatic isolines drawn where major vegetation boundaries exist.[4] The value of a classification seems to be based only on the degree of "fit" between climatic and vegetation zones. It is scarcely recognized that a significant achievement of a classification is how well it provides estimates of evapotranspiration losses that can be balanced against precipitation gains to reveal the magnitude of the moisture factor in climate.

The past century has witnessed the introduction and evolution of ideas that have successively brought greater precision and objectivity to climatic classification. First, Köppen in 1900 introduced a classification in which thermal zones were of prime importance and moisture aspects were largely treated in terms of the number of rainy days.[5] Köppen's later classifications utilized an increasingly more sophisticated moisture index (involving the ratio between mean annual precipitation and mean annual temperature plus a constant) with the thermal zones. The climatic water budget derived by Thornthwaite became the basis for his 1948 climatic classification and for his 1955 revision.[6] Fundamental to this effort was the fact that the water budget was able to combine and describe the roles of both energy and water in shaping the face of the earth more satisfactorily than earlier attempts at classification.

Thornthwaite Climatic Classification

Consider the two elements that constitute the foundation of the Thornthwaite classification, potential evapotranspiration and the moisture index. Potential evapotranspiration (PE), the estimation of the moisture that would be lost from a homogeneous surface which never suffers from a lack of water, is an energy parameter described in terms of the water that can be converted from one state to another. Potential evapotranspiration is used as an index of thermal efficiency. The moisture index (I_m), an estimation of the relative moistness or aridity of a climate, is derived from a comparison of precipitation values with the values of potential evapotranspiration. In its original form, the moisture index was expressed as $I_m = I_h - I_a$ where I_h is the humidity index ($I_h = 100S/PE$) and I_a is the aridity index ($I_a = 100D/PE$); S and D are moisture surplus and deficit respectively from the water budget. It can be shown that, on an annual basis, $S = P - AE$ and $D = PE - AE$. Substituting for $I_h - I_a$, the expression $I_m = 100 \ [(P/PE) - 1]$ results. The moisture index expresses how well the available moisture satisfies the climatic demands for water. The moisture index is positive in moist climates, negative in arid climates, and zero when precipitation equals potential evapotranspiration.

Both the annual expression of relative moistness or aridity and the occurrence of periods of aridity in moist climates or periods of moistness in arid climates are important in climatic classifications. Values of surplus and deficit from the water budget are used to determine the seasonal variation in effective moisture at a place.

The four elements that make up Thornthwaite's complete classification—moisture index, seasonal variation in effective moisture, thermal efficiency, and summer concentration of thermal efficiency—are basically derived from the two primary factors of potential evapotranspiration (water need) and precipitation (water supply) and their seasonal distribution. Four letters, both capitals and small, with subscripts and superscripts, make up the complete classification. As a result, the system is difficult to map (a separate map showing the distribution of each of the four elements is necessary) and the description of a climate by means of four letters with various super- and subscripts is somewhat awkward and unclear. For example, the climatic description of Wilmington, Delaware is B_2 $B^1_2 \ rb_2{}^1$, or humid, second mesothermal, with little or no summer water deficiency and a summer concentration of thermal efficiency equal to a second mesothermal climate.

General Climate-Soils-Vegetation Distributions

The two principal water budget factors, PE and I_m, were combined some years ago in a nonquantitative way that not only suggested major differences between climates but that also were used to describe the distributions of other systems which make up our physical environment (figure 3-1). In all three diagrams, potential evapotranspiration, the factor that expresses the distribution of available energy, increases downward on the vertical scale. The moisture index along the horizontal axis ranges from large negative values (great aridity) on the left to large positive values (great moistness) on the right. Thus, conditions change from cold and dry in the upper left to cold and wet in the upper right, to hot and dry in the lower left and hot and wet in the lower right of each of the diagrams of figure 3-1. Polar climates are found across the top of the diagram ranging from right to left from fairly moist to fairly dry. Because of the low temperatures, the air will not contain a great deal of moisture so that moisture conditions will not be extremely wet or dry. With warmer temperatures (slightly larger values of potential evapotranspiration), subpolar or so-called continental subarctic climates occur. Here, areas with mild deficits of water can be separated

24

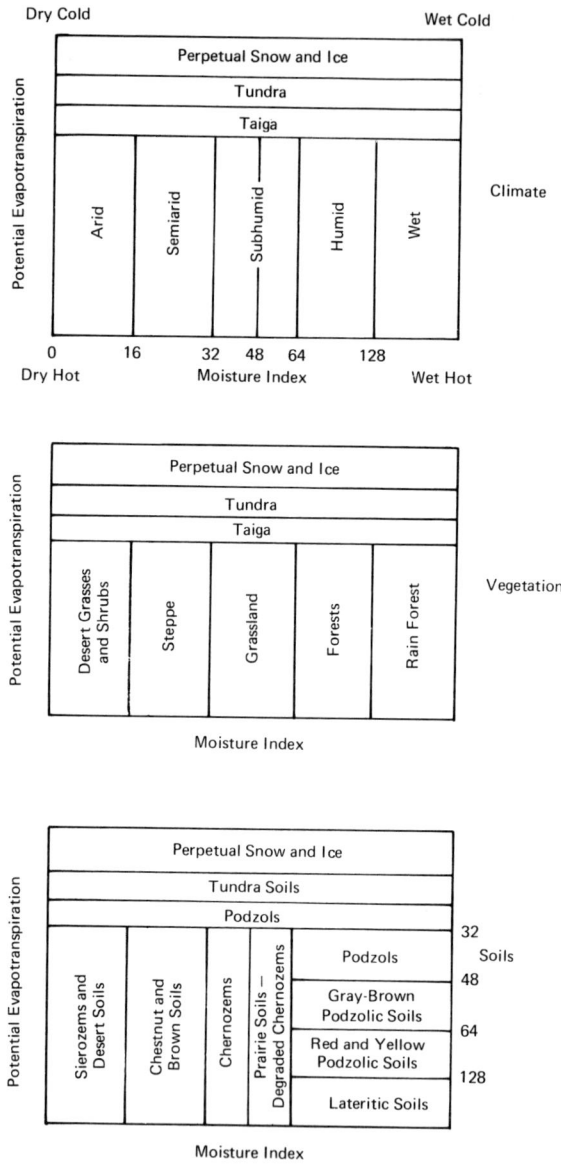

Source: D.I. Blumenstock and C.W. Thornthwaite, "Climate and the world pattern," in *Climate and Man,* Yearbook of Agriculture, U.S. Department of Agriculture, Washington, D.C. (1941).

Figure 3-1. Relation Between the Temperature or Energy Factors (Vertical Scale) and Moisture Factors (Horizontal Scale) and the Distributions of Climate, Soils, and Vegetation

from others with moderate water surpluses, although, because moisture is not a significantly limiting factor, only one continuous band of subpolar climates is shown.

Under warmer conditions, moisture becomes more significant in the distribution of climates as well as in other systems such as vegetation and soils. Thus, the schematic diagrams are divided into five areas on the basis of moisture ranging from the very dry arid or desert conditions with large negative values of the moisture index on the left through semiarid to subhumid where the moisture index passes through 0, to humid, and finally to the very moist or perhumid climates with large positive values of the moisture index on the right.

Because climate is so important in the distribution of vegetation, it is to be expected that a generalized distribution of major climatic areas would be similar to generalized distributions of vegetation and soils. The general agreement is revealed in the other two diagrams of figure 3-1. Using the names of the great soil groups included on the original figure 3-1, one finds that tundra soils and tundra vegetation, both unique subsystems of the vegetation and soil distributions, are closely related to the polar climates found across the top of the diagram. Similarly, taiga or boreal forests and podzol soils of upper mid-latitudes in the northern hemisphere are closely associated with subpolar or continental subarctic climatic conditions.

Quite distinctive types of soil and vegetation are found to be associated with temperate to hot climates ranging from very dry to very moist. Desert soils or sierozems and desert grasses or shrubs are found in the arid climatic regions; chestnut and brown soils, and steppe vegetation form under semiarid climatic regions; chernozems or prairie soils and grassland vegetation occur in subhumid climatic regions. Under humid and very humid climatic conditions, forest vegetation predominates. No real distinction between coniferous or deciduous forests is made here although the forests of perhumid climates are called rainforests as opposed to forest or mixed forests of humid climatic regions. Within humid and perhumid regions, soils are separated more on the basis of temperature than moisture conditions. Cool moist areas have gray-brown podzols, whereas warm moist areas have red-yellow podzols and tropical moist areas have latosols.

These hypothetical distributions of soils and vegetation appear quite reasonable and valid. Nevertheless, it is still desirable to see if such distributions are actually found in nature. If potential evapotranspiration and the moisture index are truly active factors in climate, we should expect these same general relations to hold using data from weather stations around the world.

Vegetation Distributions

Using maps of natural vegetation,[7] it has been possible to identify fifteen major vegetation areas across the conterminous United States and Canada in addition to the tropical rainforest.[8] Climatic stations were selected in each of the sixteen vegetation regions (in the case of discontinuous vegetation regions, some climatic stations were sought in each major segment of the vegetation association) and values of annual PE and the climatic moisture index were computed. In selecting climatic stations, those directly on vegetation borders or in transitional zones were avoided so that conditions at the stations would be representative of core vegetation areas. However, no stations were eliminated because the climatic data did not appear to fit some preconceived pattern. In the conterminous United States, PE ranged from about 500 to 1250 mm. Stations with PE values less than 500 were generally found in the boreal forest and tundra areas of Canada and Alaska. Tropical rainforest stations generally had values of PE greater than 1300 mm.

The moisture index at the different stations ranged from well over +100 in the tropical rainforest and in mountainous areas of northeastern and northwestern United States to values close to −100 in the arid areas of southwestern United States. Conspicuous by their absence were stations with I_m values of +60 or higher and PE values between 800 and 1200 mm. These warm, moist climates should be found in latitudes 30-35°N near the coastal regions where adequate moisture is present. However, these latitudes are in the subtropical belts of high pressure where drier conditions associated with the fairly permanent high pressure areas make it difficult to obtain I_m values above +50.

Using a diagram similar to those shown in figure 3-1 with potential evapotranspiration increasing downward and moisture index indicating increasing moistness to the right, a letter indicating the natural vegetation was plotted at the intersection of the PE and I_m values for each station (figure 3-2).

The distribution shown on figure 3-2 supports the idea that it is possible to locate discrete and frequently nonoverlapping vegetation areas on the basis of just the two climatic factors of PE and moisture index. The distributions clearly separate forest areas from grasslands or desert vegetation areas. Within forest areas, not only are tropical rainforests entirely separate from other forest types, but cold boreal forests of continental subarctic climates are distinct from mid-latitude forests. Even within mid-latitude forests, birch-maple appears distinct from spruce or oak-chestnut forests. Where forest types do overlap, the types are oak-chestnut, oak-hickory, and oak-pine where some degree of overlap would seem to be a reasonable expectation. Oak-pine forests also overlap loblolly pines, as would also be expected in southeastern United States.

Tundra vegetation is clearly distinctive across the colder portion of the diagram and grassland areas are found in the central part where the moisture index approximates zero ($P = PE$). This is where the grassland areas should be found according to the hypothetical scheme of figure 3-1. On the drier side of the moisture index, short or bunch grass areas, desert savanna, desert grass, sagebrush, and creosote bush vegetation areas of semiarid and arid climates occur.

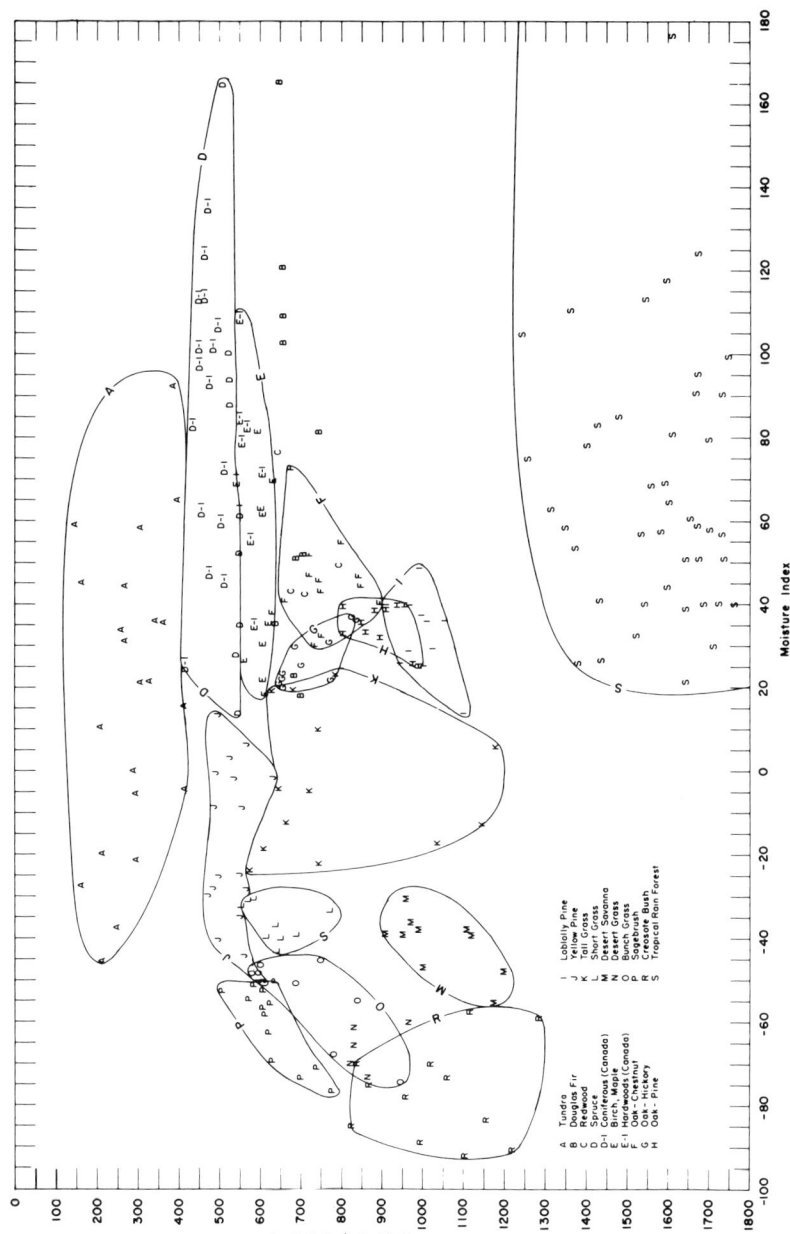

Source: J.R. Mather and G.A. Yoshioka, "The role of climate in the distribution of vegetation, *Annals of the Association of American Geographers*, vol. 58, no. 1 (1968).

Figure 3-2. Relation Between Climatic Moisture Index, Potential Evapotranspiration, and Natural Vegetation at Representative Stations in the United States, Canada, and the Tropics

Identifying such a large number of fairly discrete vegetation areas on the basis of potential evapotranspiration and moisture index data strongly reinforces the long-established idea that climate, defined by truly active factors such as *PE* and *P*, significantly influences the distribution of vegetation. One is able to speak of a grassland climate as opposed to a forest or a tundra climate and even define, with some precision, forest subtypes within the broader range of temperate forests. The relationships found do not rule out the possibility that more than one vegetation type might be able to survive and compete successfully within a given climatic range or that edaphic or other environmental factors as well as human actions might contribute to exceptions to the broad patterns found here; however, the consistency of these patterns suggests that water budget factors are quite significant in influencing the distribution of vegetation.

Using the information from figure 3-2, it is possible to determine realistic *PE* and I_m limits for the various vegetation groups suggested schematically in figure 3-1. Such quantitative limits are included in table 3-1.

These limits have been used in figure 3-3 to modify the schematic relationships of figure 3-1. Other vegetation associations can be added to make table 3-1 or figure 3-3 even more useful, but it is already clear that knowledge of *PE* and I_m for an area is sufficient to allow us to make a reasonable estimate of the natural vegetation in the area.

Soil Distributions

Climatic factors are perhaps less directly influential in the development of soils than in the development of vegetation classes. Because soils develop more slowly

Table 3-1

Ranges of Potential Evapotranspiration and Moisture Index for Different Vegetation Types and Subtypes

Vegetation	PE Range (mm)	I_m Range
Tundra	100 - 450	−50 to 100
Coniferous forests (Canada)	450 - 550	10 to 160
Hardwood forests (Canada)	550 - 600	10 to 110
Oak-chestnut, hickory, pine	600 - 1000	20 to 70
Loblolly pine	900 - 1150	20 to 50
Tropical rainforest	1250 - 1800	20 to 180
Yellow pine	450 - 600	−60 to 10
Tall grass	600 - 1200	−30 to 20
Short grass	600 - 850	−50 to −30
Desert Savanna	900 - 1250	−60 to −30
Bunch grass	600 - 950	−80 to −40
Sagebrush	500 - 750	−80 to −50
Creosote bush	850 - 1300	−90 to −60

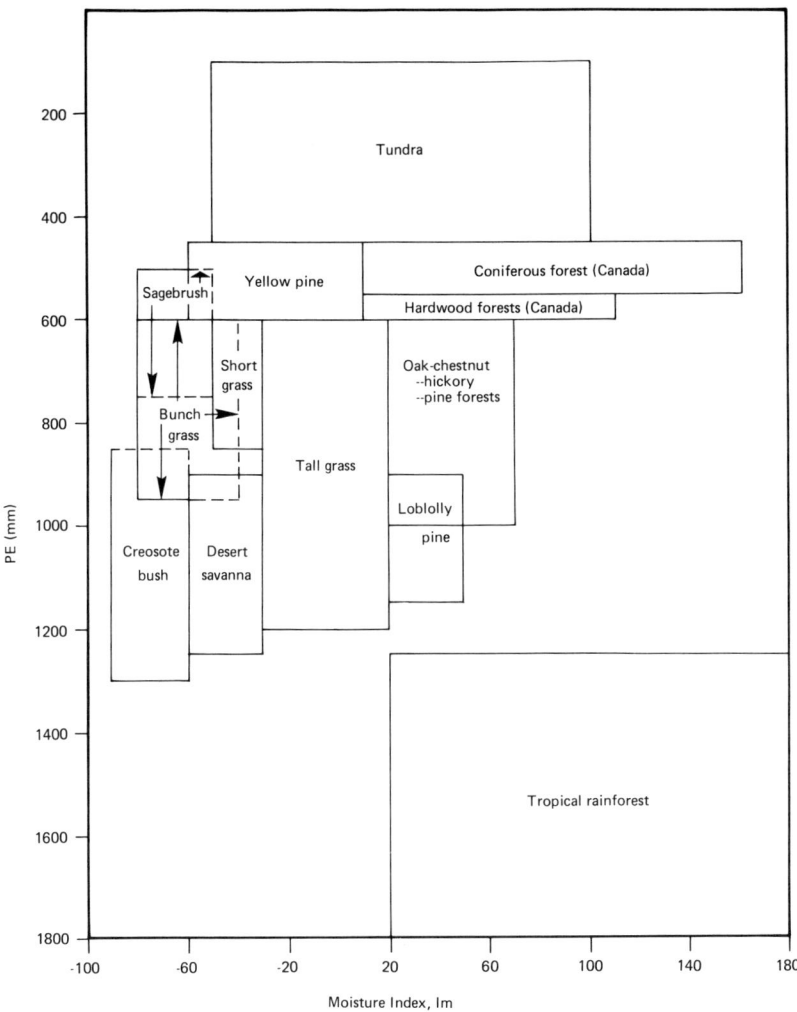

Figure 3-3. Schematic Relation Between Potential Evapotranspiration, the Moisture Index, and Natural Vegetation Regions in North America

than vegetation, and climates may vary markedly over hundreds of years, it may be more difficult to obtain significant relations between soil type and climatic factors such as potential evapotranspiration and the moisture index. Water budget factors of the past thirty years may differ from those of several hundred or several thousand years ago although those earlier climates may also have left their mark on the soils found today.

To determine the relation between the major soil groups and water budget factors, soil information from the fairly detailed soils map in the National Atlas of the United States[9] was compared with water budget information from selected stations. A significant relation between soil type and data of potential evapotranspiration and moisture index was found (figure 3-4). The results in figure 3-4, based on data from more than 200 points in the conterminous United States, are quite interesting. In all, nine distinct soil classes are represented by the climatic data from the individual stations. Though there are definite areas of overlap, there are also basic core areas for most of the soil types that are reasonably distinct from each of the other soil types. The identification of the soil groups on the basis of PE and I_m agrees reasonably well with the descriptions of the soils (see table 3-2).

Possible equivalents between the older Marbut soil terms utilized in figure 3-1 and those of the more recent U.S. comprehensive soil classification system used in figure 3-4 have been suggested.[10] Because of the differences in the way the two soil classification systems were developed, it is not possible to equate a single soil group in one system with only one soil in the other system. The recent U.S. comprehensive system is based primarily on the properties of the soil as it exists today but it also considers genesis and degree of weathering. The major soil orders in the United States are divided into suborders on the basis of physical and/or chemical properties suggesting drainage characteristics or differences resulting from variations in climate or vegetation.

U.S. Comprehensive Soil classification	Marbut Soil classification
Alfisols	gray-brown podzolic, gray wooded, degraded chernozem, noncalcic brown
Aridisols	desert, sierozem, solonchak, brown and reddish-brown, solonetz
Mollisols	chestnut, chernozem, brown, brown forest
Spodosols	podzols, brown podzolic, red-yellow podzolic, reddish-brown lateritic
Vertisols	grumusols

Generalizing the climatic information from figure 3-4 as included in table 3-2, one obtains a schematic relation among the climatic factors of potential evapotranspiration (representing heat factors) and the moisture index and soils in the conterminous United States (figure 3-5). The presentation in figure 3-5 provides quantitative values for use in estimating soil conditions in other areas from just routine water budget data.

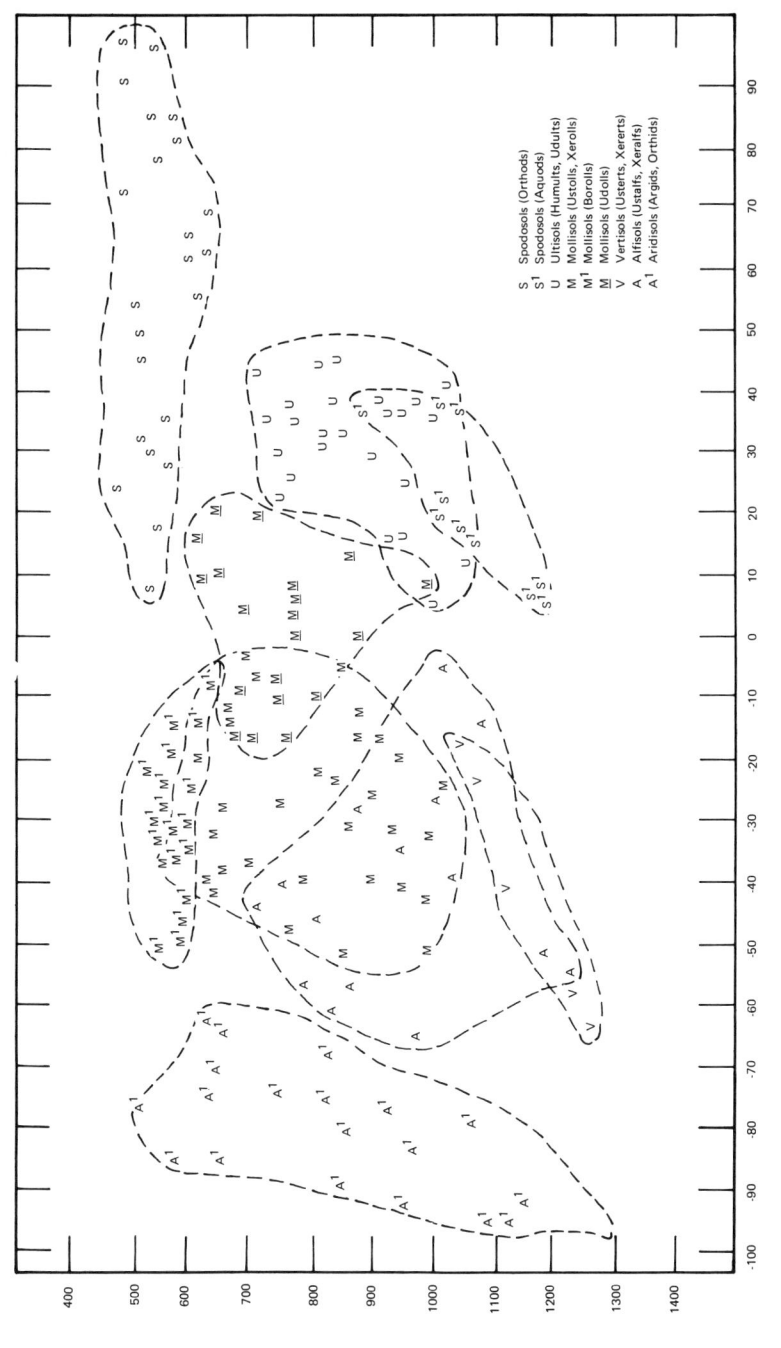

Figure 3-4. Relation Between Climatic Factors of Potential Evapotranspiration, the Moisture Index, and Selected Soil Classes in the Conterminous United States

Table 3-2

Description of Soil Groups and Potential Evapotranspiration and Moisture Index Ranges for Selected Soils in the Conterminous United States

Soil Group and Description	PE Range (mm)	I_m Range
S Spodosols (Orthods) (*Spodos* = wood ash)–mineral soils with a spodic or placic horizon cemented by iron resting on a fragipan (or first on an albic horizon). Relatively well drained with horizons of aluminum, iron and organic carbon accumulation. Cool, moist soils.	500 to 700	10 to 110
S[1] Spodosols (Aquods)–generally same as above but with characteristics associated with wetness. Only very small amounts of free iron, brownish and reddish-brown color of humus in spodic horizon may mask other colors. Warm, wet soils generally.	900 to 1200	10 to 40
U Ultisols (Humults, Udults) (*ultimos* = ultimate)– mineral soils of mid to low latitudes with a horizon of translocated silicate clays, only limited amount of bases. Humults are fairly well drained, rich in humus; Udults are fairly well drained but poorer in humus. Warm moist soils.	750 to 1100	10 to 50
M Mollisols (Udolls) (*Mollis* = soft)–mineral soils with surface mineral layer (may be overlain by surface organic layer). Soft texture, fertile, dark color. Soils lack oxic layer. Soils not dry 60 consecutive or 90 cumulative days per year. Warm, moist soils.	650 to 1000	−15 to 25
M[1] Mollisols (Borolls)–generally same as above except soils of cool or cold areas that are relatively well drained. Cool, moist soils.	500 to 650	−50 to 0
M Mollisols (Ustolls, Xerolls)–generally same as above except somewhat warmer, dryer soils. Ustoils are dry for more than 90 cumulative days per year while Xerolls are soils of Mediterranean climatic regions.	600 to 1100	−50 to 0
A Alfisols (Ustalfs, Xeralfs) (combined from al and fer)–mineral soils with horizon of layer-lattice silicate clays or with prismatic or blocky structure with some exchangeable sodium. Moderate to high base saturation. Ustalfs are mostly reddish soils of warm subhumid to semiarid climates while Xeralfs are mainly in warm semiarid Mediterranean climates. Surface massive and hard when dry with calcium layer near surface.	700 to 1200	−60 to 0

Table 3-2 (cont.)

Soil Group and Description	PE Range (mm)	I_m Range
V Vertisols (Usterts, Xererts) (*verto* = to turn)– clayey soils with deep wide cracks when dry. Usterts–soils of subtropical monsoon type climate with two rainy and two dry periods. Xererts–soils of Mediterranean climates with cool wet winters, warm dry summers.	1050 to 1250	−60 to −15
A[1] Aridisols (Argids, Orthids) (*aridus* = dry)– mineral soils with pale surface and lower horizons of silicate clays, or enrichment of calcium carbonates, calcium sulfates, exchangeable sodium, magnesium carbonates or soluble salts. Subsurface horizon could be cemented by silica. Dry, warm, soils.	500 to 1300	−95 to −55

Source for descriptions of soil groups: Donald Steila, *The Geography of Soils: Formation, Distribution and Management,* copyright 1976. Reprinted by permission of Prentice-Hall, Inc., Englewood Cliffs, New Jersey.

Annual Sea Level Changes

Oceanographic measurements have suggested that some 5.0×10^{18} gm of water are removed from the ocean between September and March each year and returned to the oceans between March and September, resulting in a change in sea level of some 1.4 cm depth when spread evenly over all world oceans. Results from the climatic water budget ought to be able to show this same movement of water from ocean to land and back again. Changes in moisture storage in the atmosphere, in vegetation, or in rivers, lakes, and reservoirs are quite small but changes in moisture storage in or on the land can be appreciable. From the water budget computation of table 2-2, large seasonal changes in soil moisture storage are found between spring and fall months.

Computations of the water budget at over 14,000 meteorologic stations worldwide have been used to evaluate monthly storage or detention of moisture in or on the land areas of the globe by 1° squares of latitude and longitude.[11] These values were later summed by 10° squares of latitude and longitude (table 3-3). The table shows maximum land storage for the world as a whole in March and minimum land storage in September, the difference being some 7.7×10^{18} gm, a value quite similar to that reported by the oceanographers to be gained by the oceans from March to September (and lost from the oceans from September to March.)

Consider the monthly values of storage on the land by hemispheres and for

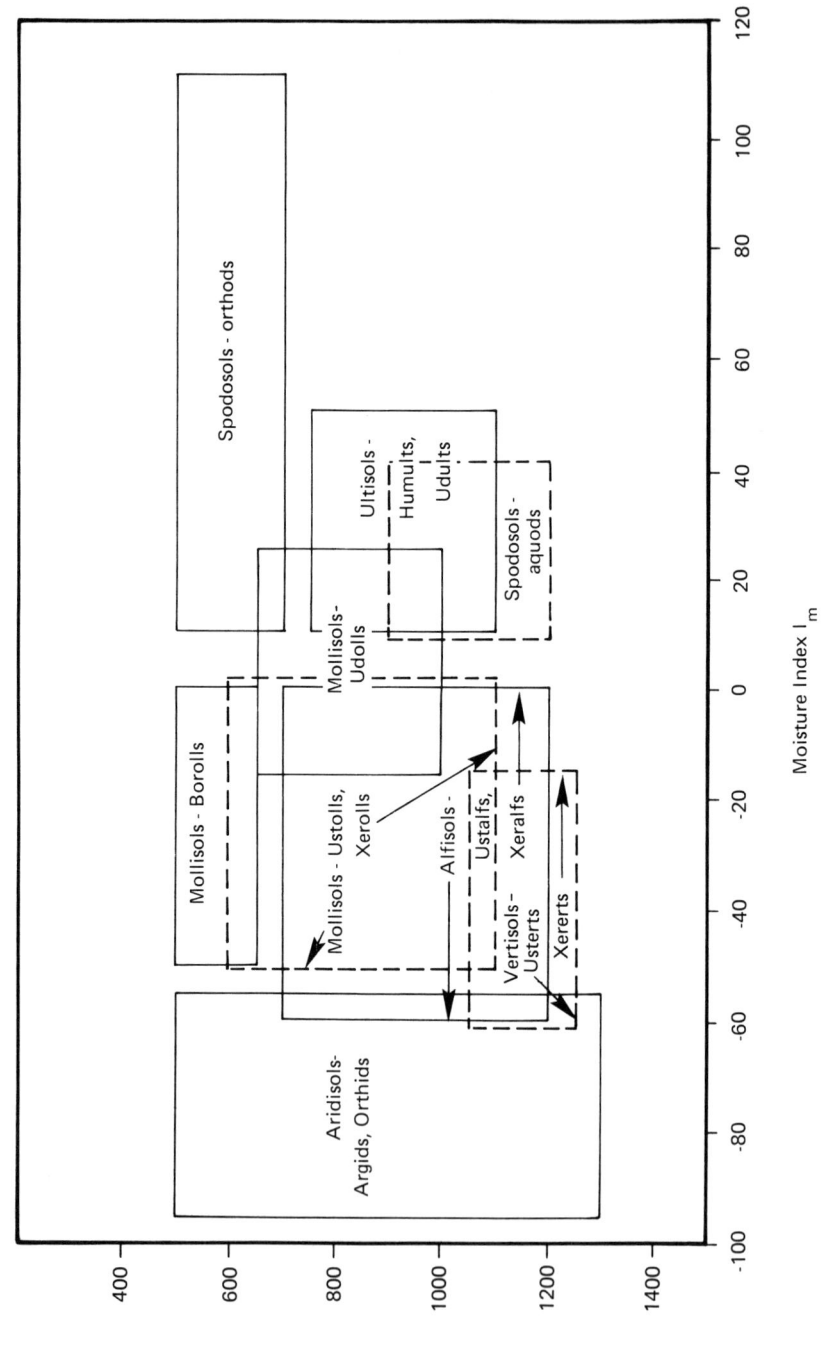

Figure 3-5. Schematic Relation Between Potential Evapotranspiration, the Moisture Index, and Selected Soil Classes in the Conterminous United States

Table 3-3
Moisture Detained in and on the Land Areas of the World by 10° Belts and by Months

		Jan. 10^{16} Grams	Feb. 10^{16} Grams	Mar. 10^{16} Grams	Apr. 10^{16} Grams	May 10^{16} Grams	June 10^{16} Grams	July 10^{16} Grams	Aug. 10^{16} Grams	Sept. 10^{16} Grams	Oct. 10^{16} Grams	Nov. 10^{16} Grams	Dec. 10^{16} Grams
Northern Latitude	60°-70°	325.3	345.7	364.3	377.2	355.6	257.4	198.8	177.6	182.3	243.0	274.5	299.6
	50°-60°	485.5	558.2	548.7	558.0	475.9	393.0	318.9	283.7	285.3	330.7	396.8	444.2
	40°-50°	397.3	437.8	472.7	458.5	397.6	333.0	267.7	225.5	222.7	247.5	296.3	353.0
	30°-40°	269.2	296.5	313.3	307.0	275.0	234.6	215.9	196.5	180.1	175.7	193.2	230.5
	20°-30°	158.8	157.6	155.5	159.4	174.5	201.3	280.8	249.9	238.2	202.1	177.0	165.0
	10°-20°	93.8	73.3	55.5	46.8	55.8	92.4	143.7	204.2	212.7	185.0	147.0	117.7
	0°-10°	215.5	191.8	189.6	212.3	245.7	273.4	297.6	316.9	318.4	307.0	281.5	246.7
Southern Latitude	0°-10°	333.3	368.2	400.3	411.6	378.1	335.9	277.6	238.8	217.4	222.0	254.5	288.9
	10°-20°	223.9	257.2	267.2	227.8	181.6	150.1	119.7	98.0	81.0	75.7	102.0	151.7
	20°-30°	84.8	87.9	88.7	85.0	82.8	84.7	81.2	76.2	74.0	72.5	73.3	77.4
	30°-40°	48.1	43.9	43.8	48.4	58.4	70.5	83.6	82.7	82.2	78.0	72.7	66.2
	40°-50°	21.7	18.2	18.3	20.1	22.0	23.9	25.4	25.5	38.1	30.2	25.8	22.5
	50°-60°	5.2	4.6	4.8	5.0	5.1	5.3	5.5	5.5	5.4	5.3	6.7	5.9
	60°-70°	28.3	23.3	21.3	24.8	27.8	31.3	33.4	34.8	39.3	42.4	45.3	30.3
North Latitude		1945.4	2060.9	2099.6	2119.2	1980.1	1785.1	1723.4	1654.3	1639.7	1691.0	1766.3	1856.7
South Latitude		745.3	803.3	844.4	822.7	755.8	701.7	626.4	561.5	537.4	526.1	580.3	642.9
Grand Total		2690.7	2864.2	2944.0	2941.9	2735.9	2486.8	2349.8	2215.8	2177.1	2217.1	2346.6	2499.6

Source: T.E.A. van Hylckama, "The water balance of the earth," *Publications in Climatology*, Laboratory of Climatology, vol. 9, no. 2 (1956).

the whole globe at the bottom of table 3-3. The course of moisture detention on land is quite similar in both the northern and southern hemispheres despite the fact that summer and winter seasons are just six months out of phase in the two hemispheres. Actual values are much smaller in the southern than the northern hemisphere because of the very much smaller total land areas in the southern hemisphere. The general agreement of storage in the two hemispheres results basically from two situations: (a) principal land masses are found in mid-latitudes in the northern hemisphere and tropical latitudes in the southern hemisphere; conditions that predominate in these areas will be strongly reflected in hemispheric totals; and (b) in mid-latitudes, maximum land storage follow a winter period of low evaporation and adequate precipitation while in tropical latitudes, maximum storage follows a summer (or high sun) period of high precipitation because evapotranspiration is fairly constant through the year. This means that maximum land storage is found in March or April in mid-latitudes in the northern hemisphere and in March or April (late summer, early fall) in tropical latitudes in the southern hemisphere.

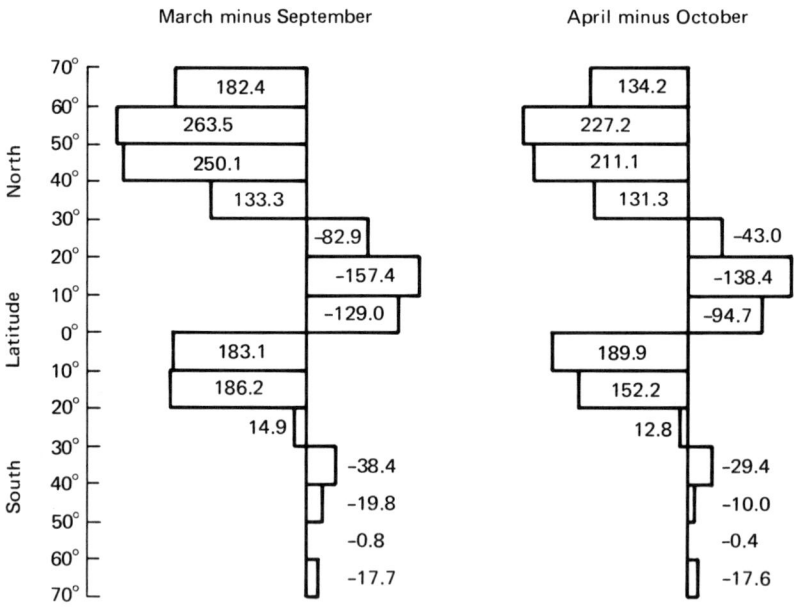

Source: T.E.A. van Hylckama, "The water balance of the earth," *Publications in Climatology*, Laboratory of Climatology, vol. 9, no. 2 (1956).

Figure 3-6. Differences in Moisture Detention on the Land Areas of the World by 10° Belts of Latitude, March Minus September, April Minus October. All values are in 10^{16} gms.

Because these two belts have the maximum land area, the pattern of moisture storage in them will dominate hemispheric results. A graphic representation of the spring minus fall storage by latitude (figure 3-6) emphasizes this point. The graph reveals that northern hemisphere tropical areas and southern hemisphere mid-latitude areas have more storage in September and October than in March or April. The less extensive land areas in these belts makes them less influential in hemispheric totals than conditions in the 30-70°N and 0-30°S belts.

The present chapter has attempted to relate water budget factors to several systems that are influential in our natural environment. Reasonable relations are found between factors such as potential evapotranspiration and the moisture index and distributions of soil and vegetation, which suggests that the water and energy factors for which they serve as surrogates play significant roles in determining such distributions. The water budget has a significant role in environmental analysis that needs to be further developed if we hope to increase our understanding of the processes involved and their interrelationships.

4 Hydrologic Studies

Because runoff is one element of the hydrologic cycle, water budget studies are of value to hydrologists and others concerned with the movement of water both overland and beneath the surface of the earth. Climatic water budget methodology can be used to provide an estimate of annual streamflow from a basin although monthly agreement between measured and computed values of surface runoff is far from exact. The problem exists because streamflow response depends on the complex interaction of many factors, including basin size and slope, vegetation cover, antecedent moisture conditions, soil properties, rainfall intensity, and subsurface characteristics; therefore it cannot be closely represented by a model that considers only precipitation, evapotranspiration, and depth of storage in the ground. But agreement on an annual basis is found, which suggests that the computational model includes factors of prime significance to surface flow. Lack of monthly agreement might argue that some local environmental factors influencing short-term stream response are still not considered.

Measured and Computed Streamflow

Measured values of streamflow from each gaging station on the Delmarva peninsula (sandy coastal plain area of Delaware and eastern shore areas of Maryland and Virginia) have been compared with runoff computed from climatic data at the closest representative station for the 1949-1964 period.[1] Results for several basins are summed in table 4-1. Correlation coefficients between annual computed and measured runoff based on sixteen years of record range from +0.94 in the case of computed runoff at Newark, Delaware, versus measured runoff in the Christina River at Cooches Bridge, to a value of +0.86 for computed runoff at Preston, Maryland, versus measured runoff in Faulkner Branch. Regression equations show considerable variation around the line $y = x$ suggesting the need for further refinement of the technique even for annual data.

Less reliable results are found when individual monthly computed and measured runoff values are compared. Table 4-2 compares computed runoff at Wilmington, Delaware, and measured runoff in Shellpot Creek draining a very small basin just outside of Wilmington.[2]

In these computations, it was assumed that 20 percent of the surplus water available for runoff in any month actually was lost by runoff, while the

Table 4-1

Annual Values of Gaged Stream Runoff and Computed Runoff at Nearby Weather Stations, Delmarva Peninsula, 1949-1964

(Values in cm depth)

Year	Milling-ton (Cal. Runoff)	Unicorn Branch (Meas. Runoff)	Newark (Cal. Runoff)	Chris-tina at Cooches Bridge (Meas. Runoff)	White Clay Creek (Meas. Runoff)	Big Elk Creek at Elk Mills (Meas. Runoff)	Preston (Cal. Runoff)	Faulkner Branch at Federals-burg (Meas. Runoff)
1949	33.4	40.8	37.4	38.8	41.5	43.4	25.7	
1950	27.7	29.6	36.2	34.5	38.4	41.2	25.3	
1951	35.4	36.3	50.7	47.9	43.2	47.7	32.4	33.8
1952	57.6	52.6	72.6	63.5	63.3	66.4	68.6	61.4
1953	46.2	44.6	57.1	54.8	55.7	56.4	42.3	43.5
1954	26.6	23.7	26.0	22.5	26.9	25.2	29.8	26.3
1955	24.4	22.0	41.1	37.6	31.1	32.4	45.1	39.3
1956	40.4	30.8	48.0	46.8	39.9	39.7	41.2	42.4
1957	40.7	29.3	39.2	41.6	34.4	35.8	39.6	36.9
1958	64.7	58.4	66.7	64.9	66.3	66.4	62.6	67.9
1959	30.9	27.1	32.6	38.4	34.0	35.3	38.1	50.2
1960	53.5	55.3	48.2	53.1	48.4	49.3	49.0	57.2
1961	49.9	57.7	40.2	49.4	45.5	48.8	52.6	56.6
1962	36.5	32.0	33.7	35.7	32.6	35.6	45.5	39.9
1963	35.2	24.4	29.0	26.7	26.1	26.4	40.1	31.4
1964	46.1	36.0	33.4	33.6	34.1	32.3	40.7	33.8

Data	Correlation Coefficient	Regression Equation
Millington vs. Unicorn Branch	0.88	$y = 0.95 \times -0.43$
Newark vs. Christina River	0.94	$y = 0.86 \times +2.28$
Newark vs. White Clay Creek	0.93	$y = 0.86 \times +1.68$
Newark vs. Big Elk Creek	0.94	$y = 0.88 \times +1.94$
Preston vs. Faulkner Branch	0.86	$y = 1.01 \times -0.35$

Source: J.R. Mather, "Factors of the climatic water balance over the Delmarva peninsula," *Publications in Climatology*, Laboratory of Climatology, vol. 22, no. 3 (1969).

remaining 80 percent was held over and added to available surplus in the following month. Annual totals are in close agreement, whereas monthly values agree fairly well except in June and November. It is possible that the overestimation of computed runoff from April through October and the underestimation from November through March are, in part, caused by problems

Table 4-2

Comparison of Monthly Computed Runoff, Wilmington, Delaware, vs. Measured Runoff, Shellpot Creek, Based on 19 Years of Data

	J	F	M	A	M	J	J	A	S	O	N	D	Yr.
Computed Wilmington runoff (mm)	42	50	56	54	44	35	28	23	18	15	18	31	414
Measured runoff Shellpot Creek (mm)	47	50	64	51	39	22	24	20	15	11	33	39	415

Source: J.R. Mather, "Factors of the climatic water balance over the Delmarva peninsula," *Publications in Climatology*, Laboratory of Climatology, vol. 22, no. 3 (1969).

associated with the seasonal nature of vegetation growth and water demand. Interception losses, which are higher in the summer season, have not been taken into account and summertime vegetation water demands may be greater than actual evapotranspiration as estimated from the climatic water budget.

Direct Overland Runoff of Intense Precipitation

Another problem not considered in the foregoing analysis is the possibility of some direct overland runoff of precipitation occurring at rates greater than the infiltration capacity of the soil. The Soil Conservation Service (SCS) has prepared simple tables and nomograms by which the amount of daily overland runoff from intense precipitation can be estimated on the basis of slope, ground cover, soil type, and antecedent precipitation.[3]

Essentially four steps are necessary to evaluate overland runoff from intense rainfall by the method developed by the Soil Conservation Service. The first step is to determine the hydrologic soil group of the particular soil to be studied from a master list of soils prepared by the SCS. All soils are classified in one of four different categories—ranked A through D on the basis of their runoff potential. Class A soils consist mostly of deep, well-drained sands and gravels with low runoff potential and high infiltration and water transmission rates. Class B soils have moderately fine to moderately coarse textures and are considered to have moderate infiltration rates when completely wet. Class C soils have moderately fine to fine textures with slow infiltration and water transmission rates. Class D soils are primarily clay soils or soils with clay pans that have very slow infiltration rates when wet. They are nearly impervious with very slow rates of water transmission.

The next step is to determine the five-day antecedent moisture condition of the particular soil from the daily precipitation record. In this case the precipitation totals that will shift the soil from one antecedent moisture class to another vary with the season of the year. One series of five-day precipitation totals is applied to the dormant season and a second series of five-day precipitation totals is used during the growing season. Table 4-3 gives the seasonal five-day accumulated rainfall limits for the three antecedent moisture condition groups.

The third step is to decide—on the basis of the land cover, the cultivation treatment, the hydrologic condition of the soil, and the hydrologic soil group of the particular soil—the actual runoff curve number to use in determining daily overland runoff from precipitation. Table 4-4 provides a list of runoff curve numbers assuming various combinations of land use and hydrologic condition.

Figure 4-1 provides information on the amount of direct overland runoff (Q) that will occur with different curve numbers with given amounts of daily rainfall (P). Because the various curves approach the X-axis at a small angle it is difficult to estimate from the graph the value of the daily P at which overland runoff will begin to occur. Table 4-5 provides the solution to the runoff equation for different curve numbers.

The fourth step is to go through the daily record of rainfall for the particular period under consideration and to identify for each rainfall episode whether the total antecedent five-day rainfall places that day's rainfall in group I, II, or III. From that information the curve number is readily read from table 4-4. If the precipitation for the day is less than the value listed in table 4-5 at which overland runoff will begin to occur for that curve number, a zero is included for overland runoff for that day. If the value of daily precipitation is greater than the starting value for runoff to occur, reference to figure 4-1 will provide information on the amount of precipitation that will run off. Summation of the overland runoff values for the month will give the monthly total, whereas subtraction of this value from the monthly precipitation will give the value of "effective" precipitation—that precipitation which enters the soil and takes part in the various steps of the water budget.

Sample computations for Seabrook, N.J., for September 1950 are given in table 4-6 to illustrate the procedure by which to calculate overland runoff. The

Table 4-3

Seasonal Five-Day Rainfall Totals for Various Antecedent Moisture Condition Groups

	Total 5-Day Antecedent Rainfall	
Antecedent Moisture Condition Group	Dormant Season Inches	Growing Season Inches
I	<0.5	<1.4
II	0.5 to 1.1	1.4 to 2.1
III	>1.1	>2.1

Source: Soil Conservation Service, *Hydrology—Section 4, National Engineering Handbook* (prepared by Victor Mockus), Hydrology Branch, SCS, U.S. Department of Agriculture, Washington, D.C. (1972).

Table 4-4

Runoff Curve Numbers for Different Hydrologic Soil-Cover-Treatment Complexes

Land Use	Cover Treatment	Hydrologic Condition	Hydrologic Soil Group			
			A	B	C	D
			(Runoff curve numbers for antecedent moisture conditions I/II/III)			
Fallow	Straight row	–	59/77/89	72/86/94	80/91/97	85/94/98
Row crops	Straight row	Poor	53/72/86	64/81/92	75/88/95	80/91/97
	Straight row	Good	47/67/83	60/78/90	70/85/94	76/89/96
	Contoured	Poor	51/70/85	62/79/91	68/84/93	75/88/95
	Contoured	Good	45/65/82	57/75/88	66/82/92	72/86/94
	Contoured & terraced	Poor	46/66/82	55/74/88	63/80/91	66/82/92
	Contoured & terraced	Good	42/62/79	52/71/86	60/78/90	64/81/92
Small grain	Straight row	Poor	45/65/82	58/76/89	68/84/93	75/88/95
	Straight row	Good	43/63/80	57/75/88	67/83/93	73/87/95
	Contoured	Poor	43/63/80	55/74/88	66/82/92	70/85/94
	Contoured	Good	41/61/78	54/73/87	64/81/92	68/84/93
	Contoured & terraced	Poor	41/61/78	53/72/86	62/79/91	66/82/92
	Contoured & terraced	Good	39/59/77	51/70/85	60/78/90	64/81/92
Closed seeded legumes or rotation meadow	Straight row	Poor	46/66/82	59/77/89	70/85/94	76/89/96
	Straight row	Good	38/58/76	53/72/86	64/81/92	70/85/94
	Contoured	Poor	44/64/81	57/75/88	67/83/93	70/85/94
	Contoured	Good	35/55/74	50/69/84	60/78/90	67/83/93
	Contoured & terraced	Poor	43/63/80	54/73/87	63/80/91	67/83/93
	Contoured & terraced	Good	31/51/70	47/67/83	58/76/89	63/80/91
Pasture or range		Poor	48/68/84	62/79/91	72/86/94	76/89/96
		Fair	30/49/69	50/69/84	62/79/91	68/84/93
		Good	21/39/59	41/61/78	55/74/88	63/80/91
	Contoured	Poor	28/47/67	47/67/83	64/81/92	75/88/95
	Contoured	Fair	12/25/43	39/59/77	57/75/88	67/83/93
	Contoured	Good	2/6/13	18/35/55	51/70/85	62/79/91
Meadow		Good	15/30/50	38/58/76	52/71/86	60/78/90
Woods		Poor	26/45/65	46/66/82	59/77/89	67/83/93
		Fair	19/36/56	40/60/78	54/73/87	62/79/91
		Good	12/25/43	35/55/74	51/70/85	59/77/89
Farmsteads			39/59/77	55/74/88	66/82/92	72/86/94
Roads (dirt)			53/72/86	66/82/92	73/87/95	76/89/96
(hard surface)			55/74/88	68/84/93	78/90/96	81/92/97

Source: Soil Conservation Service, *Hydrology–Section 4, National Engineering Handbook* (prepared by Victor Mockus), Hydrology Branch, SCS, U.S. Department of Agriculture, Washington, D.C. (1972).

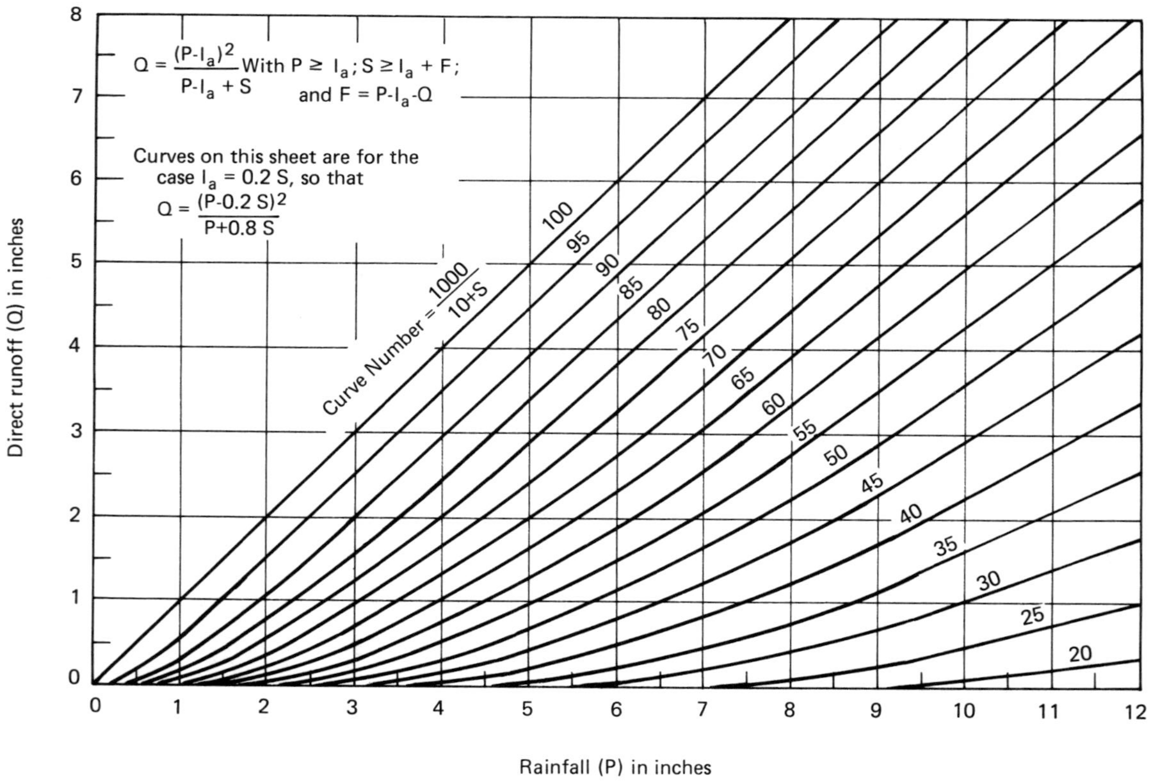

$Q = \frac{(P-I_a)^2}{P-I_a+S}$ With $P \geq I_a$; $S \geq I_a + F$; and $F = P-I_a-Q$
Curves on this sheet are for the case $I_a = 0.2\ S$, so that
$Q = \frac{(P-0.2\ S)^2}{P+0.8\ S}$
Curve Number = $\frac{1000}{10+S}$
100
95
90
85
80
75
70
65
60
55
50
45
40
35
30
25
20
Direct runoff (Q) in inches
0
1
2
3
4
5
6
7
8
Rainfall (P) in inches
0
1
2
3
4
5
6
7
8
9
10
11
12

Source: Soil Conservation Service, *Hydrology, Section 4, National Engineering Handbook*, (prepared by Victor Mockus) Hydrology Branch, SCS, US Department of Agriculture, Washington, D.C. (1972).

Figure 4-1. Relation Between Daily Rainfall Totals and Direct Overland Runoff for Various Runoff Curve Numbers

Table 4-5
Values of Daily Precipitation at Which Overland Runoff Will Begin to Occur for Different Curve Numbers

CN	Runoff Will Begin When Daily P=	CN	Runoff Will Begin When Daily P=	CN	Runoff Will Begin When Daily P=
100	0	68	.94	38	3.26
98	.04	66	1.03	36	3.56
96	.08	64	1.12	34	3.88
94	.13	62	1.23	32	4.24
92	.17	60	1.33	30	4.66
90	.22	58	1.45	25	6.00
88	.27	56	1.57	20	8.00
86	.33	54	1.70	15	11.34
84	.38	52	1.85	10	18.00
82	.44	50	2.00	5	38.00
80	.50	48	2.16		
78	.56	46	2.34		
76	.63	44	2.54		
74	.70	42	2.76		
72	.78	40	3.00		
70	.86				

Source: Soil Conservation Service, *Hydrology–Section 4, National Engineering Handbook* (prepared by Victor Mockus), Hydrology Branch, SCS, U.S. Department of Agriculture, Washington, D.C. (1972).

soil at Seabrook is Sassafras sandy loam in hydrologic soil group B and the soil is planted with small grain, the land is contoured and terraced, and the hydrologic condition of the soil is good. Thus the curve numbers for the antecedent moisture conditions of groups I, II, and III are 61, 70, and 85, respectively. Because our computations are for September, we use the precipitation values for the growing season. Table 4-6 shows that in that particularly wet September, with almost 10 inches of precipitation, just over 2 inches of overland flow occurred. Overland runoff was found on just two days with 1.55 inches occurring on September 11 when a tropical storm brought 6.66 inches of rainfall to the area. The September total of overland runoff at Seabrook was about half of the total annual overland runoff for 1950 at that station.

Application to Computed Runoff

Using the SCS technique, summed by months, the computed runoff has been obtained for an area of Cumberland County in southern New Jersey drained by

Table 4-6

Example of Computations of Direct Runoff from Precipitation, Seabrook, N.J., September 1950

Day	Precip (in)	AMC	Curve No.	Direct RO
1	0	–	–	0
2	.03	I	51	0
3	.18	I	51	0
4	0	–	–	0
5	0	–	–	0
6	0	–	–	0
7	0	–	–	0
8	0	–	–	0
9	0	–	–	0
10	0	–	–	0
11	6.66	I	51	1.55
12	0	–	–	0
13	.15	III	85	0
14	1.50	III	85	.47
15	0	–	–	0
16	0	–	–	0
17	0	–	–	0
18	0	–	–	0
19	.03	I	51	0
20	0	–	–	0
21	.05	I	51	0
22	1.15	I	51	0
23	.13	I	51	0
24	.03	I	51	0
25	0	–	–	0
26	0	–	–	0
27	0	–	–	0
28	0	–	–	0
29	0	–	–	0
30	.05	I	51	0
Totals	9.96			2.02

three small, gaged streams. The area is covered with sandy soils with forest and scrub forest vegetation interspersed with cultivated fields. Topography is flat to very gently rolling. In calculating the runoff from the climatic water budget, it was assumed that the available storage capacity in the root zone of the soil was 50 mm and that 25 percent of the available surplus water each month would run off in that month, while the remaining 75 percent would be held over and added to the surplus of the following month. The value of calculated direct overland flow was first subtracted from the value of precipitation for the month and the resulting value of "effective" precipitation (the precipitation that actually enters the soil) is carried through the steps of the climatic water budget. The monthly overland runoff is assumed to reach the surface stream and pass the gaging station in the month that the overland flow occurs. Thus, this value is added directly to the calculated streamflow from water surplus in each month that overland flow occurs.

In the area of southern New Jersey where this trial was undertaken, overland flow is small, amounting to no more than 75 mm a year out of a precipitation total of 1150 mm. It occurs in only three or four months of the year generally. Table 4-7 includes the values of computed and measured monthly runoff for a three-year period, 1950 to 1952. The measured values are obtained from records from three small, gaged basins averaged together to eliminate possible spurious results from odd distributions of precipitation, cropping practices, or gaging problems in any one of the small basins. Precipitation values were based on the average of values from a special dense network of 24 raingages in area of 1370 km^2. The three small basins whose combined areas totaled only 390 km^2 were located within this area.

Agreement between measured and computed monthly runoff is quite close and the values for total measured and computed runoff for each year and for the whole three-year period are almost identical. Figure 4-2 is a plot of the actual monthly measured and computed values showing the slope of the regression line. Using the regression equation for other prediction purposes would seem justified.

Modeling Storage-Discharge Processes for the Deschutes River, Oregon

Despite the difficulties often encountered in trying to approximate monthly runoff by means of a climatic water budget model, such a model has been used to reproduce the unique uniform monthly flow from the Deschutes River in Oregon.[4] Figure 4-3 compares the stream hydrography of the Deschutes with those of the nearby John Day and Willamette rivers, which have about the same size and climatic environment. The differences in the hydrographs are readily apparent. The Deschutes has the reputation for having the most uniform flow of any river of its size in the United States.

From a study of the stream hydrographs, it was concluded that surface runoff contributed insignificantly to the overall discharge. However, the very constant flows during drought periods suggested well-maintained groundwater discharge, whereas the slightly higher flows from January to June suggested a

Table 4-7

Comparison of Measured and Computed Streamflow, Southern New Jersey, 1950-1952

(All values in mm)

	Computed Runoff		Total Computed Streamflow	Measured Streamflow (Average of 3 basins)
	Throughflow	*Direct Overland Flow*		
1950				
J	29	0	29	27
F	41	0	41	41
M	56	0	56	48
A	44	0	44	34
M	38	0	38	37
J	28	0	28	24
J	21	6	27	28
A	16	0	16	24
S	23	25	48	42
O	17	0	17	24
N	30	38	68	55
D	39	0	39	47
Year	382	69	451	431
1951				
J	44	0	44	42
F	57	3	60	54
M	64	0	64	54
A	53	3	56	58
M	46	0	46	41
J	35	0	35	29
J	26	0	26	34
A	20	0	20	22
S	15	0	15	16
O	11	6	17	23
N	36	19	55	47
D	56	32	88	79
Year	463	63	526	499
1952				
J	74	0	74	74
F	68	0	68	67
M	81	3	84	84
A	81	9	90	72
M	67	0	67	65
J	51	0	51	54
J	38	0	38	37
A	28	32	60	71
S	21	0	21	34
O	16	0	16	25
N	25	19	44	47
D	38	0	38	57
Year	588	63	651	687
		Three-year total	1628	1617

Source: J.R. Mather, "Estimation of areal average precipitation using different network densities and averaging techniques," *Publications in Climatology*, Laboratory of Climatology, vol. 28, no. 2 (1975).

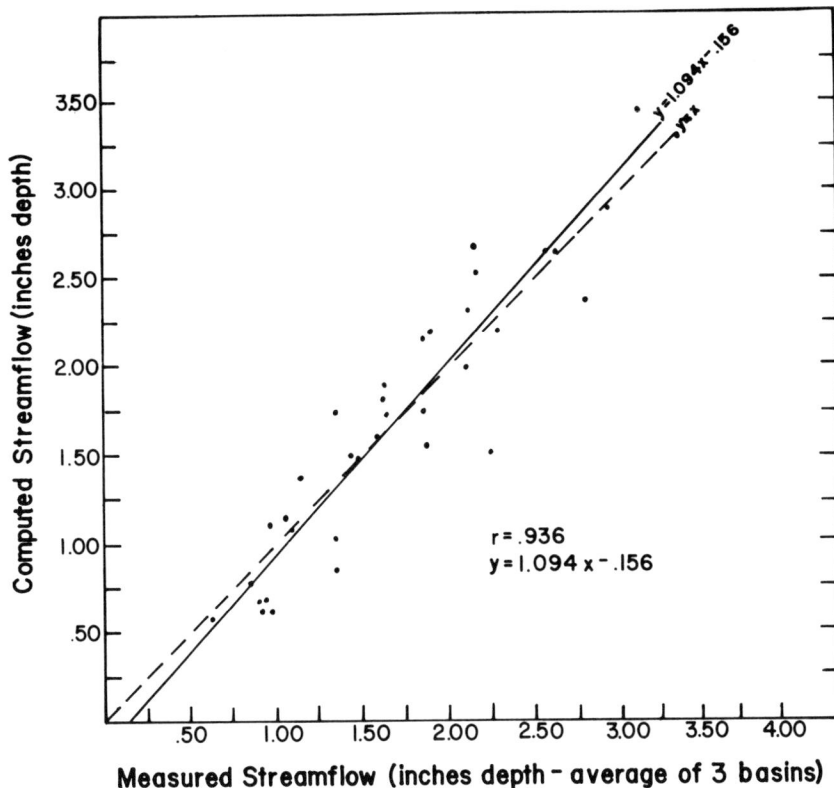

Source: J.R. Mather, "Estimation of areal average precipitation, using different network densities and averaging techniques," *Publications in Climatology,* Laboratory of Climatology, vol. 28, no. 2 (1975).

Figure 4-2. Comparison of Monthly Computed and Measured Streamflow, Southern New Jersey, 1950-1952

transient pulse of water flowing to the stream from perched water tables that drained rather rapidly. A flow-duration curve for the Deschutes River showed that a discharge of 0.4 cubic feet per second occurred more than 80 percent of the time. Discharges above this amount were assumed to come from transient storage resulting from perched water tables. The rather complex basaltic geologic formations in the Deschutes River basin could be responsible for the presence of two or three separate water tables while cracks and fissures could provide passages for water transfers through highly impermeable rock layers.

Modeling the storage-discharge process in the Deschutes River requires that the various steps be joined in series. Soil moisture recharge and storage is first accomplished, followed by a recharge to transient storage (perched water table) before any input to perennial, groundwater storage can occur. A residence time of four months for the water in transient storage was estimated on the basis of

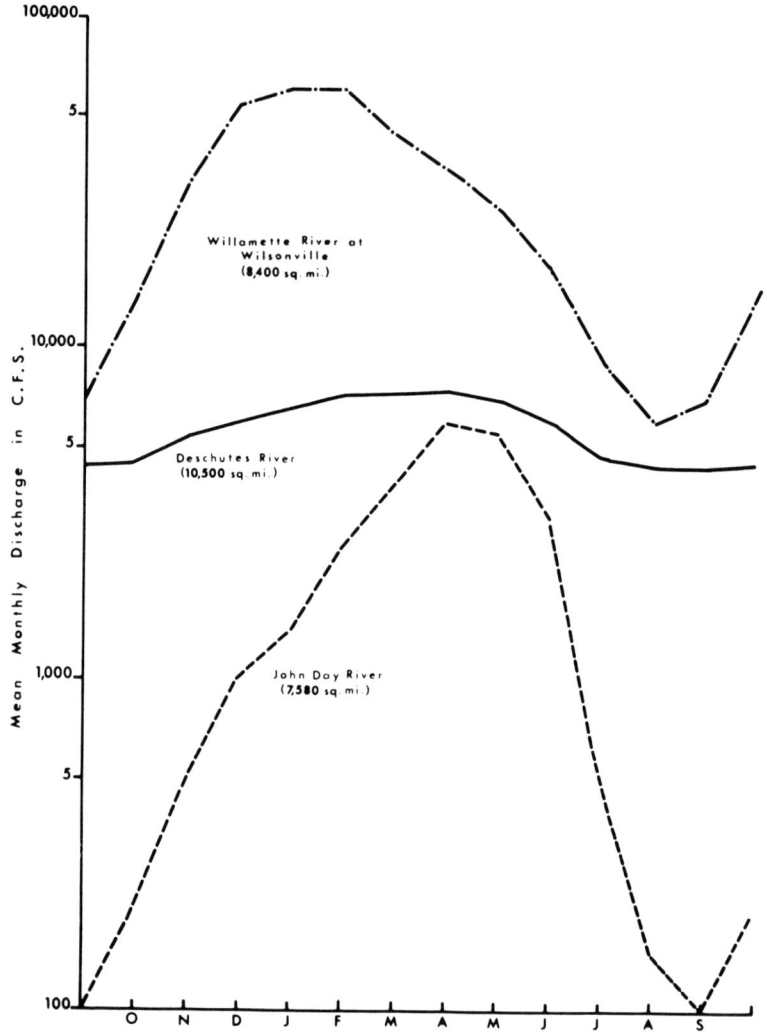

Source: M.L. Shelton, "Simulating uniform streamflow by water budget analysis," *Publications in Climatology,* Laboratory of Climatology, vol. 27, no. 2 (1974).

Figure 4-3. Discharge Hydrographs of the Deschutes, John Day, and Willamette Rivers

input-output studies. An estimate of twenty months as the residence time for water in the perennial storage was obtained by using an available volume routing procedure.[5] To make water budget modeling simpler, twenty subbasins of the main Deschutes River were identified and considered separately. It was found that discharges from the tributary basins could not be approximated with any degree of precision if it is assumed that all the input to the subbasin has to appear ultimately as discharge from that particular subbasin. Rather, some significant subsurface interbasin transfers must be postulated to account for the very large differences found between measured and computed values of streamflow in the subbasins.

To compute the monthly discharge from the Deschutes River, it was first necessary to evaluate the climatic water budget to obtain the information on water surplus that could be allocated to either transient or perennial storage. Data for the water year 1954 were used in the test although it was recognized that some errors would be introduced because of the significant water withdrawals for irrigation occurring from the basin at that time.

Water surplus was added to transient storage up to its capacity and only then made available to recharge perennial storage. The proportion of the flow in the Deschutes coming from transient storage was estimated on the basis of hydrograph analysis. Multiplying subbasin transient discharge by the area of the basin provided a weighted discharge value and the summation of these values divided by the area of the entire Deschutes basin gave a value for the flow contribution from transient storage for the whole basin (table 4-8).

Because of the long retention time in perennial storage, inputs to perennial

Table 4-8
Estimated Monthly Contributions from Transient and Perennial Storage to the Deschutes River, Oregon, as Compared with Measured Flow, 1954 Water Year

	Transient Storage Component (mm)	Perennial Storage Component (mm)	Estimated Streamflow (mm)	Measured Streamflow (mm)
October	2	10	12	13
November	4	10	14	16
December	6	11	17	22
January	6	13	19	23
February	8	14	22	25
March	8	15	23	24
April	8	15	23	21
May	7	16	23	19
June	6	15	21	17
July	5	14	19	14
August	4	14	18	14
September	3	13	16	13
Year	67	160	227	221

Source: M.L. Shelton, "Simulating uniform streamflow by water budget analysis," *Publications in Climatology*, Laboratory of Climatology, vol. 27, no. 2 (1974).

storage had to be determined for two years prior to the water year of interest. Monthly inputs were routed through the system using the twenty-month retention time for each subbasin. The same weighting and summation procedures as used for the transient storage were applied to the contributions from perennial storage to obtain monthly values of discharge from groundwater storage to the Deschutes River (table 4-8). Summation of the two discharges provided the estimated streamflow for the whole river for the year for comparison with the measured values.

Not only is annual agreement between computed and measured runoff quite good (within 0.23 inches or 3 percent) but more importantly, the monthly comparisons are reasonable, especially when it is remembered that the Deschutes River is quite unique in its own right because of its highly uniform flow. Largest differences between measured and computed runoff are found in July and August where differences of 33 and 28 percent respectively occur. In all months from May to September, computed runoff is at least 20 percent greater than measured runoff. These are the very months, of course, in which maximum diversions for irrigation would be expected. Measured streamflow should be reduced below the computed values because irrigation losses were not considered in the computational process.

Though a modification of the standard climatic water budget model to permit multiple storages and discharges has provided fair agreement between calculated and measured monthly discharge in a very unique basin, the problem still exists that monthly and annual flows from subbasins of the Deschutes were not at all well determined by the water budget model. Preliminary study of the subbasins suggests the possibility of lateral perennial storage linkages so that some of the excess computed output from one basin may contribute input to the discharge from another subbasin. Significant interbasin transfers do seem to occur. The disagreements between measured and computed flows from the subbasins might be considered not so much as failures in the model but more as evidence of the size of the groundwater linkages and as suggestions for further geomorphic and hydrologic investigations.[6]

Evapotranspiration Climatonomy

Over the past few years numerical models of evapotranspiration climatonomy have been developed that can provide reasonable approximations of different hydrologic factors such as runoff, evapotranspiration, and soil moisture storage.[7] Such models require certain inputs and involve assumptions about processes and naturally occurring feedbacks to process or input, as well as some assumptions concerning albedo and the time lag of soil moisture storage and moisture removal (figure 4-4). The components of the system are (1) the inputs of precipitation and energy (absorbed short-wave radiation) per unit of time;

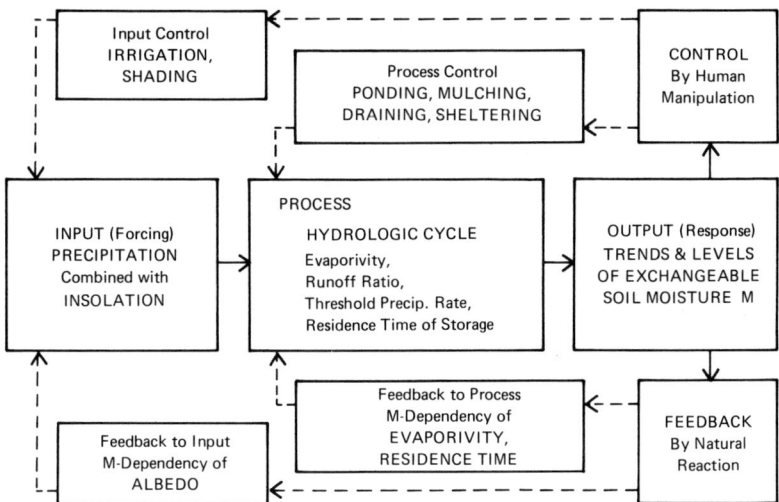

Source: H. Lettau and M.W. Baradas, "Evapotranspiration climatonomy II: Refinement of parameterization, exemplified by application to the Mabacan River watershed," *Monthly Weather Review,* vol. 101, no. 8 (1973).

Figure 4-4. Scheme of Evapotranspiration Climatonomy. The middle section shows the connection between forcing inputs of mass and energy, process and its parameterization, and the output or responses. Other boxes illustrate possible control by human activity or feedback by natural reactions which can influence either process or input.

(2) the output or response to the forcing functions of precipitation and radiation in the form of a time series of soil moisture storage; and (3) the process, involving values of runoff and evaporation. Percolation contributes to runoff and is included within that term. The factors of process, when combined with the input and output terms, provide the complete hydrologic balance:

$$P - N - E = \frac{\Delta m}{\Delta t}$$

where P is precipitation, N is runoff, E is evapotranspiration, and $\Delta m / \Delta t$ is the change in soil moisture storage over some time period. Results are usually expressed in depth/month. The model permits including such various human controls as irrigation, mulching practices, modification of cropping patterns, wind protection activities, and shading.

Clearly, evapotranspiration and runoff in any month depend not only on the immediate precipitation but also on precipitation that has fallen and been stored in previous time periods. In developing the model, therefore, it is necessary to define for a particular watershed a number of physical parameters of the immediate process as well as of the delayed process involving such things as a threshold value of the immediate precipitation needed to produce runoff in the time period under consideration (P^*), the fraction of the excess precipitation over this threshold value that will actually be involved in runoff in that time period (n^*), the fraction of the immediate precipitation that is lost as evapotranspiration and does not enter into change in soil moisture storage (immediate evaporivity, e^*), the characteristic time scale of delayed soil moisture withdrawal (t^*–a measure of the residence time of water involved in the delay process), the fraction of the evapotranspiration coming from stored soil moisture (delayed evaporivity, e^{**}), and the threshold value of exchangeable soil moisture (m^*).[8]

Naturally occurring feedbacks to input or process include the dependence of atmospheric convective instability and surface albedo on soil moisture content. With snow, below-freezing temperature, and frozen soils, there can also be significant variations in soil moisture residence time as well as in the value of immediate or overland runoff and evapotranspiration.

To apply the model to a practical example, it is first necessary to "calibrate" the particular watershed under investigation by obtaining values for the various process parameters mentioned above ($P^*, n^*, e^*, e^{**}, m^*$). Using the small (46 km^2) Mabacan River basin located about 65 km southeast of Manila in the Philippines, which has a tropical, humid climate, the following five immediate and delayed process constants were determined:[9]

n^* = 0.15

P^* = 120 mm/month

e^* = 0.25

e^{**} = 0.088

m^* = 190 mm

The change in albedo, the delay time (residence time), and the ratio of delayed evapotranspiration to the absorbed global radiation were also expressed as functions of soil moisture content. Substituting these constant and time-dependent parameters into the computer model of evapotranspiration climatonomy, monthly values of computed runoff were obtained for a three-year period and compared with gaged values. The results (table 4-9) cover a dry year (1965), a wet year (1966), and a fairly normal year (1967). The table includes monthly values of the input data on precipitation (P) and global radiation (G), exchangeable soil moisture (m), evapotranspiration (E), and both calculated and observed runoff (N).

Though the correlation coefficient between observed and computed runoff

Table 4-9

Evapoclimatonomy of the Mabacan River Watershed—Model Simulation for All Months of Three Consecutive Years (1965 relatively dry, 1966 relatively wet, and 1967 with near-normal P)

Year	Month	P	G	m	E	N	N_{obs}
1965	J	34	173	580	34	105	116
	F	10	228	480	28	77	82
	M	20	262	392	25	76	88
	A	80	302	336	42	74	91
	M	134	248	324	47	80	84
	J	91	238	313	34	82	89
	J	238	202	349	60	98	88
	A	107	238	375	45	78	81
	S	123	222	370	44	76	84
	O	84	211	358	32	77	73
	N	174	176	372	44	87	47
	D	122	160	396	34	80	71
1966	J	36	200	364	21	79	63
	F	24	245	299	16	74	51
	M	22	284	236	11	72	59
	A	4	331	174	1	64	56
	M	442	219	278	98	121	90
	J	194	258	396	72	84	66
	J	168	219	429	59	81	70
	A	199	238	464	76	82	71
	S	202	191	506	66	97	100
	O	140	181	523	52	91	99
	N	410	174	606	106	156	126
	D	423	150	742	102	203	233
1967	J	174	149	760	64	174	110
	F	12	201	652	40	111	79
	M	11	241	532	35	79	76
	A	17	292	439	33	68	60
	M	21	285	358	24	75	60
	J	233	232	363	70	96	82
	J	126	220	394	47	78	71
	A	297	162	463	67	106	94
	S	268	213	554	92	115	107
	O	178	198	582	71	108	74
	N	428	152	666	99	184	365
	D	37	160	656	70	100	84

Source: H. Lettau and M.W. Baradas, "Evapotranspiration climatonomy. II. Refinement of parameterization, exemplified by application to the Mabacan River watershed," *Monthly Weather Review*, vol. 101, no. 8 (1973).

for these three years is reasonable, $r = .785$ (regression equation $y = 0.46x + 53.9$) it can be seen that computed runoff may, at times, differ appreciably from the observed values. Extreme differences were found in January and November 1967 with departures of -64 and $+181$ mm, respectively. However, the agreement seems quite good in view of the fact that precipitation and radiation data were available at only one lowland station near, but not within, the basin and that part of the basin is as high as 700 m above the observing station. Orographic influences could easily be the cause of many of the discrepancies found. Certainly, the model produces results that are significant enough to justify further testing and refinement.

A Two-Layer Model for Streamflow from Small Basins

A simple, self-calibrating four-parameter model to compute monthly runoff from small watersheds has been developed and tested.[10] The model recognizes that the moisture-holding and moisture-transmitting characteristics of the soil as well as rainfall intensity are prime factors regulating runoff from small basins. The soil is separated into two layers in terms of moisture-availability characteristics, an upper layer in which moisture is easily available for evapotranspiration and a lower layer from which evapotranspiration is less probable. The water holding capacity of the upper layer is taken to be 1 inch. If both layers are at field capacity, it is assumed that no infiltration into the soil occurs, whereas if one or both of the soil layers is holding less than its capacity, the infiltration rate will be determined by the rate of precipitation or the maximum possible infiltration rate, whichever is smaller.

Daily evapotranspiration loss will equal the potential loss whenever the upper soil layer has sufficient moisture in storage to meet this demand; when this upper layer has no water, the rate of evapotranspiration is determined by the ratio of actual moisture content in the lower layer to total moisture content in that layer. Whenever there is precipitation, the calculated value of evapotranspiration is reduced by half because of cloudy conditions and low solar radiation. No surface runoff will occur if the precipitation is less than the infiltration capacity of the soil, whereas runoff will equal precipitation minus the infiltration rate if the precipitation rate exceeds the infiltration rate. Deep seepage of water to the water table is assumed to equal the maximum possible seepage rate multiplied by the ratio of available water in the lower layer to maximum water-holding capacity of that layer. A proportion of deep seepage is allowed to return as surface flow within the watershed. That value must be estimated along with factors of maximum infiltration rate, maximum deep seepage rate, and water-holding capacity of the lower soil layer.

Short-period precipitation intensity is a necessary input to the model. Because this figure is seldom known, except where recording raingages are

57

available, the daily value of precipitation has been divided into 24-hourly values[11] and then further subdivided into 6-minute intervals.[12] This procedure produces a wavy rainfall distribution through the day so that timing of runoff on a daily basis is not possible but the model is designed to predict only monthly runoff. Without using computers, distributing daily rainfall into 6-minute segments is very time-consuming.

The model self-calibrates by selecting values of the four estimated parameters—maximum infiltration (f max), maximum deep seepage (S max), moisture holding content of the lower layer (C), and fraction of deep seepage that appears as stream runoff (F)—that will minimize the sum of squares of deviations between observed and simulated monthly runoff volumes. Of course, values of the estimated parameters are a function of the particular year used in estimating the parameters.

The model was tested against runoff from seven small watersheds, three near Clemson, South Carolina, and four in Kentucky. Characteristics of the seven basins are given in table 4-10. Despite the differences in the basins, using different assumptions concerning hourly rainfall had very little influence on the final monthly runoff totals. The results from the seven watersheds are briefly summarized in table 4-11, which gives not only the values of measured and computed runoff but also the correlation coefficients between measured and computed runoff and the optimized values of f_{max}, S_{max}, C, and F for each

Table 4-10
Characteristics of South Carolina and Kentucky Basins Used to Test Two-Layer Model

Basin	Location	Area (acres)	Average Land Slope (%)	Stream Length (feet)	Predominant Land Use
Clemson 1	Near Clemson, S.C.	33	11	2000	74% pine, 22% pasture
Clemson 2	Near Clemson, S.C.	561	12.6	9350	60% woods, 30% scrub
Clemson 3	Near Clemson, S.C.	28	8	1600	75% grass, 25% pine & scrub
Cave Creek	North-Central Ky.	1619	7	13730	approx. 100% pasture
Cane Branch	Southeast Ky.	429	21	5755	75% forested, 25% strip mined
Helton Branch	Southeast Ky.	544	23	6810	98% forested
Perry Creek	Southwest Ky.	1101	5	9980	90% agricultural, 10% wooded

Source: C.T. Haan, "A water yield model for small watersheds," *Water Resources Research*, vol. 8, no. 1, Table 4, pp. 63, 66 (1972). Copyrighted by American Geophysical Union.

Table 4-11
Relation Between Measured and Computed Runoff and Optimum Values of Estimated Parameters for Seven Selected Basins in South Carolina and Kentucky

Watershed	Years Used for Optimum	Optimum Values				No. of Years Simulated	Correlation Coefficient	Slope	Observed Mean V_t	Simulated Mean V_t
		Maximum Infiltration Rate	Maximum Deep Seepage	Moist. Hold. Capacity in Lower Layers	Fraction Deep Seepage That Goes to RO					
Clemson 1	1964, 1965	0.70	0.210	2.95	0.20	6	0.97	1.04	9.75	10.63
Clemson 2	1964, 1965	0.30	0.185	3.75	0.40	6	0.95	1.02	17.42	17.53
Clemson 3	1965, 1966	0.90	0.125	2.75	0.00	5	0.95	1.02	7.35	7.35
Cave Creek	1953, 1961, 1962	0.95	0.200	5.00	0.10	16	0.93	1.04	14.63	15.14
Perry Creek	1953, 1959, 1960	0.95	0.065	4.75	0.00	13	0.95	1.04	13.04	12.85
Cane Branch	1957, 1958	3.20	0.030	10.00	0.35	10	0.96	1.02	17.25	18.11
Helton Branch	1957, 1958	2.80	0.050	9.40	0.35	12	0.94	1.05	17.48	16.93
Perry Creek[a]	1953, 1954	1.25	0.085	6.05	0.10	13	0.94	0.89	13.04	10.97[a]

Source: C.T. Haan, "A water yield model for small watersheds," *Water Resources Research*, vol. 8, no. 1, Table 6, p. 67 (1972). Copyrighted by American Geophysical Union.

[a]Shown to illustrate the inadequacy of the correlation coefficient as a measure for evaluating the model.

basin. A graph of the seasonal course of monthly computed and measured runoff is given in figure 4-5. Though it is clear that the model can be improved, many of the improvements would eliminate its major advantage—its simplicity and ease of application.

Water Budget of the Nile Basin

Runoff to the Nile River comes from two principal sources: from the Ethiopian highlands, and from the Lake Victoria plateau area and northward along the highland border of Sudan. Drainage from this latter, more equatorial area, is quite chaotic because of the nature of the terrain. The best organized river systems draining this area include the Victoria Nile, the Albert Nile, and the Bahr el Jebel. This last stream is greatly altered in the Sudd swamps and is artificially connected with a competing stream, the Bahr el Zeraf. Other streams, mainly the Bahr el Ghazel, Jur, Lol, and Maridi drain from other portions of the equatorial highlands into the Sudd swamps where all lose appreciable water as well as most of their identities. Below the Sudd swamps, the Sobat joins to form the White Nile near Malakal. The Sobat seems to receive most of its water from the Ethiopian highlands but some may come from the equatorial highlands as well.

The Blue Nile is the major drainage system from the Ethiopian highlands although the Atbara also contributes significantly to the Nile flow. Figure 4-6 locates most of these major tributaries to the Nile River and provides measured values of the average annual flow at different places along the river.[13] There are no stream measurements of the total water originating in the equatorial

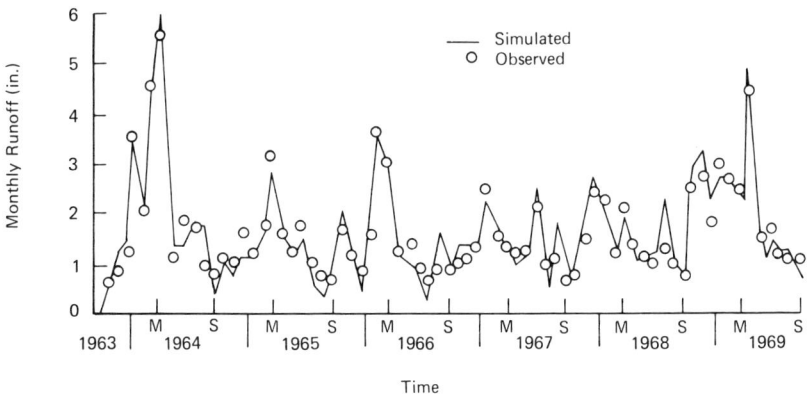

Source: C.T. Haan, "A water yield model for small watersheds," *Water Resources Research*, vol. 8, no. 1 (1972):68. Copyrighted by the American Geophysical Union.

Figure 4-5. Results of Simulation of Mean Stream Runoff on Clemson 2 Watershed

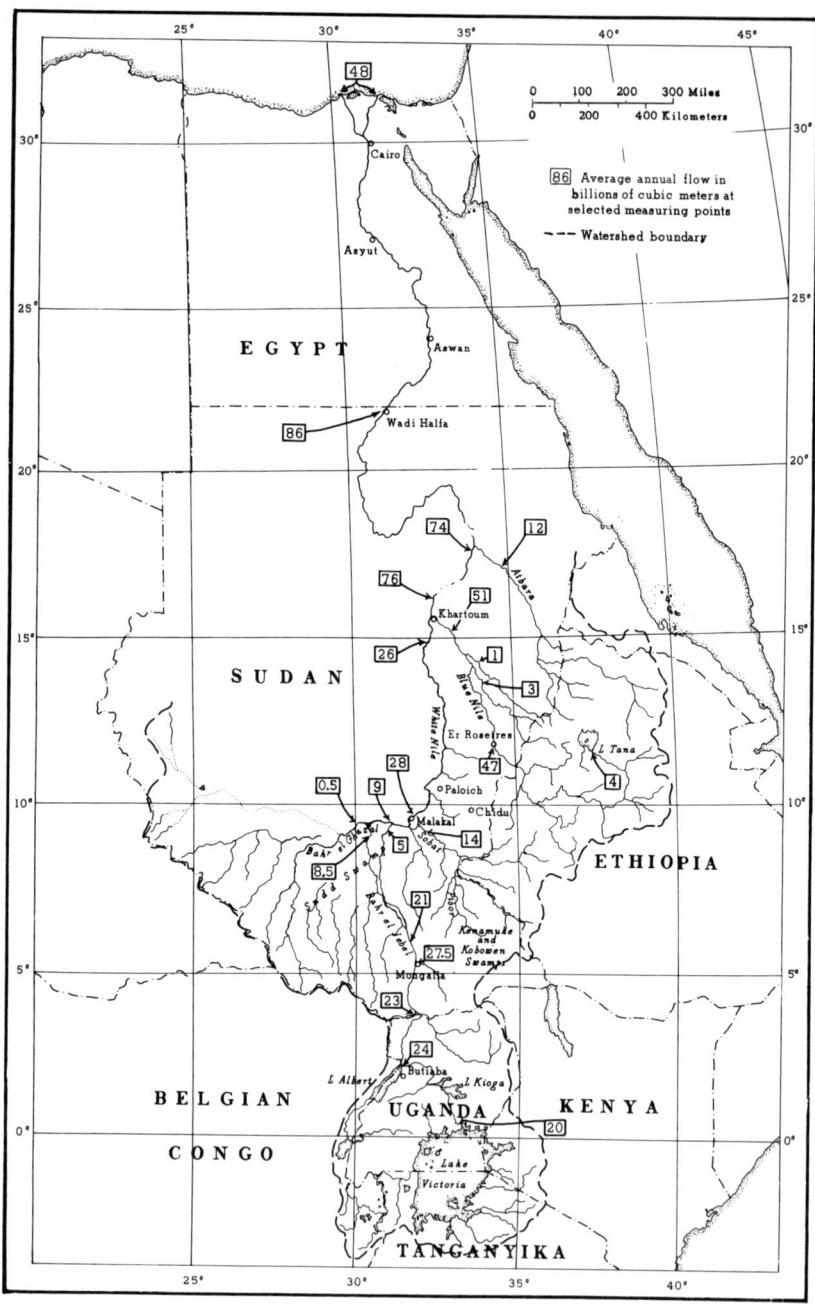

Source: D.B. Carter, "The water balance of the Mediterranean and Black Seas," *Publications in Climatology,* Laboratory of Climatology, vol. 9, no. 3, 1956. Discharge data from H.E. Hurst, "The Sudd region of the Nile," *Journal of the Royal Society of Arts,* vol. 81 (1933).

Figure 4-6. Average Annual Discharges of the Nile River

highlands. Even at the most upstream gaging stations, large evapotranspiration losses have already occurred. By the time the Nile reaches Malakal all the streams draining the equatorial highlands have finally come together. The measured flow of 28 billion cubic meters at Malakal is made up of 14 billion cubic meters from the Sobat and an equal amount from the equatorial highlands. This flow is extremely small from such a large drainage area because of the large evapotranspiration losses encountered by all tributaries in passing the Sudd swamps. The flow from the Ethiopian highlands is not subject to such severe attrition because of the presence of fewer swamps.

It is possible to use a climatic water budgeting approach to estimate the water yields from the two highland source regions of the Nile as well as the evapotranspiration losses in transit.[14] Computed monthly runoff (table 4-12) from the equatorial highlands is much less variable than from the Ethiopian highlands although total annual runoff is much greater from the Ethiopian highlands. Note that almost one-third of the entire water yield of the Nile basin comes from these highlands in just August and September. A tremendous attrition of water occurs in the Nile system; of this total 154 billion cubic meters, only 48 billion cubic meters reaches the mouth of the Nile according to measurements (figure 4-6).

Water budgets at representative stations in the Nile basin show that moisture deficits increase northward from the headwaters regions. But loss of water from the Nile depends not only on increasing water deficits but also on the excessive evapotranspiration from swamps and other areas of standing water, irrigation demands, and losses to phreatophyte vegetation. The major losses have been estimated on the basis of actual areas of water surface, computed potential evapotranspiration, and tabulated areas under irrigation as follows:[15]

		(billions m^3)
1.	Lakes, rivers, and swamps in the area above Mongalla	8.7
2.	Sudd swamp	≈ 40
3.	Kenamuke and Kabowen swamps	1.1
4.	Pibor swamps (area near Chidu, Paloich, Er Roseires)	≈ 11
5.	Irrigated area, Gezira, Sudan	3.4
6.	Riparian losses, Malakal to Aswan	4.0
7.	Irrigated area, Egypt	32.8
	Total Nile basin losses	101.0

If the losses through evapotranspiration and irrigation are subtracted from the total water input or surplus from the two headwaters regions (154 billion m^3) a difference of 53 billion cubic meters is found. In view of the uncertainties in the data and the estimations made, this value is in fairly close agreement with the measured total at the mouth of the Nile of 48 billion m^3.

Table 4-12

Average Monthly and Annual Runoff of the Nile Basin

(Billions of cubic meters)

	J	F	M	A	M	J	J	A	S	O	N	D	Year
Equatorial highlands	1.4	1.5	1.9	5.0	6.5	3.1	3.6	9.0	13.1	9.1	5.2	2.9	62.3
Ethiopian highlands	1.5	1.2	0.7	0.4	0.3	0.3	7.6	28.1	26.3	13.8	7.6	3.9	91.7

Source: D.B. Carter, "The water balance of the Mediterranean and Black Seas," *Publications in Climatology*, Laboratory of Climatology, vol. 9, no. 3 (1956).

The major unknowns occur in the Sudd swamp. Though it can be assumed that water will be lost at the potential rate throughout the year, the exact size of the swamp area is difficult to determine. The area fluctuates markedly from season to season as well as from year to year being possibly as large as 100,000 km^2 in the wet season and only a fifth of that size in the dry season. Because of the presence of islands and seasonal fluctuations in swamp size, effective swamp area may be 70 to 80 percent of its total area. Multiplying the effective area by a representative water deficiency for the area suggested a value of water loss of somewhere between 35 and 50 billion m^3 in the Sudd swamp area.[16]

Loss of water to irrigation in Egypt of just over 32 billion m^3 was based on a pre-Aswan High Dam estimate of 26,000 km^2 of irrigated area. However, efficiency of irrigation is unknown and some of this water may find its way back into the river as subsurface flow so again this figure may be in error by more than ±10 percent.

Certain checks on the data are possible as a result of the few measured values that do exist in the basin. For example, losses upstream from Malakal are estimated at 48.7 billion m^3 (items 1, 2 in previous list). The flow at Malakal is 28 billion m^3 of which 14 billion m^3 comes from the Sobat. Thus, 14 billion m^3 comes from the equatorial highlands. Computed runoff from that area of 62.3 billion m^3 less the evapotranspiration losses of 48.7 billion m^3 results in a river flow at Malakal from the equatorial highlands of 13.6 billion m^3. The estimates of evapotranspiration losses in the swamps seem reasonable. Measured flow in the Sobat, Blue Nile, and Atbara from the Ethiopian highlands totals 77 billion m^3 just before these rivers enter the Nile. Losses in the total water volume originating in the Ethiopian highlands (91.7 billion m^3) have been estimated at 15.5 billion m^3 (items 3-5 in previous list). The difference in these two values, 76.6 billion m^3, agrees well with the total measured runoff from the Sobat, Blue Nile, and Atbara rivers. Thus, the water budget technique provides rather good estimates of what has happened to the precipitation over this part of Africa. The method, which is independent of stream measurements, provides reliable data for an area with rather limited data of both climatic and hydrologic factors.

Possible Effects of Canalization in the Sudd Region

A current water development scheme in the Sudd area has led to sharp arguments between developers and conservationists. The scheme is not new; it was briefly described in a 1933 report as something that had been long talked about although not technologically feasible at that time.[17] The scheme now being proposed is to construct a 170-mile canal from just above Malakal to the Bahr el Gebel at Jonglei, located some miles downstream of Mongalla where the river enters the Sudd Swamps. The canal would be designed to carry about a quarter of the total inflow of the White Nile, estimated to be about 27.5 billion cubic meters at Mongalla and 21 billion cubic meters at Bor downstream from Mongalla (figure 4-6) but still some distance upstream from Jonglei. Thus, the canal should prevent the loss by seepage and evapotranspiration of some 4 to 5 billion cubic meters of water annually and make this additional water volume available for irrigation use in upper Sudan and Egypt.

Conservationists argue that this canalization of the eastern portion of the Sudd swamp area will disrupt rainfall patterns over the Sudan as well as over central Africa and lead to a rapid increase in desertification. The argument hinges on whether the amount of water that would not be evaporated or transpired from the Sudd area as a result of the canal scheme is significant in the whole pattern of precipitation over the area. Clearly, it is a matter of considerable significance to a large region and a question that cannot be answered with assurance without further detailed study. However, certain suggestions can be gained from our knowledge of the operation of the hydrologic cycle as well as from the previously described water budget study.

Studies in both the central United States and western Russia have shown that about 10 to 11 percent of local pcipitation comes from local land-base evapotranspiration.[18] Whether such a figure might also be valid for central Africa is not known. At the same time, the figure of some 4 to 5 billion cubic meters of water that could not go through the swamp because of the proposed canal is only about 10 percent of the estimated water loss from the whole swamp based on water budget computations. Thus, one might wonder about the argument of the conservationists that the removal of this relatively small amount of evapotranspiration from the local hydrologic cycle would seriously modify the climate of the area. It might be argued that the lost evapotranspiration contributes only in a very small way to the total moisture for precipitation in the central African region and, of course, the lost evapotranspiration from the Sudd Swamps will be put back into the air in northern Sudan or in Egypt as a result of increased use of the water for supplemental irrigation and as evaporation from the reservoir behind the Aswan High Dam. This new reservoir, which will extend from Aswan at the first cataract on the Nile to Delgo near the third cataract at about 20°N latitude, will store about three times the amount of water now stored in Lake Mead behind Hoover Dam.

The conservationists might seriously argue that because the canal will change the swamp locally it will also modify vegetation, soils, and animal life locally. The canal will certainly lead to a drying of a portion of the swamp. Water budget considerations might suggest, however, that the decrease in evapotranspiration in the whole area will be small in relation to the total amount of moisture in the air and that little change in local precipitation should result. Just as increasing local evapotranspiration by creating reservoirs, lakes, and forested tracts will not significantly increase local precipitation, so small reductions in local evapotranspiration losses should not significantly decrease local precipitation.

Determining Inflow-Outflow Relations of Lake Maracaibo, Venezuela

Another example of the use of a water budget technique in hydrology is the determination of the inflow or outflow of water to Lake Maracaibo in Venezuela, a large coastal lake linked to the ocean by a narrow channel.[19] Few stream gaging stations exist in the area. The water budget procedure provides a way by which stream runoff can be evaluated from available climatic data. The sum of precipitation (P) onto the lake surface plus runoff (RO) from surrounding land areas less evaporation (E) from the lake surface should provide quantitatively an estimate of net inflow or outflow of water to the lake needed to maintain a constant lake level. During the 1946-1953 period, total precipitation plus land runoff exceeded evaporation from the lake in most months so that there was a net outflow to the ocean although a few times, evaporation losses exceeded gains by precipitation and runoff resulting in the need for salt water inflow to maintain the level of the lake. Inflow from the Gulf of Venezuela to Lake Maracaibo occurred at least once every year from 1946 to 1953 except in the very moist 1950. Net monthly outflow-inflow of the Maracaibo Basin for the 1946-1953 period is illustrated in figure 4-7.

Lake Levels and Net Basin Supply

To determine the so-called net basin supply or the water contributed to the Great Lakes system by a particular lake basin, a climatic water budget approach has been used with some success.[20] The net basin supply (NBS) can be evaluated simply from the relation

$$NBS = R + P - E$$

where R is runoff from the basin around the lake; P is over-water precipitation; and E is evaporation from the lake surface.

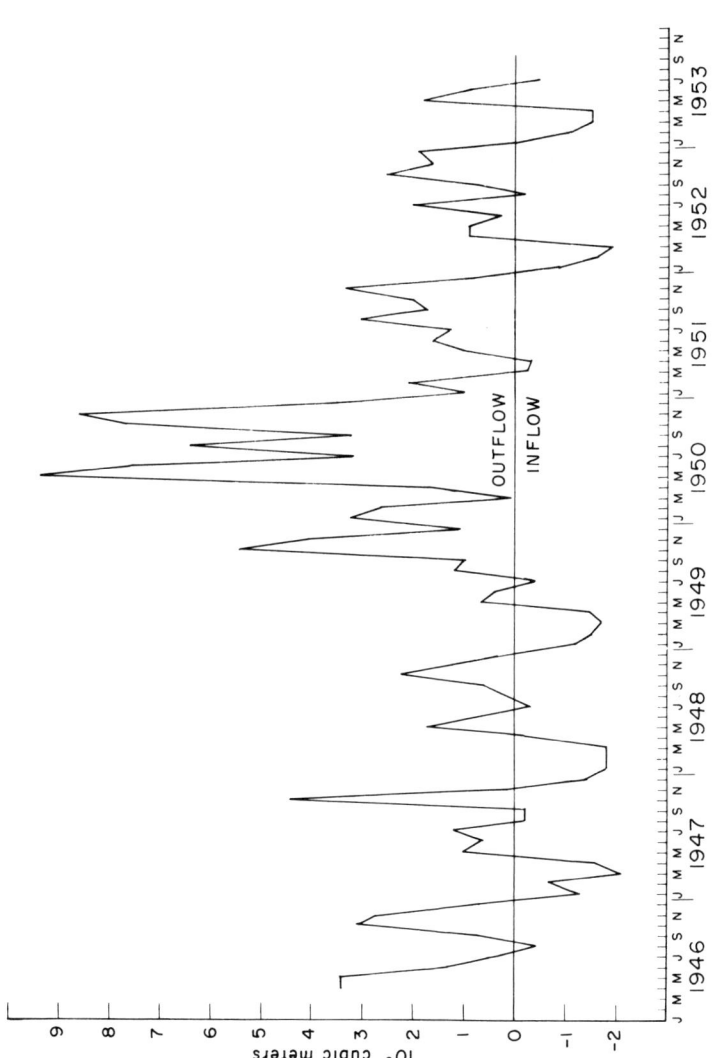

Source: D.B. Carter, "The water balance of the Lake Maracaibo Basin during 1946-53," *Publications in Climatology*, Laboratory of Climatology, vol. 8, no. 3 (1955).

Figure 4-7. Net Outflow-Inflow of the Maracaibo Basin, 1946-1953

The water budget can be used to determine R, and P can be determined from isolines drawn on the basis of data from perimeter stations. E can be evaluated as the only unknown in the following water budget equation for the lake

$$E = I - O \pm \Delta S + P + R$$

where I is water inflow from upper lakes; O is water outflow to lower lakes; and ΔS is change in storage in the lake.

A clear relation between the change in water level of Lake Erie and the net basin supply is revealed in figure 4-8. Inflow from lakes above is quite constant over the years so that the lake level is directly related to changes in net basin supply. During the 1959-1963 period, lake levels rose for the first three years and fell for the last two years with changes in the net basin supply.

The present chapter, while suggesting many applications of the water budget to hydrologic problems, has, by no means, exhausted all possible examples. Though a Thornthwaite-type climatic water budget approach has been stressed, more detailed or complex budget approaches are also possible. In selecting examples for discussion, budgets that could be evaluated from readily available data were used in order to make possible their wider applicability. Improvements in our current water budget models are needed but if these improvements also add factors that limit their general usefulness, each investigator must then determine the type of water budget approach to use depending on the nature of the results he wishes to achieve.

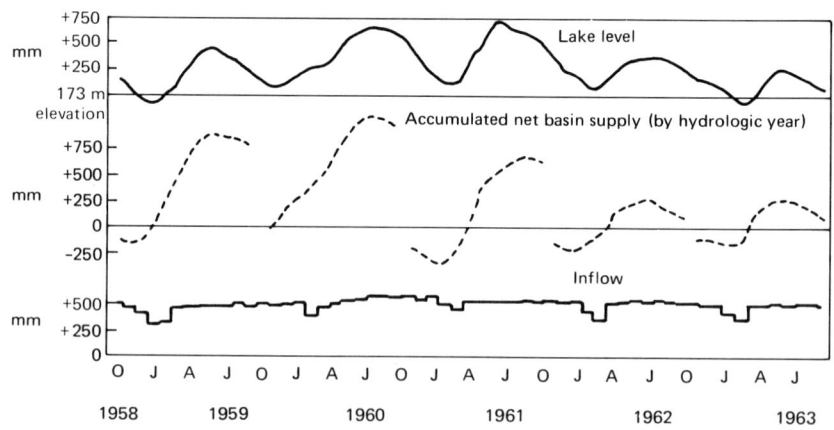

Source: M. Sanderson, "A climatic water balance of the Lake Erie basin, 1958-1963," *Publications in Climatology,* Laboratory of Climatology, vol. 19, no. 1 (1966).

Figure 4-8. Relation of Inflow, Net Basin Supply, and Lake Levels, Lake Erie Basin, 1958-1963

5 Agriculture

Farmers have long known that the various factors of the water budget influence their day-to-day operations. Crops need water to grow and if that water is not available naturally, recourse to irrigation must be considered. Water leaching through the soil dissolves and removes needed fertilizers so that some farmers regularly add fertilizer with the irrigation water. Floods or excessive amounts of water prevent the farmer from working his fields when he would like to and may even harm growing crops and reduce yields. Finally, water supplies for his crops, animals, and even for domestic uses often depend on groundwater storage and its fluctuations through time.

Determining Soil Moisture Content

A useful climatic model to determine soil moisture content was first suggested some three decades ago and developed over the following years.[1] The approach is to treat all precipitation in excess of current plant needs (positive values of $P-PE$) as soil moisture storage until the field capacity of the soil is reached. Precipitation in excess of current plant needs occurring when the soil moisture storage is full does not enter into the moisture budget but is lost by runoff and percolation. As long as some water remains in storage in the soil, it is removed at a rate dependent on the potential evapotranspiration multiplied by the ratio of actual soil moisture content to the moisture content at field capacity. Both horizontal subsurface and overland flow of intense precipitation are neglected. More recently, some investigators[2] have employed "effective" precipitation, which is defined as the precipitation that actually infiltrates the root zone of the soil, in water budget computations with improved results. The Soil Conservation Service method (described in chapter 4) can be used to determine overland runoff from daily rainfall values based on knowledge of soil and vegetation conditions in the area. Deducting the monthly total of such overland runoff from monthly precipitation provides the "effective" precipitation.

In the water budget computations (see table 2-2), the soil moisture storage at the end of the month is only one part of the value for total moisture detention found in the last line of the bookkeeping procedure. Actual moisture conditions in the soil at any time must be made up of more than just the capillary water held in the soil because gravitational water in the process of moving out of the soil and snow stored on the surface both represent a form of very temporary moisture storage.

67

68

The test of any model comes when it is compared to reality. Over the years, the Thornthwaite climatic water budget model has been used repeatedly to provide values of soil moisture storage that can be compared with actual measured values. For example, figures 5-1 and 5-2 show the results of a test of measured and computed soil moisture content at Coshocton, Ohio, for 1943 and 1944 using a soil profile that contained 290 mm of water at field capacity.[3] In the computations, it was assumed that 93 percent of available gravitational water was detained in the soil each day and that no percolation occurred on days when mean air temperature was below −1°C.

Considering the necessary assumptions and approximations, agreement between measured and computed soil moisture is quite satisfactory. Note that the discrepancy between measured and computed soil moisture at the end of 1943 was not adjusted but rather the values of soil moisture content determined then were carried over to begin 1944. Despite this, results for 1944 were quite close, the largest disagreements occurring during the winter period when temperatures were below freezing, and snow and high soil moisture contents all added to the problems of calculating soil moisture content.

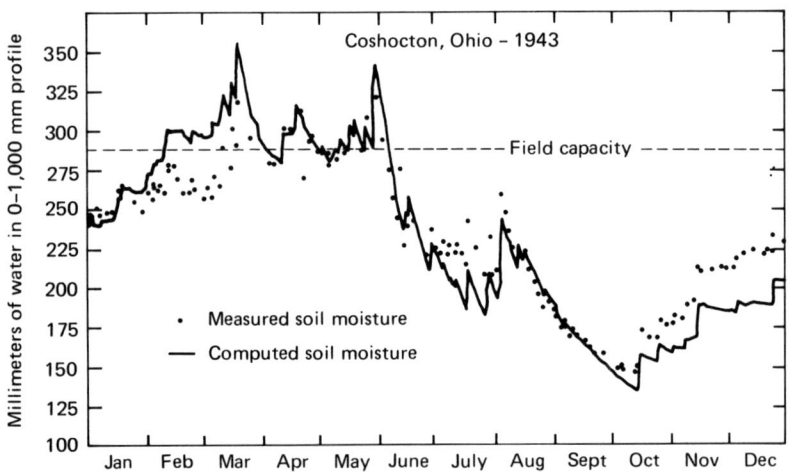

Source: C.W. Thornthwaite, "Estimating soil tractionability from climatic data," *Publications in Climatology,* Laboratory of Climatology, vol. 7, no. 3 (1954).

Figure 5-1. Comparison of Measured and Computed Soil Moisture Content at Coshocton, Ohio, 1943. Soil moisture in 0-1 m profile on watershed Y102; measured values obtained by Soil Conservation Service from soil samples and weighing lysimeter. Computed values from climatic data using water budget method.

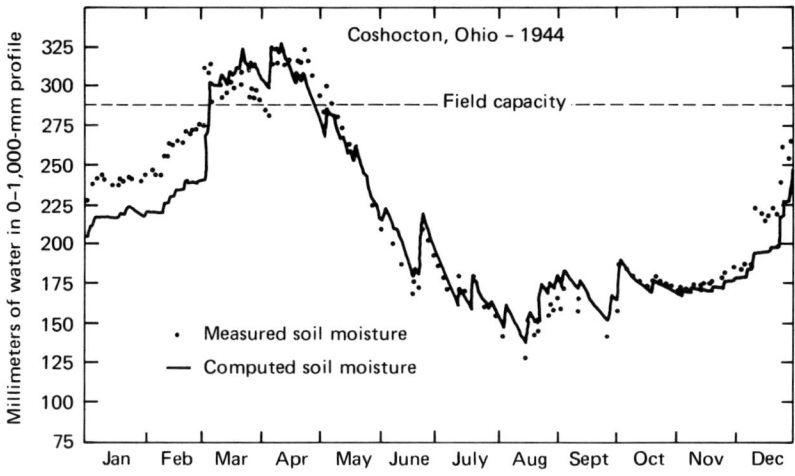

Source: C.W. Thornthwaite, "Estimating soil tractionability from climatic data," *Publications in Climatology*, Laboratory of Climatology, vol. 7, no. 3 (1954).

Figure 5-2. Comparison of Measured and Computed Soil Moisture Content at Coshocton, Ohio, 1944. (See figure 5-1 for legend information.)

Measured-Computed Soil Moisture in Sand and Clay Soils

A water budget technique has been used to compute soil moisture storage under pine and mixed oak forests in the coastal plains sands in southern New Jersey and under a natural stand of mixed hardwoods and pines on clay soil in the South Carolina piedmont.[4] In the first case, soil moisture data were available from gravimetric measurements taken weekly to a depth of 1.5 m. Available moisture storage in this depth was estimated to be 125 mm of water. Computed soil moisture withdrawals were obtained from the following assumptions: (1) with current soil moisture storage equal to or above 25 percent of total storage, actual evapotranspiration (soil moisture depletion) equaled computed potential evapotranspiration; (2) with soil moisture storage less than 25 percent of total storage, actual evapotranspiration (soil moisture depletion) equaled potential evapotranspiration times 0.5 (current soil moisture/total storage). The results of these assumptions are shown in figure 5-3, in which the values of computed and measured soil moisture are compared during the 1955 growing season. Agreement is quite close even though the assumptions concerning soil moisture depletion are reasonably simplistic.

Four years of measured values of soil moisture content taken with fiberglass electrical resistance units were available to a depth of 1.5 m in clay forest soils of

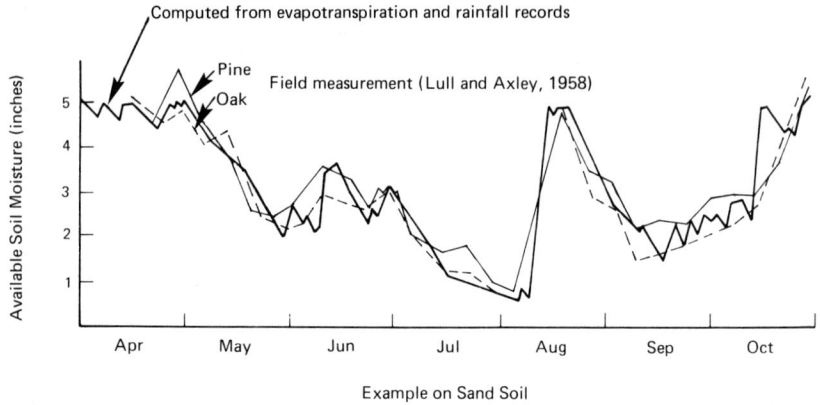

Example on Sand Soil

Source: R. Zahner, "Refinement in empirical functions for realistic soil-moisture regimes under forest cover," in *Forest Hydrology,* ed. W.E. Sopper and H.W. Lull, Proceedings NSF Advanced Science Seminar, Penn. State Univ., Aug. 29-Sept. 10, 1965, Pergamon Press Ltd., Oxford (1967). Measured trends from H.W. Lull and J.H. Axley, "Forest soil-moisture relations in the Coastal Plain sands of Southern New Jersey," *Forest Science* 4 (1958):2-19.

Figure 5-3. Comparison of Measured Versus Computed Soil Moisture Regimes for Sand Soils.

South Carolina. It was found that about 175 mm of available water storage could be held in the root zones of these soils. Because of the low infiltration rates on the clay soils, the precipitation records first had to be corrected for the amount of direct overland runoff from individual storms.[5] This correction assumed that all the small volume storms became soil moisture recharge, although only about 30 percent of the largest volume storms might go to recharge. Depletion of storage was considered to be at the potential evapotranspiration rate as long as soil moisture content was at or above 67 percent of total storage. With storage between 67 and 33 percent of total storage, daily depletion was assumed to equal potential evapotranspiration times the ratio (current soil moisture/total storage). Agreement between computed and measured soil moisture storage was quite reasonable (figure 5-4) in view of the many assumptions that had to be made on these heavier clay soils. Reliable daily or weekly computations of soil moisture content are possible from relatively uncomplicated bookkeeping procedures.

Measured-Computed Soil Moisture in a Semiarid Climate

Another model for estimating soil moisture content has been tested against weekly measured values of soil moisture for a three-year period in a semiarid climate at Sidney, Montana.[6] First, potential evapotranspiration is estimated by using the Penman combination method (chapter 2). Daily values are accumu-

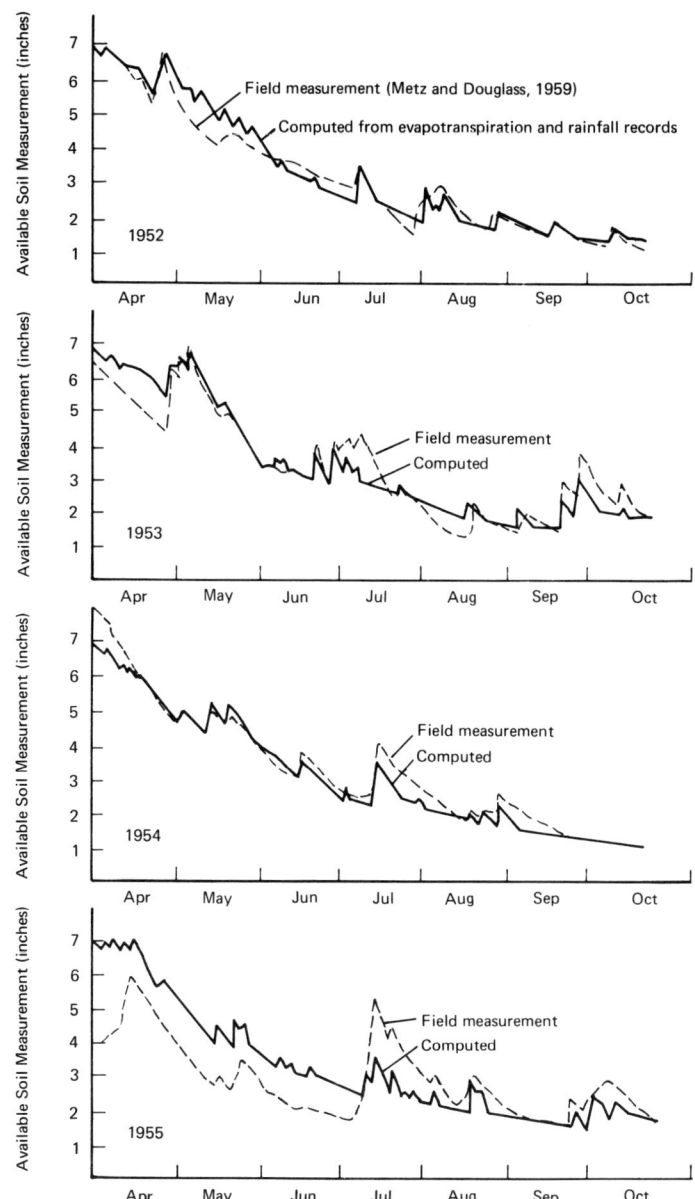

Source: R. Zahner, "Refinement in empirical functions for realistic soil-moisture regions under forest cover," in *Forest Hydrology,* eds., W.E. Sopper and H.W. Lull, Proceedings NSF Advanced Science Seminar, Penn State Univ., Aug. 29-Sept. 10, 1965, Pergamon Press Ltd., Oxford (1967). Measured curve from L.J. Metz and J.E. Douglass, "Soil moisture depletion under several Piedmont cover types," *Forest Service Technical Bulletin 1207* (Washington, D.C.: U.S. Department of Agriculture, 1959).

Figure 5-4. Comparison of Measured Versus Computed Soil Moisture Regimes for Clay Soils.

lated to provide weekly totals. Next, potential evapotranspiration is converted to actual evapotranspiration by multiplying by an adjusted plant growth coefficient. A plant growth coefficient is obtained from a growth curve derived from the average upstretched leaf lengths of the dominant forage crop. A value of 0.5 corresponds to the maximum height of the estimated growth curve since the maximum ground cover did not exceed 50 percent in the experimental area. The plant growth coefficient curve was extrapolated back to emergence and forward to senescence.

Because water is limited in the semiarid climate in which the study took place, the plant growth coefficient was then adjusted by multiplying it by a soil water coefficient, W_1, and adding the extra evaporation that will occur after rain storms to this product. W_1 equals $\log ({}^{100W}a/W_c + 1)/\log 101$ where W_a is the water storage in the root zone above the permanent wilting point and W_c is the amount of water in the soil at field capacity above the permanent wilting point. A 150 cm soil profile was used because it agreed with the maximum depth of soil water removal in the area.

Precipitation not lost immediately by evaporation was considered to be added to soil storage while moisture was removed from storage by actual evapotranspiration. Although data points ranged all the way from the wilting point to field capacity (figure 5-5), the computed and measured values agreed within 15 percent of the line of unity in all but seven weekly periods during the three growing seasons. The method would appear to predict soil moisture content sufficiently well for use by rangeland managers.

Measured-Computed Soil Moisture Using a Two-Layer Water Budget Model

A two-layer water budget in which the soil moisture content is assumed to be uniform within each zone has also proved useful in determining moisture content in the soils of three pastures in northern Australia.[7] The upper zone or layer corresponds to the A soil horizon. With drying of the soil, the rainfall of the previous day is assumed to be evaporated at the potential rate (determined as $0.8 \times$ Class A pan evaporation). Potential water demands, not satisfied by rainfall, are apportioned to the two soil layers on the basis of the relative root densities in each layer. To satisfy potential demands, available water is first withdrawn from the upper, and then from the lower layer. Availability of water in each layer is a function of the fractional storage.

In this example, three different soils were considered; soils 1 and 2 had 50 mm and 70 mm of storage capacity respectively in the upper soil layer and 30 mm and 80 mm in the lower soil layer. Soil 3 had 25 mm of storage capacity in the upper layer and 155 mm in the lower layer. In soils 1 and 2, an AE/PE ratio of unity was assumed until soil moisture content reached 50 percent of field

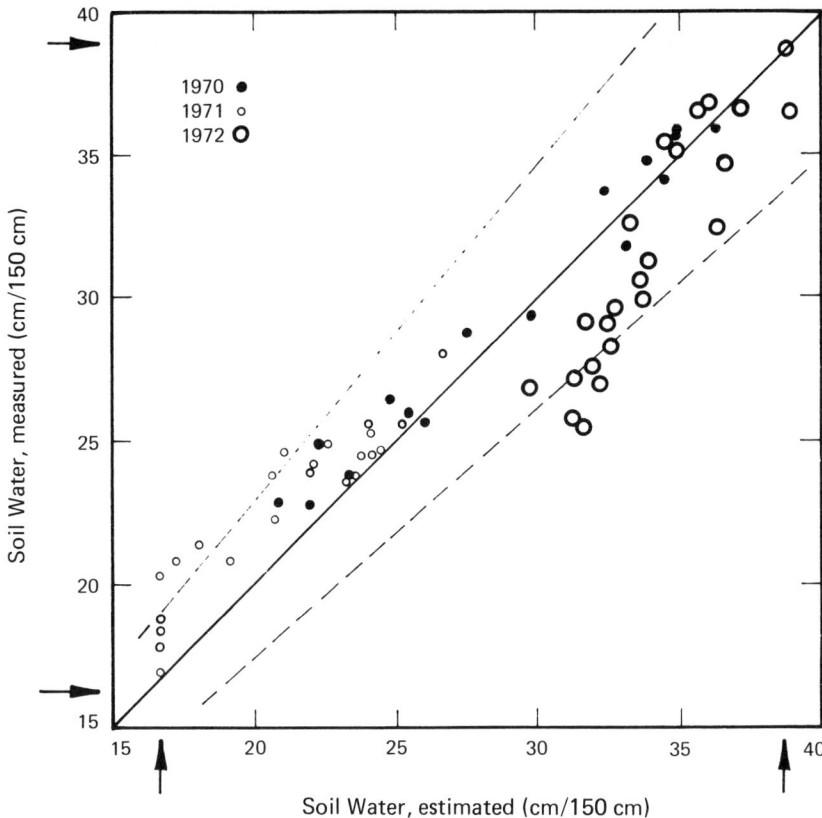

Source: J.K. Aase, J.R. Wight, and F.H. Siddoway, "Estimating soil water content on native rangeland," *Agricultural Meteorology*, vol. 12 (1973):185-191, Elsevier Scientific Publishing Co., Amsterdam.

Figure 5-5. Calculated Soil Moisture Compared with Measured Soil Moisture Content for 1970-1972 Seasons near Sidney, Montana. Solid line is $y = x$; dashed lines indicate a difference of ±15 percent. Arrows indicate wilting point and field capacity.

capacity with a linear decline in the ratio after that, while in soil 3 an AE/PE ratio proportional to fractional storage over the whole range of soil moisture values was assumed. With remoistening, the upper layer must first be brought back to field capacity before the second layer received any moisture. When both layers reach field capacity, water is available for runoff and throughflow. Simulated and measured soil moisture storage for a portion of two years, 1968 and 1971, for all three soils are shown in figure 5-6. The results indicate that it is

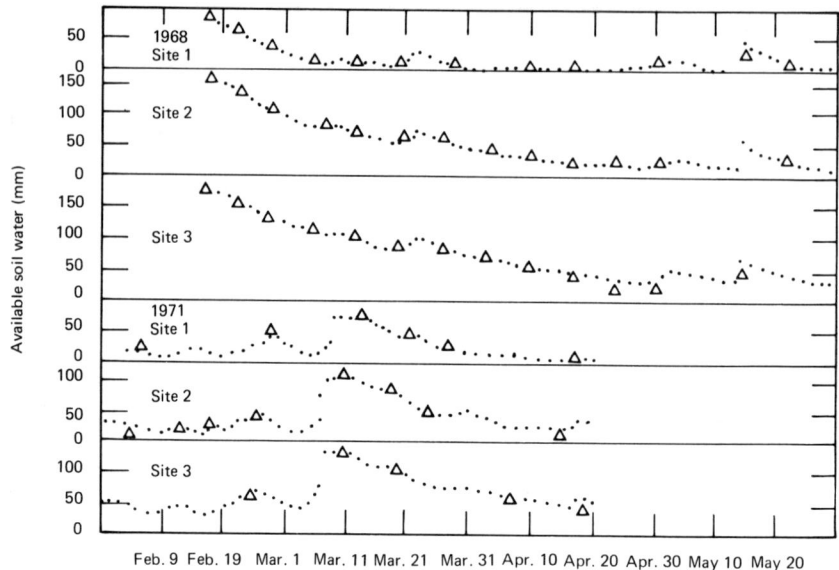

Available water storage in 1968 and 1971. Measured (Δ) and simulated (•).

Source: R.L. McCown, "An evaluation of the influence of available soil moisture storage capacity on growing season length and yield of tropical pastures using simple water balance models," *Agricultural Meteorology,* vol. 11 (1973):53-63, Elsevier Scientific Publishing Co., Amsterdam.

Figure 5-6. Measured (Δ) and Computed (·) Available Soil Moisture Storage in a Solodized Solonetz (site 1), Solodic Soil (site 2), and a Levee Soil with Good Internal Drainage (site 3) in Northern Australia in 1968 and 1971

quite possible to predict soil moisture storage from bookkeeping techniques using readily available meteorologic and soil information.

Irrigation Scheduling

Farmers have increasingly turned to irrigation to solve the problem of poor distribution of moisture for crops, but scientific irrigation involves more than just installing equipment and turning on water. For optimum yields, timing and quantity of irrigation applications must be such that plants never suffer from a lack of water; applications must also not result in the occurrence of gravitational water in the soil to leach fertilizers and other plant nutrients from the soil.

Farmers who think of irrigation as merely "crop insurance," used only as a last resort, often employ no rational method to determine when and how much to irrigate. They look at the soil and crop, as well as local weather forecasts, and are swayed in their judgment by many different and sometimes conflicting bits of evidence. Watching soil or plants and judging the timing of an irrigation application on the feel of the soil, or on the degree of wilting or color changes in plant leaves, will usually result in irrigation well after growth and yield have been reduced. Such irrigation will serve only to mitigate a real economic disaster. Plants often do not show signs of wilting or color change until they have experienced a considerable deficiency in their moisture requirements which may have already limited yields.

Another approach to the problem of determining time and amount of irrigation is the use of different soil moisture measuring devices to provide a continuous record of the day-to-day changes in soil moisture content. These devices often do not provide the information that the farmer really needs. Samples are obtained at only one particular spot and the assumption must be made that the response of the sensor to changes in soil moisture is similar in all respects to that of the soil itself. The climatological approach to the problem of determining soil moisture content, described in the previous section, is simple and useful. It avoids errors involved in calibration and exposure of measuring instruments and can provide average values over good-sized areas depending on the climatic data used.

An irrigation schedule is a natural outgrowth of the method of computing soil moisture content. One can set limits below which soil moisture should not be allowed to fall for any particular crop and depth of root zone. By keeping daily account of how much water has been lost from the soil, one can determine exactly when the predetermined level of soil moisture depletion is reached and know just how much to irrigate to bring the moisture level back to a safe value. Shallow-rooted crops will have to be irrigated more frequently but with smaller amounts of water than will deeper-rooted pastures or orchards.

If irrigation is scheduled by keeping continuous account of the soil moisture, no great moisture deficiency can develop in the soil to limit growth or yield and there will be no overirrigation to damage both soil and crop with a wasteful misuse of water. The predetermined level of soil moisture content before irrigation is begun will depend on the crop being irrigated, other competing demands for water, the amount of irrigation equipment or labor available, and the degree of drought which the irrigator feels the crop can survive without significant reduction in yield.

Hypothetical Irrigation Schedules for Seabrook, N.J.

Two hypothetical irrigation schedules have been evaluated for Seabrook, New Jersey, using data for July and August, 1965 (figure 5-7). The two programs are

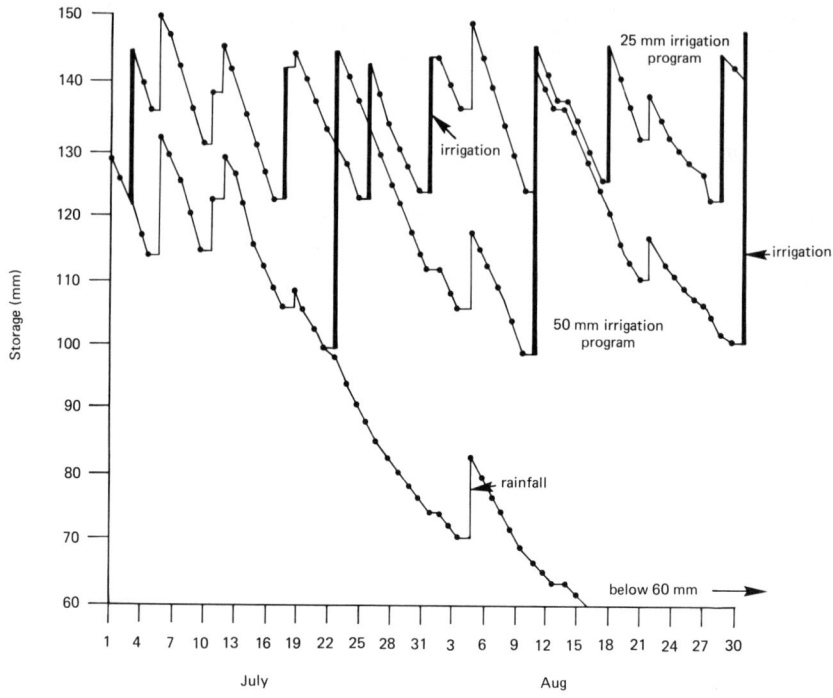

Figure 5-7. Two Hypothetical Irrigation Schedules, Seabrook, N.J., July-August, 1965.

(1) irrigation of 25 mm depth every time soil moisture storage is less than 125 mm; and (2) irrigation of 50 mm depth every time soil moisture storage is less than 100 mm. In daily water budget computations, irrigation is treated in the same manner as 25 or 50 mm of precipitation. It has been assumed that 150 mm of water can be stored in the root zone of the sandy loam soil in the area.

From figure 5-7 it is clear that permitting a greater degree of drying of the soil to occur before irrigation (and, thus, a greater depth of irrigation at each application) will require less frequent irrigations but also result in a greater water deficit during the season. Leaching of soils should be less under the 50-mm irrigation program because the soil will be refilled almost to field capacity less often. At those times a rain might bring the soil moisture content to over field capacity and result in leaching. The two programs of irrigation result in nearly the same amount of water stored in the soil at the end of August 1965, although there have been seven irrigations under the program calling for 25 mm per irrigation and only three irrigations under the program calling for 50 mm per irrigation. The course of soil moisture storage under the natural rainfall distribution (and without irrigation) is also included for comparison in figure 5-7.

The 25-mm irrigation program consistently keeps soil moisture storage near field capacity. No large deficits develop so that yields should not suffer. However, seven irrigations within two months results in no more than six or seven days between irrigations. A farmer using such a program, especially one with many fields to irrigate, would be quite busy with just the irrigation aspect of his farming program. Both irrigation programs were designed to bring soil moisture storage almost to field capacity to allow some opportunity for unanticipated precipitation after the end of irrigation to be stored in the soil. This will reduce the opportunity for leaching of the soil.

Evaluation of the water budget for each day of the fifteen-year period 1947-1961 at Seabrook, New Jersey, has provided a series of values of deficit, surplus, storage, and actual evapotranspiration. Deficit is of principal interest here. Monthly values of water deficit for this period at Seabrook are summed in table 5-1, with average monthly values included at the bottom. During this period, no moisture deficit occurred in the winter months, December through March. Only once did a deficit occur in April, and it was too small to influence the average. Water deficit increased from an average value of 5 mm in May to a

Table 5-1
Water Deficit by Months, Seabrook, N.J., 1947-1961, as Computed from Daily Climatic Water Budget (Sandy loam soil with 150 mm of moisture held in root zone of the soil at field capacity)

	J	F	M	A	M	J	J	A	S	O	N	D	Year
1947	0	0	0	0	0	10	48	94	58	41	2	0	253
1948	0	0	0	0	0	5	38	8	28	18	5	0	102
1949	0	0	0	0	5	46	84	84	23	15	0	0	257
1950	0	0	0	0	2	10	25	51	23	5	5	0	121
1951	0	0	0	0	5	15	41	51	30	10	0	0	152
1952	0	0	0	0	2	25	76	23	13	8	2	0	149
1953	0	0	0	0	0	23	51	36	38	20	0	0	168
1954	0	0	0	0	2	51	99	48	8	18	0	0	226
1955	0	0	0	0	23	10	81	33	25	2	0	0	174
1956	0	0	0	0	2	15	23	18	5	0	0	0	63
1957	0	0	0	0	23	43	96	86	28	5	0	0	281
1958	0	0	0	0	0	18	13	13	18	2	0	0	64
1959	0	0	0	0	10	33	23	23	20	18	0	0	127
1960	0	0	0	5	2	30	49	23	15	2	0	0	126
1961	0	0	0	0	2	18	48	25	41	5	2	0	141
Avg.	0	0	0	0	5	23	54	41	25	11	1	0	160

Source: J.R. Mather, "Irrigation agriculture in humid areas," *Eclectic Climatology*, Yearbook of the Association of Pacific Coast Geographers, vol. 30 (1968), Oregon State University Press.

peak value of 54 mm in July. Total annual water deficit varied from a high value of 281 mm in 1957 to low values of 63 and 75 mm in 1956 and 1958 respectively. Average water deficit for the fifteen years is 160 mm annually.

The data in table 5-1 have been obtained from daily computations of the climatic water budget assuming a water-holding capacity in the soil root zone of 150 mm and no irrigation. Hypothetical irrigation programs can now be evaluated merely by selecting reasonable lower limits of soil moisture content at which irrigation should begin. The number of irrigations and the quantity of water applied can readily be determined for each year by going through the daily computations once more.

Using the fifteen years of data from Seabrook, two irrigation programs that were quite similar to those used in the previously discussed study were evaluated: (1) application of 25 mm whenever 50 mm of moisture were removed from the soil or when the soil moisture content dropped to 66 percent of field capacity; and (2) application of 50 mm of water whenever 75 mm of moisture were removed from the soil or when the soil moisture content reached 50 percent of field capacity. Table 5-2 shows the results of the application of the two irrigation programs. The first program requires irrigation in each of the 15 years; the average is 148 mm but it varies from 50 mm in moist 1958 to 250 mm in dry 1957. Most of the need occurs in June, July, August, and September, with the greatest average need of 62 mm in July. The second program shows an average irrigation need of 90 mm per year, ranging from 0 in 1956 and 1958 to a maximum of 150 mm in five different years. Peak months were July, August, and September.

Both programs allow some drying of the soil to occur before irrigation is applied. This is the reason for the difference between irrigation requirements and actual values of deficit in table 5-1. With more frequent irrigations (less drying of the soil), computed irrigation needs should agree closely with computed water deficit. Each program calls for only enough irrigation to return soil moisture content to just over 80 percent of field capacity to allow for the possible occurrence of rain just after completion of irrigation.

For actual planning purposes, values of irrigation need (table 5-2) can provide quantitative information on amounts of water which might be needed even before an irrigation system is designed or laid out. In addition, these values can be used to recommend pump capacities, or estimate operating costs since expectancies of equipment needs and pumping hours can be determined.

Estimating Probability of Irrigation Need

A computer-based bookkeeping procedure for estimating the probability of irrigation requirements from climatic data has been developed in Canada.[8] In this approach daily latent evaporation is estimated by means of a regression

Table 5-2

Computed Irrigation Need, Seabrook, N.J., 1947-1961, Under Two Hypothetical Irrigation Programs

(In mm)

Year	Program a) – 25 mm irrigation when 50 mm removed						Program b) – 50 mm irrigation when 75 mm removed					
	M	J	J	A	S	Total	M	J	J	A	S	Total
1947	0	0	75	100	50	225	0	0	50	50	50	150
1948	0	0	50	0	50	100	0	0	0	0	50	50
1949	0	75	75	75	0	225	0	50	50	50	0	150
1950	0	0	25	75	25	125	0	0	0	50	50	100
1951	0	0	50	50	0	100	0	0	0	50	0	50
1952	0	25	100	0	0	125	0	0	100	0	0	100
1953	0	25	50	25	25	125	0	0	50	0	0	50
1954	0	75	100	25	0	200	0	50	100	0	0	150
1955	25	0	125	25	50	225	0	0	100	0	50	150
1956	0	0	50	0	25	75	0	0	0	0	0	0
1957	25	50	100	75	0	250	0	50	50	50	0	150
1958	0	25	0	0	25	50	0	0	0	0	0	0
1959	0	50	25	25	25	125	0	0	50	0	0	50
1960	0	50	25	25	25	125	0	0	50	0	50	100
1961	0	0	75	25	50	150	0	0	50	0	50	100
Avg.	3	25	62	35	23	148	0	10	43	17	20	90

Source: J.R. Mather, "Irrigation agriculture in humid areas," *Eclectic Climatology*, Yearbook of the Association of Pacific Coast Geographers, vol. 30 (1968), Oregon State University Press.

technique (see table 2-1). This value is adjusted by multiplying by a consumptive use factor and the result is subtracted from any precipitation that has occurred. The difference is the change in soil moisture storage from one day to the next.

If a crop is actively transpiring, completely covers the ground, and has all the water it needs, the consumptive use factor will be 1.0 ($AE = PE$). The consumptive use factor may exceed 1.0 if the crop has all the water it needs and is spaced in rows. Under those conditions, energy can reach lower portions of the plant so that the exposed surface area is greater than with a closed vegetation surface. Normally, with short plants not covering all the surface and not supplied with all the water they need, the consumptive use factor will be less than 1.0 ($AE < PE$).

The soil moisture content on any day is merely the sum of the previous day's storage plus any change in storage from that day to the present not to exceed the water-holding capacity of the soil. If the sum of yesterday's soil moisture storage and soil moisture changes in the past 24 hours exceeds 0 then no irrigation is required, whereas if this sum is 0 irrigation is required, the amount depending on the storage capacity of the soil.[9]

Because soils and vegetation conditions vary appreciably even within short distances, tables of the supplemental irrigation requirements for various water-holding capacities, different consumptive use factors, different probability levels, different weather stations, and different weeks of the growing season have been prepared. For example, table 5-3 lists irrigation requirements for Ottawa, Canada, for the first week of August under different soil (storage capacity) and vegetation (CU factor) conditions. For this particular week near Ottawa, the irrigation requirements for moist soils with a 3-inch (75 mm) storage capacity with actively growing vegetation will not exceed 0.92 inches (23 mm) 80 percent of the time. On the average (50 percent probability), irrigation requirements under such conditions will equal 0.38 inches (10 mm). The availability of these data not only at a point but over geographical areas as well makes possible the rational development of water resources programs for large regions of a country.

Leaching of Calcium

Water surplus, as defined in many water budgets, is the water in the soil over and above that needed to satisfy evapotranspiration demands or to recharge the soil moisture to field capacity in the time period under consideration. This is the water that will percolate downward through the soil and will take part in the leaching of the soil. It has been possible to develop a mathematical model to describe the downward leaching or movement of material in the soil under the action of gravitational water.[10] The model considers the movement of water and material downward in a series of cycles. A cycle can be defined as completed when 10 percent of the original concentration of the material in any half-inch layer in the soil has moved downward to the next lower half-inch layer. The leaching efficiency in the soil is defined as the number of cycles of vertical movement per unit quantity of surplus water. This quantity depends, in large measure, on the cation exchange capacity of the soil and the chemical composition of the leaching solution.

Using a relation between the climatic moisture index

$$Im = 100 \left(\frac{P}{PE} - 1 \right)$$

where Im is the annual moisture index, P is the annual precipitation, and PE is the annual potential evapotranspiration, and the cation exchange capacity of different soils, a generalized relation between the moisture index and leaching efficiency for four different types of soil was developed (figure 5-8). Under very

Table 5-3

Supplemental Irrigation Requirements for Different Storage Capacities and Consumptive Use Factors at Ottawa During First Week of August

Storage Capacity	CU Factor	Probability, %							
		25	50	75	80	85	90	95	99
		in.	in.	in.	in.	in.	in.	in.	in.
1.00	0.25	0.00	0.00	0.00	0.00	0.00	0.00	0.00	0.00
	0.50	0.00	0.00	0.11	0.19	0.28	0.40	0.57	0.89
	0.75	0.00	0.24	0.54	0.62	0.71	0.82	0.99	1.30
	1.00	0.20	0.54	0.89	0.97	1.08	1.20	1.38	1.74
3.00	0.25	0.00	0.00	0.00	0.00	0.00	0.00	0.00	0.00
	0.50	0.00	0.00	0.00	0.00	0.00	0.00	0.04	0.20
	0.75	0.00	0.00	0.28	0.41	0.56	0.74	1.01	1.52
	1.00	0.00	0.38	0.81	0.92	1.04	1.20	1.43	1.87
5.00	0.25	0.00	0.00	0.00	0.00	0.00	0.00	0.00	0.00
	0.50	0.00	0.00	0.00	0.00	0.00	0.00	0.00	0.00
	0.75	0.00	0.00	0.00	0.00	0.00	0.27	0.69	1.49
	1.00	0.00	0.14	0.68	0.82	0.98	1.17	1.46	2.01

Source: W. Baier and G.W. Robertson, "Estimating supplemental irrigation water requirements for climatological data," *Canadian Agricultural Engineering*, vol. 9 (1967).

dry conditions ($Im = -80$) leaching efficiency is uniformly low ranging from about 1.2 cycles per inch of surplus water for sand to less than 0.2 cycles per inch for clay soils. Under moist conditions ($Im = 100$) the leaching efficiency in sands has increased to nearly 6 cycles per inch of surplus water while for clays the value has risen to only about 0.5 cycles per inch.

The mathematical model has been applied to the problem of calcium leaching from a battery of four-foot deep lysimeters at Cornell University. The lysimeters were filled with Petoskey gritty sandy loam. Based on the available soil analyses, the initial concentration of calcium in the tanks was calculated to be as follows:[11]

Depth	Calcium Concentration (lb/acre/half-inch layer)
1st foot	92
2nd foot	150
3rd foot	100
4th foot	158

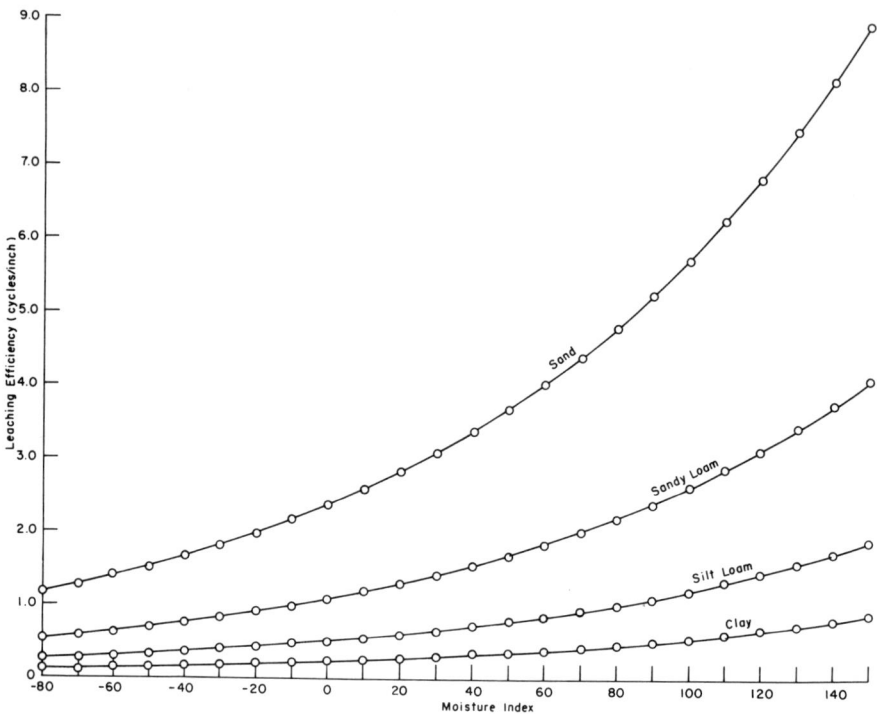

Source: J.R. Mather and J.K. Nakamura, "The climatic and hydrologic factors affecting the redistribution of strontium in soils," *Publications in Climatology*, Laboratory of Climatology, vol. 15, no. 1 (1962).

Figure 5-8. Relation Between Leaching Efficiency and Moisture Index for Different Soil Types

To simplify the calculation process, it was decided to consider one-inch layers rather than half-inch layers so that a cycle of leaching would be defined as completed when one-twentieth (5 percent) of the concentration of material in a one-inch layer had moved downward to the next lower one-inch layer. Further, the concentration of calcium in each foot was rounded off as 100 lb/acre/half-inch layer in the first and third foot and 150 lb/acre/half-inch layer in the second and fourth foot. The distribution of calcium in the soil of the lysimeter after different numbers of cycles of leaching is shown diagramatically in figure 5-9.

After 120 cycles of leaching practically all the original concentration of calcium in the top foot had been leached out and the heavy concentration of calcium in the second foot had moved downward into the third foot. The lower concentration of calcium in the third foot originally had moved into the fourth

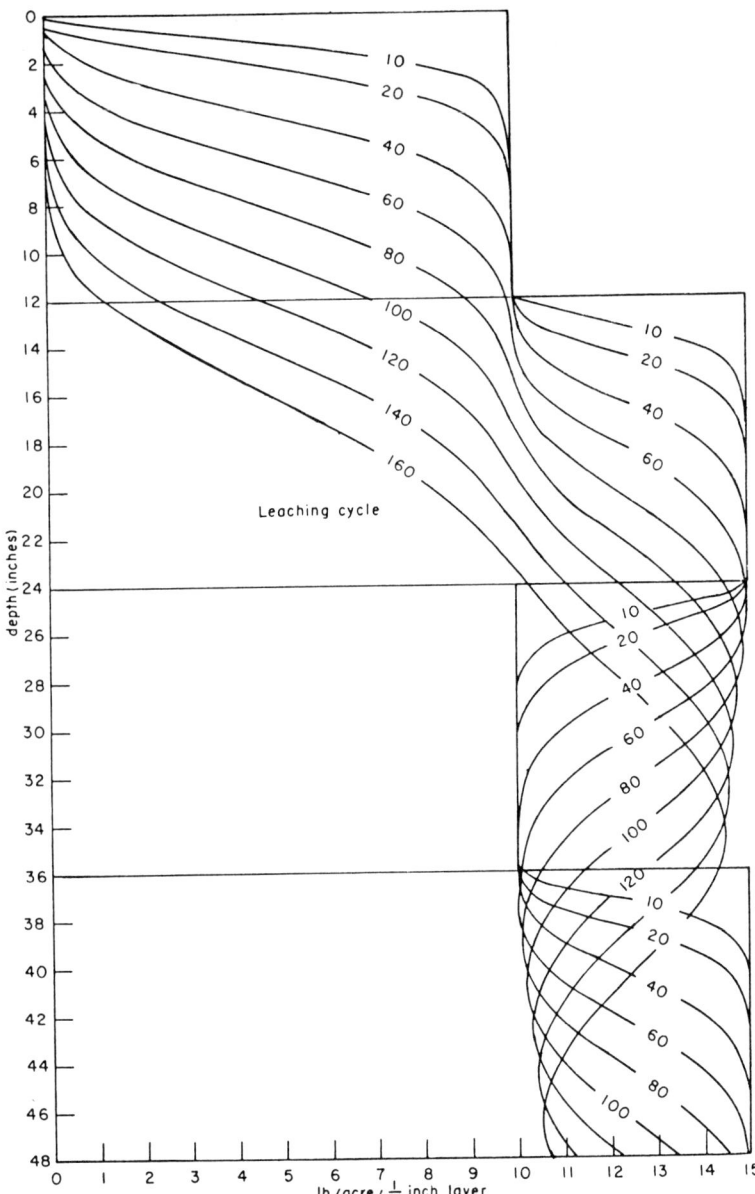

Source: J.R. Mather and J.K. Nakamura, "The climatic and hydrologic factors affecting the redistribution of strontium in soils," *Publications in Climatology*, Laboratory of Climatology, vol. 15, no. 1 (1962).

Figure 5-9. Distribution of Calcium in Lysimeter Soil After Various Cycles of Leaching

foot and a significant amount of calcium originally in the fourth foot had been leached out of the lysimeter. If the leaching continued, it was estimated that by cycle 240 the bulge of calcium originally in the second foot would have been located in the middle of the fourth foot while by cycle 300 it would have been leached out of the fourth foot entirely.[12]

To test the result, annual calculated leaching from the four-foot deep lysimeters was compared with the values actually obtained by measurement on the lysimeters.[13] Using the climatic water budget it is possible to compute the yearly amount of surplus water on the lysimeters. The calculated water surplus approximated quite well the total measured percolation from the lysimeters. The leaching efficiency for the sandy loam soil in the lysimeters was estimated to be 1.5 cycles per inch of surplus water. Both the calculated surplus and the measured percolation were used with this value of leaching efficiency to compute the amount of leaching. The number of cycles of leaching each year was obtained by multiplying the annual water surplus by the leaching efficiency.

The leaching experiment was carried out for eleven years. In four years, additional amounts of calcium were applied to the surface as fertilizer and turned under. It was assumed that this additional calcium was well mixed in the upper 6 inches of the soil. Figure 5-10 compares the annual values of measured and computed leaching year by year, the computed values being obtained both from the calculated water surplus and from the measured percolate. Agreement is poor in 1922, the first year of the study, and again in 1924, 1925, and 1927, but appears to be reasonable in the other seven years. Total leaching over the eleven years amounted to 1902 lb/acre using the calculated water surplus and 1977 lb/acre using the measured percolate whereas the actual measured calcium lost from the lysimeters was 2007 lb/acre. A difference in total leaching loss of just over 100 lbs/acre after eleven years would seem to be reasonable in view of the assumptions that had to be made about initial calcium distribution and cation exchange capacity and its relation to soil type. The mathematical model for leaching using calculated water surplus might have further usefulness not only in the study of leaching of other materials but also in the whole problem of soil formation, the development of hardpans, and the formation of distinctive soil profiles.

Depth of the Caliche Layer

In another study of leaching, it has been shown that there is a significant positive linear relationship between the depth of the caliche layer in arid and semiarid soils (layer of accumulation of calcium carbonate in unconsolidated sediments), the depth of moisture movement into the soil and soil texture.[14] While altitude was also included as a possible variable, it was concluded that this parameter added little to the value of the coefficient of determination (R^2). It was found

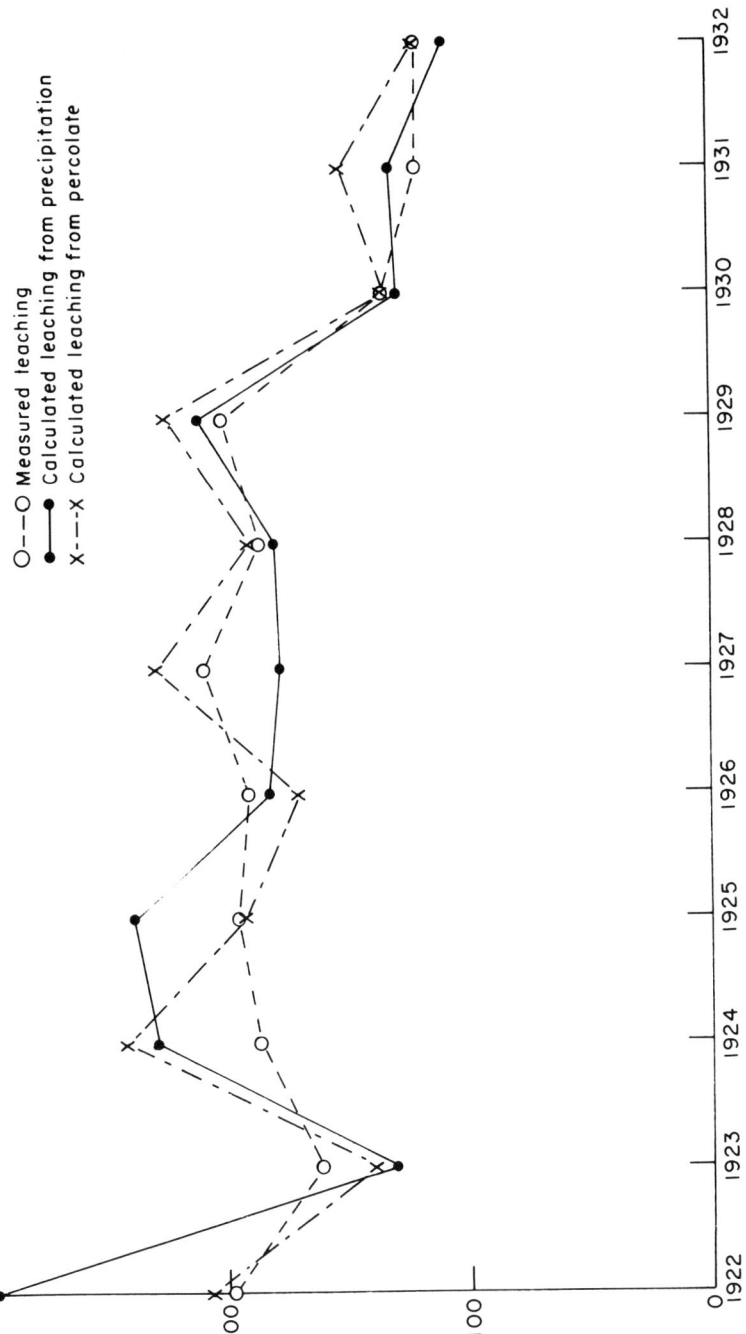

Source: J.R. Mather and J.K. Nakamura, "The climatic and hydrologic factors affecting the redistribution of strontium in soils," *Publications in Climatology*, Laboratory of Climatology, vol. 15, no. 1 (1962).

Figure 5-10. Annual Loss of Calcium in Drainage Water from Lysimeter, Cornell University, Ithaca, N.Y.

that some 98 percent of the variation in depth of caliche in clay loam soils could be explained on the basis of moisture penetration. On loams and loamy sands some 96 and 94 percent respectively of the variation in depth of caliche could be explained on the basis of moisture penetration information while poorest relations were found with silt loam and sandy loam soils on which just 79 and 71 percent respectively of the variation in caliche depth could be predicted from moisture penetration data. Moisture penetration in this particular study was determined from the sum of the positive values of $P - AE$ from water budget computations.

Crop Yield Studies

Though information on soil moisture is basic to a rational irrigation schedule, it also has a real role in the determination of crop yields whether or not irrigation is involved. The concept of moisture deficit, expressed as "stress index," "moisture stress," or even "grass-growing days" has been related to the yield of different crops. In such uses, sometimes the word *deficit* refers to the difference between plant water loss under always adequate moisture conditions and the actual plant water loss, or $PE - AE$, while at other times it refers simply to the difference between actual soil moisture content and that existing at field capacity. In both cases, it reflects the fact that moisture is not adequate for plant needs so that additional water must be supplied, either by irrigation or precipitation, to eliminate the condition of deficiency. Moisture deficit is, thus, closely linked with the previously discussed factor of soil moisture storage.

Crop yields are related to a combination of climatic factors that express how satisfactorily the plant's requirements for moisture and energy have been satisfied. Water deficit gives, in quantitative terms, a measure of how well the plant's water needs have been fulfilled. If plants grow better and produce higher yields when they do not suffer a lack of water, a significant correlation should exist between yield and water deficit. For example, a correlation coefficient of −0.71 was found between sugar cane yield in Barbados and the climatic water deficit $(PE - AE)$, computed monthly.[15] This indicates a decrease in sugar yields as total moisture deficit for the crop-growing season increases.

Average annual yields of corn and soybeans in Cumberland County in southern New Jersey from 1947 through 1961 have been compared with water deficit $(PE - AE)$ computed for a single, centrally located station, Bridgeton.[16] The results are shown in figure 5-11 along with the calculated regression line. Correlation coefficients were −0.85 for corn yield and −0.75 for soybean yield. In each case crop yield was reduced as total water deficit for the growing season increased.

In considering these results, several factors are important. First, over the period studied, remarkable advances have occurred in the production of more

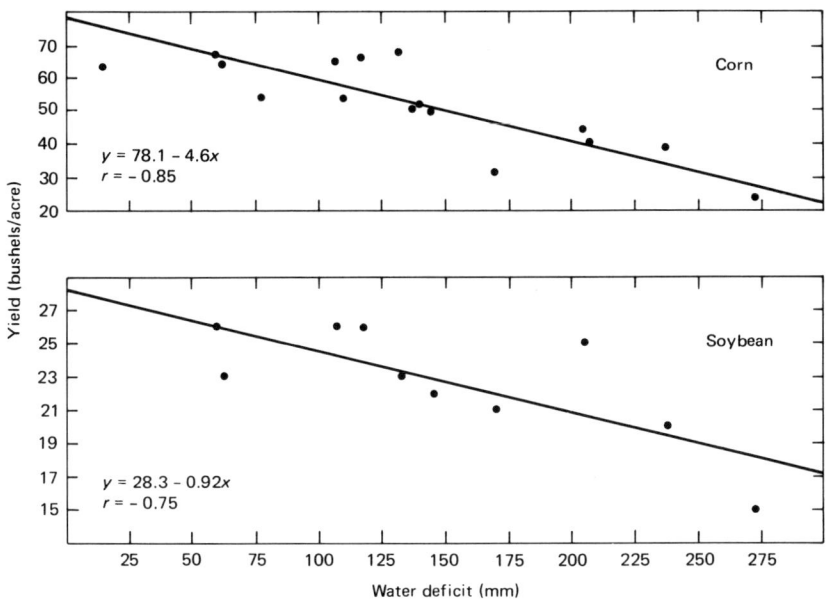

Source: J.R. Mather, "Irrigation agriculture in humid areas," in *Eclectic Climatology*, ed., A. Court, Yearbook of the Association of Pacific Coast Geographers, vol. 30, Oregon State University Press (1968).

Figure 5-11. Relation Between Corn and Soybean Yield and Water Deficit, Seabrook, N.J., 1947-1961

viable and higher yielding seeds; new fertilizers have become available; cultivation, soil conservation, and crop rotation techniques have all improved. The effect of these advances in seeds and farming techniques have not been removed from the relationship found in figure 5-11. Even without correcting for these outside influences, it is clear that water deficit is closely related to crop yield.

Some investigators have suggested that the ratio AE/PE would be a more useful indicator of actual yield than either AE or deficit.[17] This ratio has been used to achieve a generalized relationship to yield (figure 5-12). When actual and potential evapotranspiration are equal ($AE/PE = 1$, soil at field capacity) actual yield in vegetative crops is found to approach that potentially possible. When $AE/PE = 0.1$, actual yield is approximately 0.1 of potentially possible yield. Large variations are found to occur in the middle portion of the relation between evapotranspiration and yield as a result of the timing of rainfall or of drought periods, and the efficiency of irrigation. Irrigation at the correct time and in the proper amount to prevent the AE/PE ratio from dropping to values of 0.4, 0.5, or 0.6 at critical times in the life cycle of the crop could result in the doubling of yield. It is not so much the absolute total of precipitation or

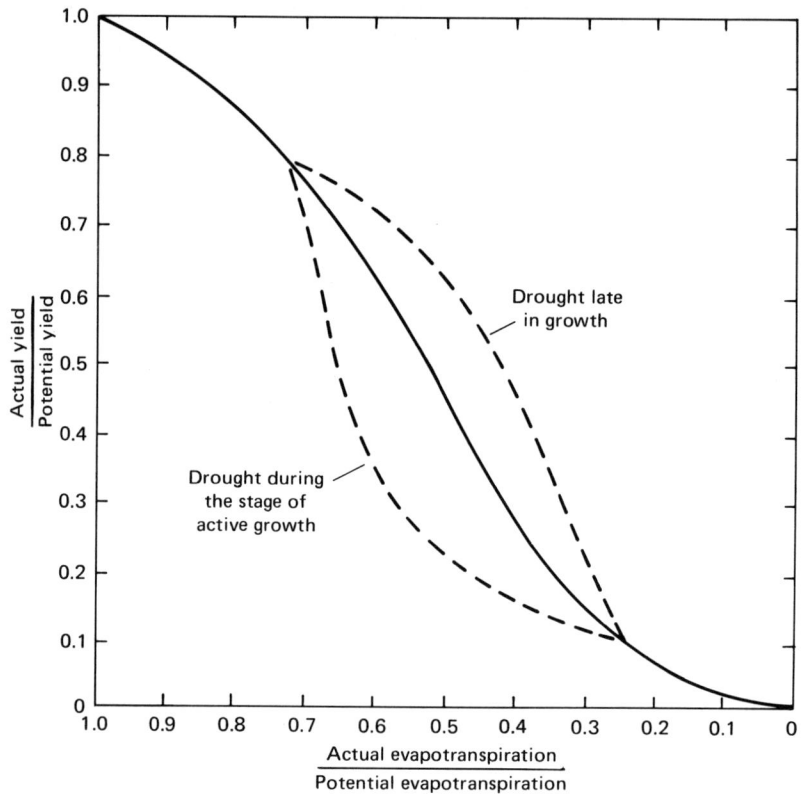

Source: Reproduced from Jen-hu Chang, R.B. Campbell, and F.E. Robinson, "On the relationship between water and sugar cane yield in Hawaii," *Agronomy Journal*, vol. 55, no. 5 (1963):450-453, by permission of the American Society of Agronomy.

Figure 5-12. Generalized Relationship Between Yield and Adequacy of Water Application

irrigation that seems to be important but rather the availability of water to meet the plant's requirements at the time they are most critical.

Hay and Grass Yields

A grass-growing day, defined as a day during the April-September growing season that had a soil moisture deficit of less than 2 inches (50 mm), has been found to be related to milk production.[18] Deficit here means the difference in soil moisture storage for the day from the moisture storage at field capacity. Hay transpiration and hay yield are known to be related whenever deficits are smaller than 2 inches.[19] Computing soil moisture deficit by means of a simple water budget based on available weather data, it is found that the western part of England as well as Wales experiences more than 170 grass-growing days whereas the drier southeastern portion of England has less than 130 such days. Milk production by section of the country was quite closely correlated ($r = -0.91$) with number of grass-growing days lost as a result of high soil moisture deficits.[20]

In a more recent study of the growth of Townsville stylo pasture[21] in northern Australia, a fairly close relationship was found between dry matter production and actual evapotranspiration as long as phosphate nutrition was considered (figure 5-13). The curves for different values of superphosphate application ($P = 1$ through 6 on the graph) were based on actual data for $P = 2$ obtained experimentally.[22] The break in the relation found at an accumulated actual evapotranspiration of 263 mm for $P = 2$ was assumed to be present for all rates of phosphate application as well.

Wheat Yields

In another study, a water stress day was defined as one in which the soil-water deficit of the main root zone (0-90 cm depth) reached 100 mm.[23] Available moisture in this soil depth at the Gilat Experiment Station in the northern Negev, Israel, was 140 mm. Some 80 to 90 percent of the moisture extracted by wheat occurred from the top 90 cm of the soil profile. The "stress index" was merely the total number of water stress days during the growing season.

The potential yield for the particular wheat variety used at the Gilat Experiment Station was determined under different irrigation treatments. Under the climate and soil conditions existing there this was found to be 420 kg du^{-1} (1 dunam = 1000 m^2). The potential yield assumed that the critical level of water stress used approximates reality and that water is the limiting factor in wheat production. The stress index merely takes into account the number of stress days during the December-May growing season without giving any special emphasis to stress days occurring during special "critical" times in the life of the crop. A correlation coefficient of -0.864 was found between yield and stress index (figure 5-14) with the regression equation $Y = 100 - 0.59x$, expressing the percentage reduction of yield from the potential (Y) for the number of stress days (x) in the growing season.[24] For each day of stress, yield is reduced by just over one-half of a percent from the potential.

A particularly detailed study of wheat yield and soil moisture deficit has been carried out in Canada.[25] Using a modulated soil moisture budget[26] a moisture stress index (actually $PE - AE$ or moisture deficit) was computed. Wheat yield from experimental plots was compared with various measured and

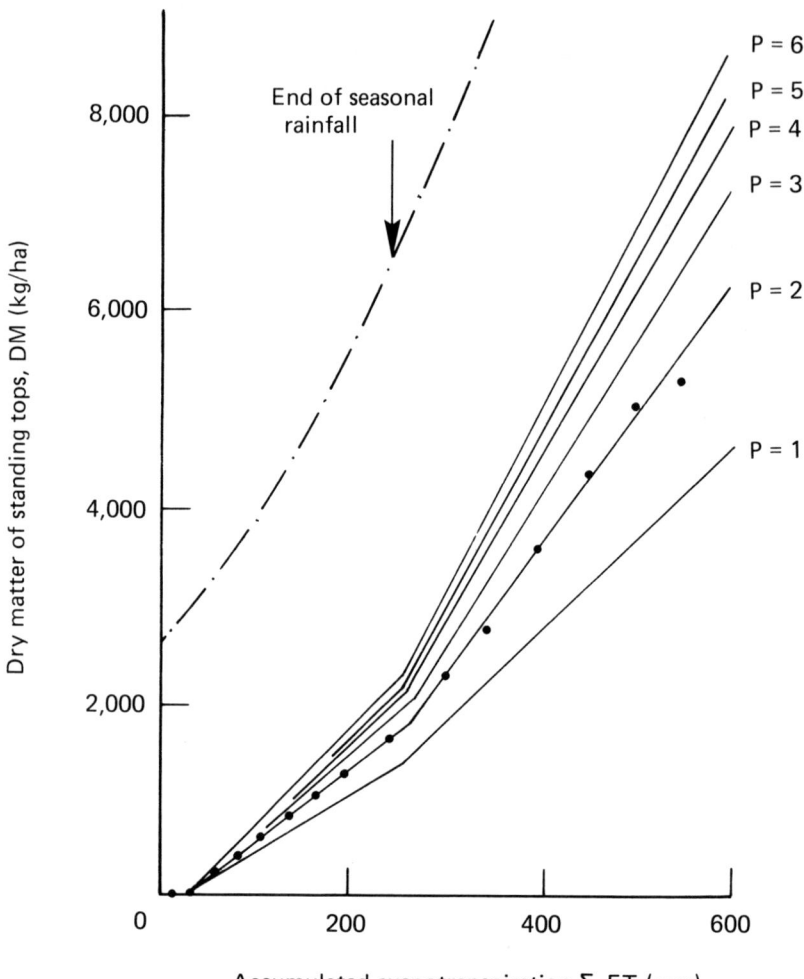

Source: C.W. Rose, J.E. Begg, G.F. Byrne, B.W.R. Torssell, and J.H. Goncz, "A simulation model of growth-field environment relationships for Townsville stylo pasture," *Agricultural Meteorology*, vol. 10 (1972):161-183, Elsevier Scientific Publishing Co., Amsterdam.

Figure 5-13. Relationships Between Dry Matter of Standing Tops of Townsville Stylo and Accumulated Evapotranspiration (solid curves). *P* is equivalent rate of superphosphate applied prior to season (in cwt/acre units). Points are based on experimental data. Dashed curve refers to data from a later experiment (with displaced zero abscissa).

derived weather factors. It was found that the moisture stress index $(PE - AE)$ was more closely correlated with wheat yield $(r = -0.83)$ than was seasonal precipitation $(r = 0.62)$; potential evapotranspiration $(r = -0.59)$; the ratio AE/PE $(r = 0.78)$; or degree-days $(r = 0.59)$.

Because moisture stress during one developmental stage of the wheat plant might be more limiting than during another stage, the wheat growing period was separated into five shorter periods (emergence to third leaf, third leaf to fifth leaf, fifth leaf to shot-blade, shot-blade to soft-dough, soft-dough to harvest) and the relation of moisture stress was evaluated at each of these times to final yield. Average yield was reduced by 156 ± 40 kg/ha per cm of water deficit using the whole period from emergence to harvest. However, yield was reduced by 311 kg/ha per cm of water deficit from the fifth leaf to the soft-dough stage but only 69.1 kg/ha per cm of deficit from the soft-dough to harvest stage.[27] More of the variation in yield could be explained by using values of moisture deficit for particular periods of growth than by using the single moisture deficit value for the whole growing period.

The ratio AE/PE has been employed as an indicator of the yield of wheat and grain sorghum in Australia.[28] In the study, it was stressed that limited soil moisture at certain critical periods in the life of the plant (from ear emergence to early grain filling) was more highly related to yield than was a moisture deficit at other times. The AE/PE ratio was found to account for 60 to 83 percent of the variation in the yield of the wheat and grain sorghum varieties tested in Australia.

Copra Yields

Soil water deficit has been related to the yield of copra in Trinidad.[29] Weekly values of deficit were computed by means of the climatic water budget using a linear relation between AE and PE. To determine what factors were most closely related to yield a series of correlation analyses between copra yield and various meteorological factors summed over different time periods (table 5-4) were undertaken.

The period between inflorescence and the dropping of the nut is almost 29 months. Highest correlations were found with both rainfall and integrated soil moisture deficit using a 29-month period of accumulation before harvest. Use of soil moisture deficit rather than rainfall improved the yield relation from +0.64 to −0.81. Rainfall by itself is not as directly related to ultimate copra yield as is the derived factor of soil moisture deficit.

The Failure of the Groundnut Scheme

The well-known East African groundnut (peanut) enterprise of the late 1940s might be considered a prime example of a costly failure of a major agricultural

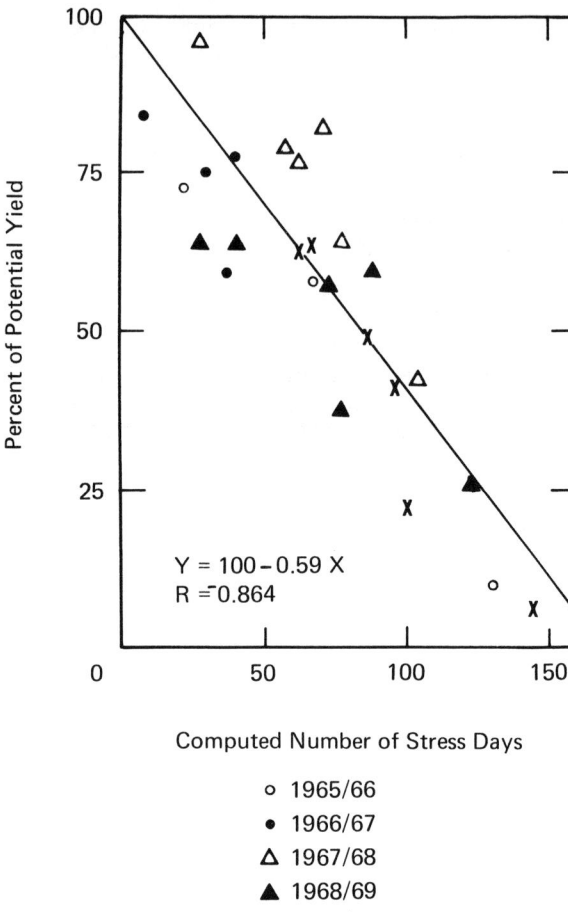

Source: J. Lewin, "A simple soil water simulation model for assessing the irrigation requirements of wheat," *Israel Journal of Agricultural Research*, vol. 22, no. 4 (1972).

Figure 5-14. Computed Total Number of Stress Days and Actual Wheat Yields Obtained at Gilat, Israel, 1965-1970

program due to the lack of consideration of available water budget information. Groundnuts require sufficient soil moisture in all portions of the root zone, particularly in a critical eight- to ten-week middle growing period when water requirements are greatest. The groundnut needs only small (approximately 25 mm per week) amounts of water in the first six to seven weeks of growth and again only little water during the final few weeks of growth; moisture deficit in the critical two-month period of active growth is highly detrimental to yield.[30]

Table 5-4

Correlation Coefficients Between Yield of Copra, Rainfall, and Integrated Soil Water Deficit, Perseverance Estate, Cedros, Trinidad

Correlation coefficient between yield and:	
Total rainfall, year before harvesting	+0.32
Total rainfall, second year before harvesting	+0.25
Total rainfall, first and second year before harvesting	+0.44
Jan-May rainfall, year before harvesting	+0.66
Jan-May rainfall, second year before harvesting	+0.10
Sum Jan-May rainfall, first and second year before harvesting	+0.72
Total rainfall, 29 months before harvesting	+0.64
Integrated soil water deficit, year before harvesting	−0.75
Integrated soil water deficit, second year before harvesting	−0.38
Integrated soil water deficit, first and second year before harvesting	−0.78
Integrated soil water deficit, Jan-May, year before harvesting	−0.68
Integrated soil water deficit, Jan-May, second year before harvesting	−0.29
Sum integrated soil water deficit, Jan-May, first and second year before harvesting	−0.70
Integrated soil water deficit, 29 months before harvesting	−0.81

Source: G.W. Smith, "The relation between rainfall, soil water and yield of copra on a coconut estate in Trinidad," *Journal of Applied Ecology,* vol. 3 (1966), Blackwell Scientific Publications, Ltd.

The British government, faced with a critical shortage of oils and fats, attempted to relieve this shortage by clearing extensive land areas to grow groundnuts in Tanzania in the late 1940s. Temperature conditions are favorable for groundnut production in Tanzania but precipitation conditions are anything but propitious. A simple water budget study to compare the distribution of periods without precipitation or with low soil moisture storage in Tanzania with similar conditions in other areas where groundnuts grow successfully, would have revealed the low probability of success in Tanzania. Had this been done, the scheme probably would never have been attempted.

Using a two-layer water budget model in which water is removed from the top layer at the potential evapotranspiration rate until its capacity (25 mm) is exhausted, the frequency of occurrence of different length periods with dry topsoil (no water in the top layer of the two-layer model) for one proposed groundnut area in Tanzania and two present growing areas in the United States has been determined (table 5-5).[31] While Tifton, Georgia, and Norfolk, Virginia,

Table 5-5

Frequency of Occurrence of Various Durations of Dry Topsoil for Dodoma (1936-1965), Norfolk, and Tifton (1940-1969)[a]

Duration (days)	Number of Occurrences[b]			Frequency (%)		
	Dodoma	Norfolk	Tifton	Dodoma	Norfolk	Tifton
6-10	18	16	27	60	53	90
11-15	19	4	4	63	13	13
16-20	7	0	0	23	0	0
21-25	6	0	0	20	0	0
>26	5	0	0	17	0	0

Source: A.Y.M. Yao, "Evaluating climatic limitations for a specific agricultural enterprise," *Agricultural Meteorology*, vol. 12 (1973) Elsevier Scientific Publishing Co., Amsterdam.
[a]Mid-January—mid-April at Dodoma, mid-May—mid-August at Norfolk and Tifton.
[b]Includes no more than one occurrence in each duration class each year.

in the United States had about the same frequency of short periods (6 to 10 days) of dry conditions as Dodoma, Tanzania, they had many fewer occurrences of longer dry periods. These longer dry periods result in significant decreases in yield without the use of irrigation. In Dodoma, 63 percent of the years had dry periods lasting 11 to 15 days, whereas Tifton and Norfolk experienced dry periods of this length in only 13 percent of the years. Twenty-three percent of the years had dry periods lasting 16 to 20 days in Dodoma but there were no dry periods of this length in either Norfolk or Tifton. One out of five years will have a dry period lasting 21 days or more (two-thirds of the month) in Tanzania; without irrigation the crop would suffer severe to total loss of yield.

Similar figures were obtained when the ratio AE/PE was evaluated using both layers of the root zone profile. Assuming irrigation would have been necessary whenever this ratio dropped below 60 percent and that no stress existed when this ratio was above 90 percent, the probability of AE/PE less than 0.60 was 0.37 in Dodoma in January and only 0.01 and 0.05 in Norfolk and Tifton respectively in May (the corresponding month for U.S. groundnut production).[32] The probability of AE/PE greater than 0.90 was 0.26 in Dodoma in January and 0.77 and 0.73 in Norfolk and Tifton respectively in May. During the five-month growing season, the frequency of occurrence of one or more times with AE/PE less than 0.60 is 76 percent at Dodoma and only 10 percent at Norfolk and Tifton. Irrigation would be needed three years out of four in Dodoma but only one year out of ten in southeastern United States to maintain an adequate groundnut yield.

Such water budget studies make clear that groundnut production without irrigation in Tanzania would be a most risky proposition. Planning such a multimillion dollar program without adequate climatic study became a costly nightmare; consideration of water budget factors should have been sufficient to indicate the perilous nature of the scheme long before the program got to the field trial stage.

Economic Feasibility of Irrigation

In any study of climate and changing crop yields over time, it is first necessary to remove the influence of changing technology, improved varieties of seeds, better farming practices, and increased use of fertilizers from the data of yield. If these other changes have been gradual so that a fairly continuous trend of increasing yields has resulted, it is possible to develop the trend line of yield and to use it as the line that best indicates the effect of improved farming operations on yield. The effect of climatic conditions would therefore be assumed to be represented by the deviations of the individual yearly values of yield from the steady trend line.

Figure 5-15 presents the information on changing annual corn yields in

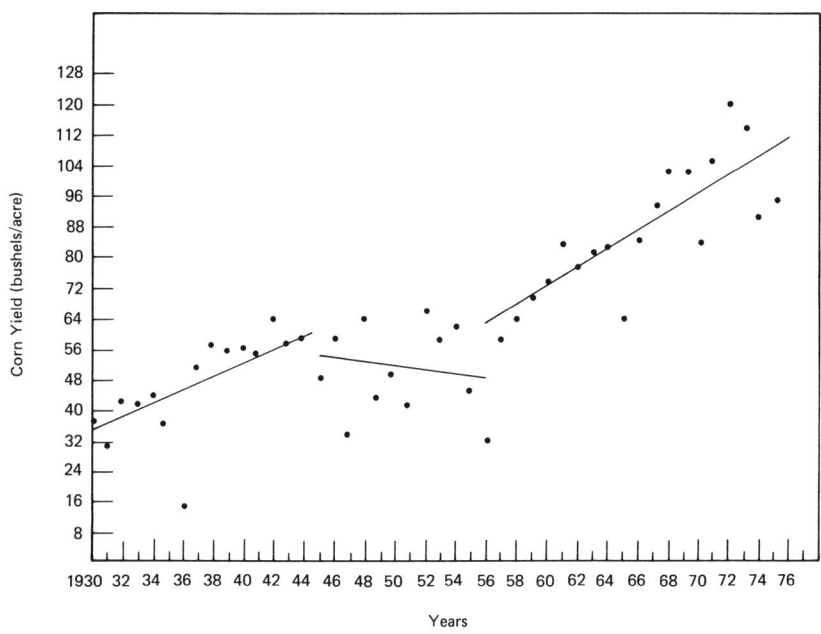

Source: Yield data from Iowa State Farm Census and from official U.S.D.A. Statistical Reporting Service county estimates, courtesy Iowa Crop and Livestock Reporting Service.

Figure 5-15. Annual Corn Yields in Bushels per Acre, Northwestern Iowa, 1930-1975

northwestern Iowa for the 1930-1975 period. Possibly three distinct periods or trends in the record are revealed. From 1930 to 1945 there appears to be a marked increase in yields associated with improved farming practices and better seeds. From 1946 through 1956 little in the way of an increasing trend occurs. The early 1950s were a period of rather dry conditions and it is possible that this period of drought effectively masked any trend caused by improved farming operations. The year 1957 appears to mark the beginning of a second prolonged period of increasing yields, which has continued through the last year of record, 1975.

Using just the yield data for the 1957-1975 period, the regression equation that best fits the distribution of yields is found to be $y = 2.48x - 77.01$ where x is the last two digits of the year. Using the regression line as the line that best expresses the effect of technology on yield, it is possible to obtain the deviations of individual yearly yield values from the trend line. These yearly deviations, considered to be a function of the deviation of climate from "normal," are listed in table 5-6 along with values of the accumulated soil moisture deficit $(PE - AE)$ during the July-August period of peak plant growth. The period from silking to early ear development has been found to be one of great sensitivity to moisture stress for the corn plant. This comes in late July and early August in the Iowa area.

The correlation between corn yield and water deficit in northwestern Iowa is found to be -0.74. Slightly over half the variations in annual corn yield in northwestern Iowa can be explained on the basis of accumulated soil water deficit for July and August. Based on the regression equation between deficit and deviation of corn yield from the trend line $y = -7.06x + 16.22$ where y is

Table 5-6
Accumulated Soil Moisture Deficit July, August (inches) and Deviation of Annual Corn Yield from Trend Line, Northwestern Iowa, 1957-1975

Year	Soil Moist. Deficit (in)	Deviation Corn Yield from Trend Line (bushels/acre)	Year	Soil Moist. Deficit (in)	Deviation Corn Yield from Trend Line (bushels/acre)
1957	1.97	−5.35	1967	1.75	+4.25
1958	1.68	−3.23	1968	1.65	+11.17
1959	3.11	−0.21	1969	1.23	+7.89
1960	1.37	+1.81	1970	4.05	−12.59
1961	1.99	+8.83	1971	1.71	+6.43
1962	1.32	+1.05	1972	0.88	+18.45
1963	2.42	+2.27	1973	2.20	+9.10
1964	1.90	+1.19	1974	2.29	−14.31
1965	4.39	−20.29	1975	3.71	−13.39
1966	3.89	−1.87			

the deviation from the trend and x is the accumulated July-August deficit, it can be seen that maximum possible increases in yields over normal (average climatic conditions, average farming operations) would be 16 bushels per acre if all soil moisture deficits were eliminated by supplemental irrigation. If the irrigation program still allowed 1 inch of deficit to develop in the July-August period, yields would increase only about 9 bushels per acre over normal.

The information on possible increases in crop yields caused by soil moisture deficit provides the data needed to evaluate the economic feasibility of supplemental irrigation. If the overall costs of irrigation in northwestern Iowa are about $25 per acre (for pumps, laterals, labor, power, and so on), and corn brings $2.00 per bushel, clearly supplemental irrigation would not be economically feasible if deficits of 1 inch or more still existed even with the use of irrigation. However, if deficits could be reduced below 1 inch (or to 0) so that yields were increased by at least 13 bushels per acre then it would be economically feasible to use supplemental irrigation.

Clearly in years that are drier than normal, supplemental irrigation may prove economically feasible even if deficits exceed 1 inch but in wetter than normal years, any use of irrigation might not actually increase dollar returns at all. The analysis does suggest certain limits within which the farmer can operate to maximize his use of supplemental irrigation even though all the parameters are not precisely defined given the present state of our knowledge.

6 Forest Ecosystems

Tree growth, productivity, vigor against attacks of insects and fungi, susceptibility to fires, and rates of accumulation and breakdown of leaf litter and forest
duff are all related to the water budget. Foresters have long studied moisture
relationships within forests, focusing on such problems as the effect of forest
cover on the increase or decrease of precipitation, the effect of clear cutting or
partial tree removal on runoff, and the relation between climatic conditions
(especially moisture) and actual distribution of different vegetation species.
More recent work has dealt, in part, with water relationships of individual trees,
including movement of water from soil to roots and within the trunk to the
leaves, problems of water stress in individual trees, and the relation of stress to
tree vitality. Several different factors of the water budget have been employed in
the search for data that are clearly related to the response of forest ecosystems.

Net Above-Ground Productivity

Primary productivity can be defined as the rate at which organic matter is
photosynthetically created per unit of surface and time. Because energy is
required for photosynthesis, the rate of primary productivity may be expressed
either in kilogram calories or in grams per unit area per time. Because
productivity is a rate, it must be considered separately from the biomass or
standing vegetation already present at the beginning of the period being studied.
Of course, green plants use some of the organic material they have created in the
process of respiration, so that net primary productivity may be defined as the
organic matter produced per unit area and time after losses by respiration have
been taken into account. It is the net primary productivity that is available for
use by humans or other animals.

Investigators have long attempted to find ways to express net primary
productivity in terms of more readily measured quantities so that areal estimates
can be achieved. Both water and temperature factors have been studied and used
as surrogates for net primary productivity. Plants use large amounts of water in
transpiration and food manufacture. Under environments in which water is fairly
limited, natural plant selection results in the spread of plants that conserve more
of their water supplies while in the more humid climates wider variations in
water use per unit of production occur from one species to another. Figure 6-1
relates a large number of values of net primary productivity to values of annual

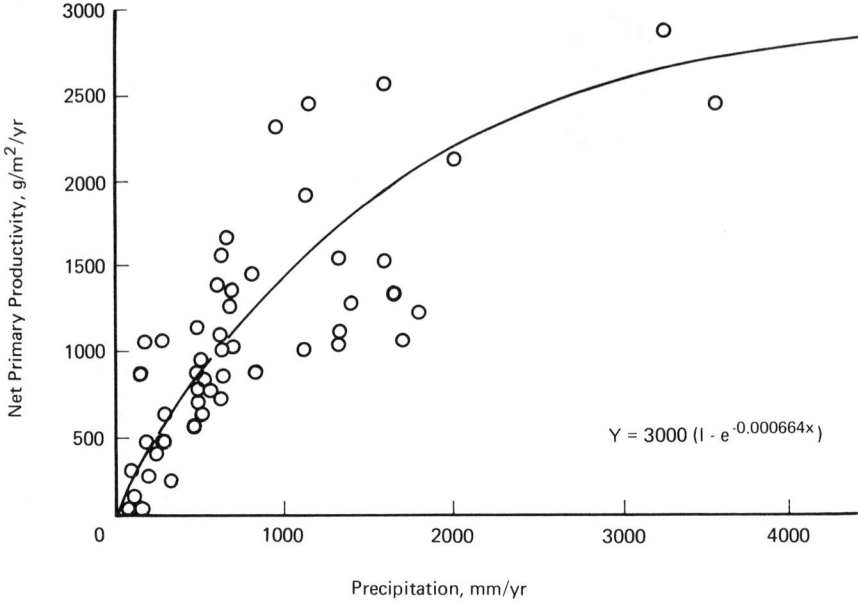

Source: H. Lieth and E. Box, "Evapotranspiration and primary productivity: C.W. Thornthwaite Memorial Model," *Publications in Climatology*, Laboratory of Climatology, vol. 25, no. 3 (1972); also H. Lieth, "Modelling the primary productivity of the world," *Nature and Resources* (UNESCO Paris), vol. 8, 1972.

Figure 6-1. Annual Dry Matter Production, Above and Below Ground, in Relation to Average Annual Precipitation

precipitation. It shows a fairly linear relation with values of precipitation less than about 500 mm/year. A curvilinear relation is found with higher precipitation values and the scatter of points is such that the exact shape of the curve is in doubt. Above about 2000 mm/year productivity seems to level off so that it is fairly independent of precipitation.

The leveling off in productivity is evidently related to energy factors; when net primary productivity is compared with mean annual temperature (figure 6-2) a stretched out S-shaped relationship is found. Net primary productivity increases from less than 200 g/m^2/yr with annual temperatures of $-10°C$ to values approaching 2500 g/m^2/yr with annual temperatures between 25 and 30°C. The excessive scatter of the data points with both temperature and precipitation is undoubtedly an indication that neither factor individually is an adequate surrogate of productivity, although both considered together might offer a much closer approximation.

The ratio of actual evapotranspiration to potential evapotranspiration (AE/PE) has been used as an index of dry matter production or yield although it

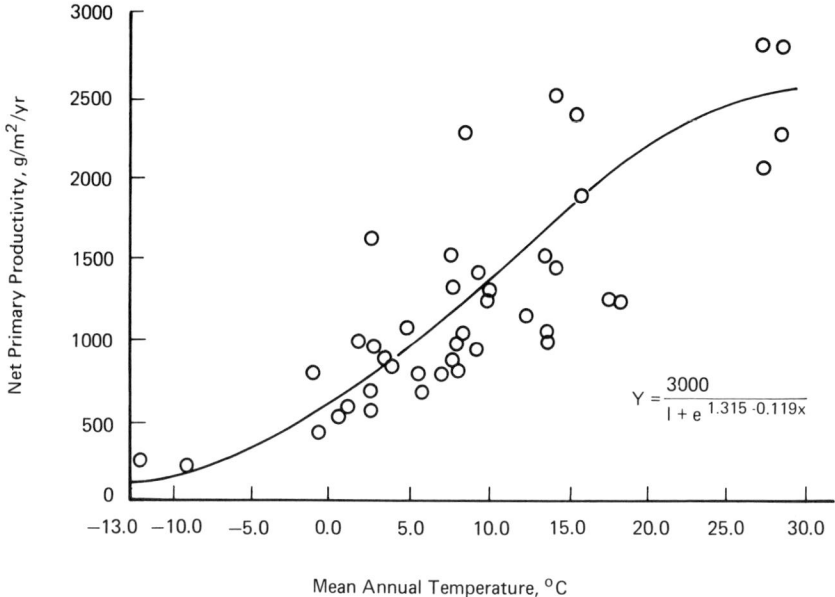

$$Y = \frac{3000}{1 + e^{1.315 - 0.119x}}$$

Source: H. Lieth and E. Box, "Evapotranspiration and primary productivity: C.W. Thornthwaite Memorial Model," *Publications in Climatology*, Laboratory of Climatology, vol. 25, no. 3 (1972); also H. Lieth, "Modelling the primary productivity of the world," *Nature and Resources*, (UNESCO, Paris), vol. 8 (1972).

Figure 6-2. Annual Dry Matter Production, Above and Below Ground, in Relation to Average Annual Temperature

has also been suggested that vascular plant activity and growth might be related directly to actual evapotranspiration.[1] Using net above-ground productivity data from diverse vegetation and geographic areas, a productivity prediction relation (including 5 percent confidence intervals for slope and intercept) has been developed:[2]

$$\log_{10} NAAP = (1.66 \pm 0.27) \log_{10} AE - (1.66 \pm 0.07)$$

where *NAAP* is net annual above-ground productivity in grams per square meter and *AE* is annual actual evapotranspiration in mm.

Figure 6-3 illustrates the results of a worldwide survey of vegetation, the letters on the graph indicating particular sites. Actual evapotranspiration would seem to be a good predictor of net annual above-ground productivity in mature plant communities, possibly resulting from the fact that *AE* reflects the simultaneous availability of two of the important resources limiting photosyn-

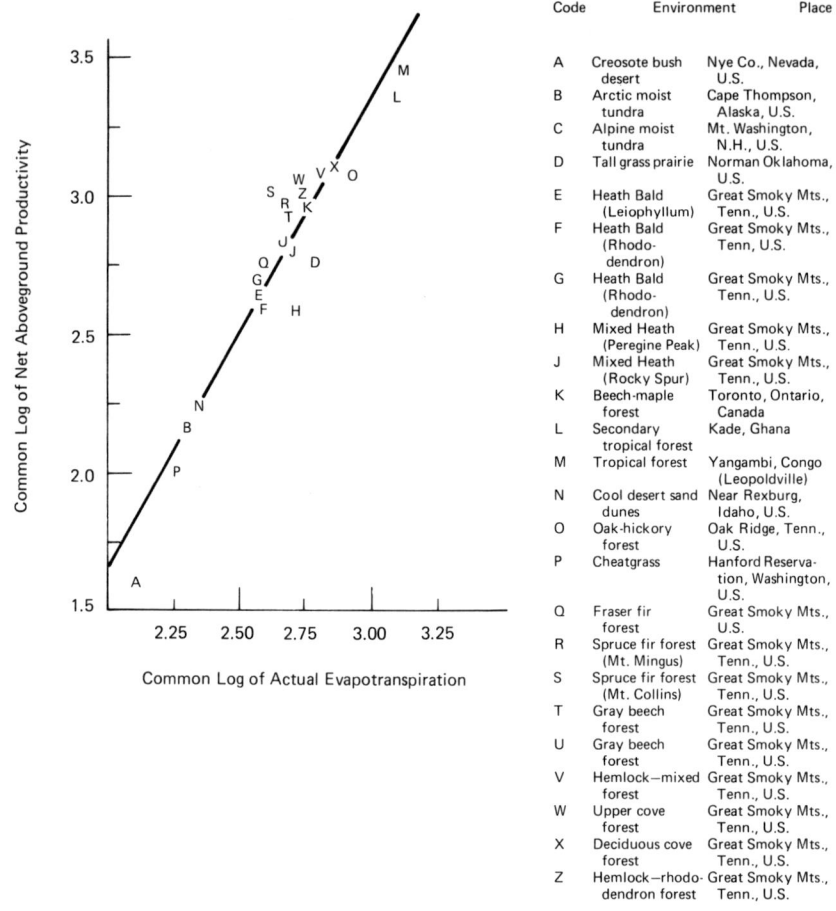

Code	Environment	Place
A	Creosote bush desert	Nye Co., Nevada, U.S.
B	Arctic moist tundra	Cape Thompson, Alaska, U.S.
C	Alpine moist tundra	Mt. Washington, N.H., U.S.
D	Tall grass prairie	Norman Oklahoma, U.S.
E	Heath Bald (Leiophyllum)	Great Smoky Mts., Tenn., U.S.
F	Heath Bald (Rhodo-dendron)	Great Smoky Mts., Tenn, U.S.
G	Heath Bald (Rhodo-dendron)	Great Smoky Mts., Tenn., U.S.
H	Mixed Heath (Peregine Peak)	Great Smoky Mts., Tenn., U.S.
J	Mixed Heath (Rocky Spur)	Great Smoky Mts., Tenn., U.S.
K	Beech-maple forest	Toronto, Ontario, Canada
L	Secondary tropical forest	Kade, Ghana
M	Tropical forest	Yangambi, Congo (Leopoldville)
N	Cool desert sand dunes	Near Rexburg, Idaho, U.S.
O	Oak-hickory forest	Oak Ridge, Tenn., U.S.
P	Cheatgrass	Hanford Reservation, Washington, U.S.
Q	Fraser fir forest	Great Smoky Mts., U.S.
R	Spruce fir forest (Mt. Mingus)	Great Smoky Mts., Tenn., U.S.
S	Spruce fir forest (Mt. Collins)	Great Smoky Mts., Tenn., U.S.
T	Gray beech forest	Great Smoky Mts., Tenn., U.S.
U	Gray beech forest	Great Smoky Mts., Tenn., U.S.
V	Hemlock—mixed forest	Great Smoky Mts., Tenn., U.S.
W	Upper cove forest	Great Smoky Mts., Tenn., U.S.
X	Deciduous cove forest	Great Smoky Mts., Tenn., U.S.
Z	Hemlock—rhodo-dendron forest	Great Smoky Mts., Tenn., U.S.

Source: M.L. Rosenzweig, "Net primary productivity of terrestrial communities: Prediction from climatological data," *The American Naturalist*, vol. 102, no. 923 (1968) reprinted by permission of the University of Chicago Press.

Figure 6-3. Net Above-Ground Productivity in Grams of Dry Matter per Square Meter in Relation to Actual Evapotranspiration in Millimeters. The regression line is indicated. (Letters refer to list indicating vegetation environment and location.)

thesis, water and solar energy. CO_2, the third important element in photosynthesis, remains fairly constant.[3]

Geographical Representation of Primary Productivity

Various relations between climatic factors and primary productivity have been brought together to produce a computer-generated map of world terrestrial productivity.[4] Preliminary world maps on a SYMAP map module had been based on a relation between average annual temperature and annual total precipitation.[5] Later computer maps attempted to use a relation with evapotranspiration rather than temperature and precipitation since this quantity expresses both the energy and water relationships influencing plant growth. For example, the relation shown in figure 6-3 has been used although not without problems. Any relation between primary productivity and climatic factors should approach but not exceed as an upper limiting value one suggested by Mitscherlich's yield law.[6] The results shown in figure 6-3 do not provide such an upper limiting value.

To correct this problem a computer simulation of Geiger's excellent world map of actual evapotranspiration[7] was prepared. Comparing the values of actual evapotranspiration, so obtained, with values of primary productivity, the following new relation was developed:

$$P = 3000 \left[1 - e^{-0.0009695(E-20)} \right]$$

where P is productivity in $g/m^2/yr$; E is actual evapotranspiration in mm/yr; and e is the base of the natural logarithms. Using this relation and Geiger's values of evapotranspiration, a new computer-generated map of net terrestrial primary productivity was produced (figure 6-4).[8] Though the map was dedicated to Thornthwaite because of his interest in evapotranspiration, the data actually used were from Geiger's map. More basic data on primary productivity are still needed to fill certain gaps clearly evident in the estimates from many individual regions.

Tree Ring Growth and Climate

Trees grown in areas in which climate is frequently limiting (in the semiarid forest border, for example) often provide the best indication of any climate-growth ring relationship.[9] In those areas, precipitation plays a more obvious role in size of rings produced and there is greater relative variation in yearly ring width. A schematic model starting with low precipitation and high temperature (which would result in low actual evapotranspiration) is useful in describing the various interrelationships of activities that would ultimately lead to the formation of a narrow tree ring (figure 6-5). The double set of arrows indicates a possible primary sequence of events. Precipitation (as it affects both soil moisture and water available for actual evapotranspiration) and temperature (through its effect on rate of evapotranspiration) are controlling factors in yearly ring width.

A climatic model has also been used to determine how much the lack of available soil moisture limits the diameter growth of loblolly pines in the southern United States.[10] Such a model can also be used to determine whether it would be economically feasible to irrigate such forests to eliminate soil

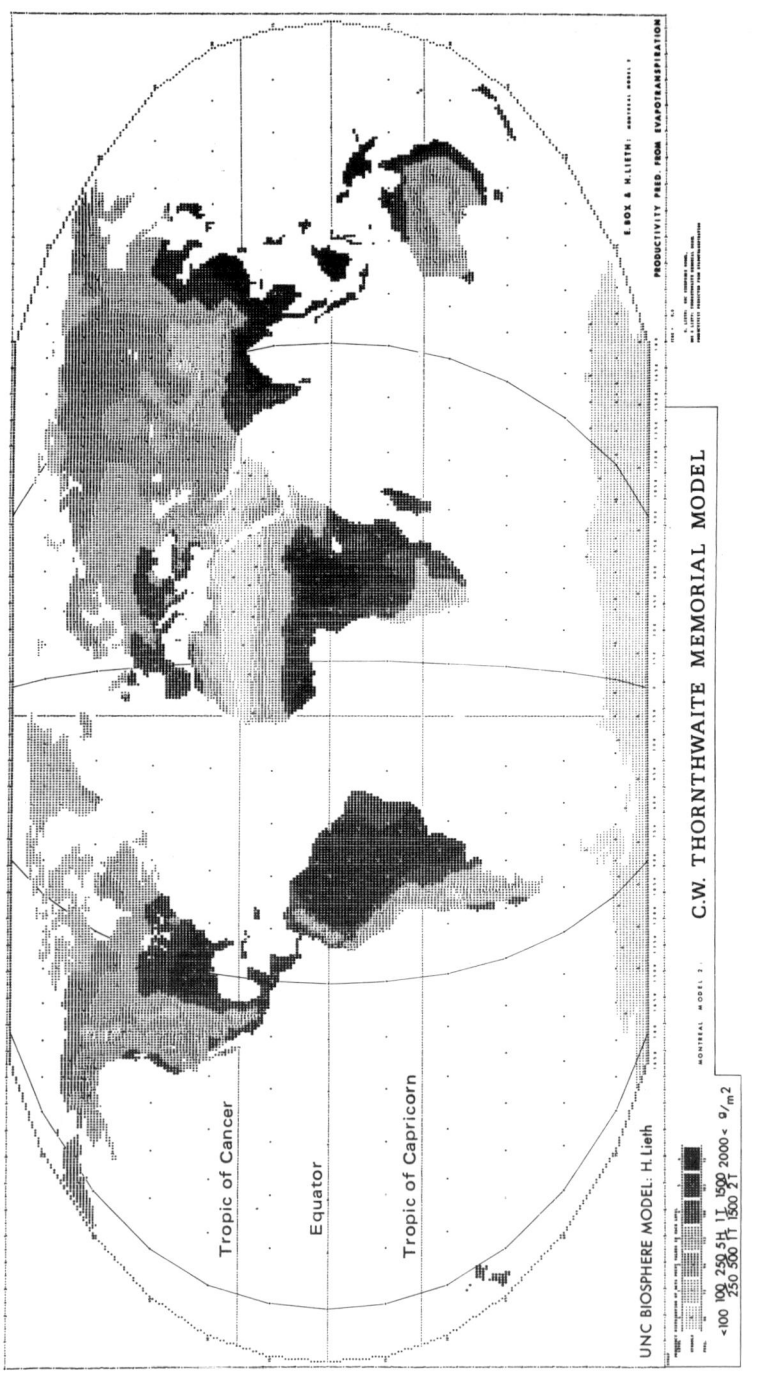

Source: H. Lieth and E. Box, "Evapotranspiration and primary productivity: C.W. Thornthwaite Memorial Model," *Publications in Climatology*, Laboratory of Climatology, vol. 25, no. 3 (1972).

Figure 6-4. The C.W. Thornthwaite Memorial Model. The primary productivity of the land areas predicted from actual evapotranspiration using the Box-Lieth model to convert Geiger's evapotranspiration map into a productivity map

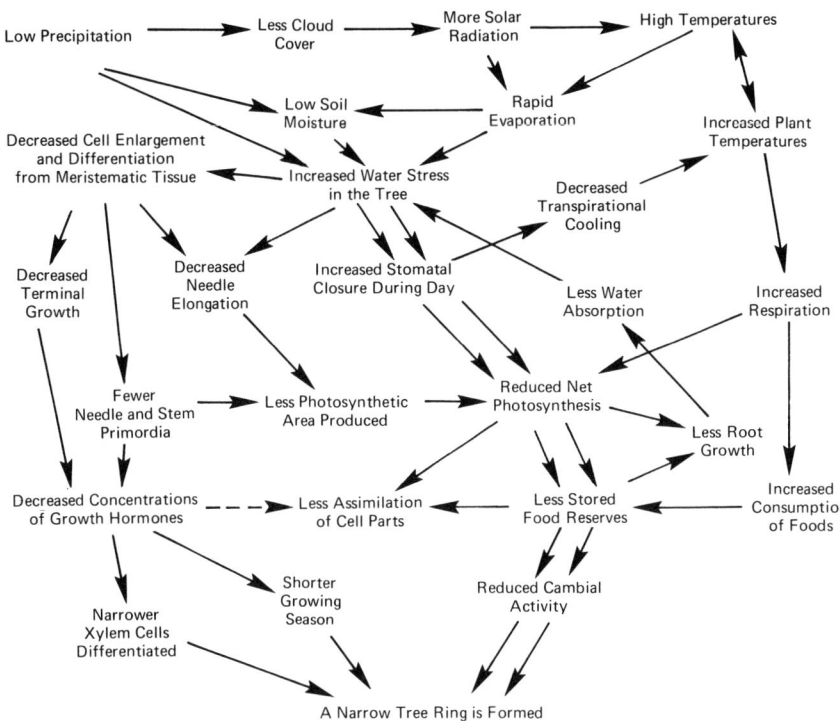

Source: H.C. Fritts,"Growth-rings of trees: their correlation with climate," *Science*, vol. 154, no. 3752 (25 November 1966):973-979, figure 4. Copyright 1966 by the American Association for the Advancement of Science.

Figure 6-5. Diagram of a Hypothetical Model for the Relationship Between Low Precipitation and High Temperature Leading to the Production of a Narrow Tree Ring

moisture deficits. Relating monthly diameter growth increments to seventeen variables based on the weather elements of temperature, precipitation, water budget factors, age, stand density, and site index, only six were found to contribute directly to the prediction of growth. These were combined in the following relation

$$G = 3.034 + 0.123 \, (X_1) - 0.120 \, (X_2) - 0.067 \, (X_3)$$

$$- 0.101 \, (X_4) - 0.032 \, (X_5) - 0.015 \, (X_6)$$

where G is the monthly diameter growth of loblolly pines (sq. ft. of basal area per acre); X_1 is the calculated actual evapotranspiration (inches) for current month; X_2 is the calculated actual evapotranspiration (inches) for previous month; X_3 is calculated actual evapotranspiration (inches) for previous June-November period; X_4 is soil moisture deficit (inches) for current month; X_5 is calculated actual evapotranspiration (inches) for previous three months; and X_6 is the age of trees in years.[11] The predictive model was found to explain 81 percent of the growth variation in trees.

Using available climatic data in the predictive model, the additional growth (in cords per acre per year) that could be produced at various places throughout the southeastern part of the country using a hypothetical program of irrigation to eliminate soil moisture deficit for thirty continuous years was calculated. In the example, it was assumed that the trees were then fifty years old. Comparing these values with the growth possible under the actual conditions of soil moisture deficit, values of the increase in wood production possible through elimination of soil moisture deficit conditions were obtained. The values ranged from 0.07 to 0.26 additional cords per acre per year in the coastal states from Florida to Virginia, and from 0.23 to 0.56 cords per acre per year in the drier Texas and Arkansas area.

Based on 1973 pulpwood prices, it would not have been economically feasible to irrigate southeastern pine forests.[12] Because feasibility is related to both costs of operating irrigation systems and pulpwood prices, the occurrence of either future technological changes (including the possibility of effective cloud seeding operations) or higher pulpwood prices might justify efforts to eliminate moisture deficit and so increase forest production in the South.

In another study of loblolly pine growth in relation to climatic factors, a two-layer climatic water budget model was used to determine the distribution of moisture in the upper soil layers.[13] Gravitational water was assumed to move downward from the upper layer to the layer below whenever the moisture content in the layer above exceeded the moisture-holding capacity of that layer. Moisture was removed from the first soil layer until its moisture content equaled that of the next layer; then the two layers were combined and moisture was lost from both together. These assumptions create a series of soil layers with moisture contents decreasing with depth. Soil moisture deficit was defined as the difference between the computed soil moisture content and the value at the moisture holding capacity of the soil.

Annual growth of loblolly pines can be separated into two seasonal periods—earlywood and latewood growth. Though it is difficult to define exactly when these two growth periods begin or end in loblolly pines growing on well-drained sites in North Carolina, earlywood growth probably begins in late March and ends in June or early July. July soil moisture deficits do not seem to be related to either earlywood or latewood growth. Latewood growth may start in July or August, possibly running through October. These dates are tentative because of the possible influence of such factors as height of the sampling point, tree size, or other climatic growth parameters.

A significant curvilinear relation is found between annual latewood volume and soil moisture deficit.[14] By plotting the reciprocal of the latewood volume against the August-October moisture deficits (figure 6-6) an approximate straight line relation results. The regression equation is

$$Y_1 = 0.0244 + 0.0241X$$

where Y_1 is the reciprocal of the mean annual latewood volume (m^{-3}) and X is the sum of August-October moisture deficits (cm).

Earlywood volume was found to be related to more than just soil moisture deficit. Testing twenty-one independent variables, five were found to be related significantly to the variation in earlywood volume. From a stepwise regression analysis, the following equation was developed

$$Y_e = 0.1412 - 0.002683X_1 - 0.00000488X_2 - 0.002127X_3$$

$$+ 0.0002132X_4 + 0.0009218X_5$$

where Y_e is the reciprocal of the annual earlywood volume (m^{-3}); X_1 is mean temperature of June (°C); X_2 is moisture deficit of May (cm); X_3 is mean temperature, previous October (°C); X_4 is percent sunshine, previous November; and X_5 is mean temperature, March (°C). The multiple correlation coefficient of the equation is 0.90; partial correlation coefficients are all significant at the 1 percent level.[15]

Interestingly, age and tree height exerted only little influence on early or latewood volume. Also no clear correlation was found between earlywood and latewood production in the same year. Light and temperature were not limiting factors in the August to October period although they were in the spring period. Temperature was most limiting to earlywood production whereas soil moisture deficit was most influential in latewood production.

Water Use By Pine and Fir Trees

There have been an increasing number of studies of the water relations of individual trees or of tree species. They have included study of water stress in trees and its effect on such aspects as growth, tree vigor, and susceptibility to disease or insect attack. For example, the water use of two different tree species, Corsican pine and Douglas fir, was studied in southeastern England.[16] Comparing total evaporation from each of these tree stands with Penman's estimates of open water evaporation, both species were found to be quite similar. Both tree species were essentially forty years of age, the mean height of the pine being 21.3 m and of the fir 23.7 m. Tree density was 655 per hectare for the pine and

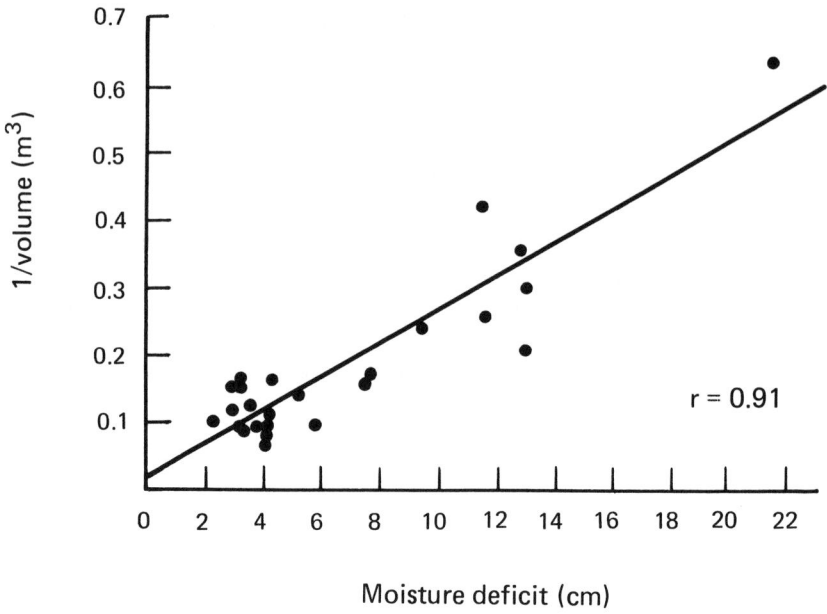

Source: F.M. Buckingham and F.W. Woods, "Loblolly pine as influenced by soil moisture and other environmental factors," *Journal of Applied Ecology*, vol. 6 (1969), Blackwell Scientific Publications Ltd.

Figure 6-6. Relationship Between the Reciprocal of Latewood Volume and Combined Moisture Deficits of August, September, and October

642 per hectare for the fir. The trees were growing on moderately podzolized sandy loam soil some 60 cm deep under the pine and about 150 cm deep under the fir. The upper layer was underlain with sandy clay loam in each case. Observation sites were in the middle of larger plantations of similar trees extending nearly 1 km in all directions.

Estimates of evapotranspiration were made by assuming that all precipitation was lost as evapotranspiration from the last time in spring when the soil moisture tension (measured indirectly through the use of gypsum resistance blocks) was steady (soil at or near field capacity) until it returned to this same point in the fall or winter. Table 6-1 shows the results for four replicate sites under each tree species for five years, 1962-1967. Values for Penman open water evaporation for the same time periods are also included along with values of the ratio of estimated actual evaporation to calculated open water evaporation.

The results suggest clearly that during periods when soil moisture is limited, Corsican pine will use more water than will Douglas fir. Differences in various site factors, such as depths to the water table, heights of capillary rise, deep percolation, soil water deficits, or heights of the tree plantations were investi-

Table 6-1

Estimates of Actual Evapotranspiration (E) and Calculated Open Water Evaporation (Penman Eo) from Corsican Pine and Douglas Fir Plots During Periods of Water Deficit, Southeast England, 1962-1967

Date		Corsican Pine				Douglas Fir			
		1	*2*	*3*	*4*	*1*	*2*	*3*	*4*
1962-63	E	51.5	51.5	52.1	51.5	23.9	24.0	26.8	30.4
	Eo	41.9	41.9	43.9	41.9	30.1	35.6	37.2	37.4
	E/Eo	1.12	1.12	1.06	1.12	0.79	0.68	0.72	0.81
1963-64	E	56.2	54.0	53.6	53.6	–	19.6	21.5	21.5
	Eo	39.8	39.3	36.4	36.4	–	28.9	33.9	33.9
	E/Eo	1.41	1.37	1.47	1.47	–	0.68	0.64	0.64
1964-65	E	101.0	100.4	99.6	100.1	22.4	24.2	24.7	26.6
	Eo	100.8	97.4	96.1	98.2	23.9	28.6	28.8	36.7
	E/Eo	1.00	1.03	1.04	1.02	0.94	0.86	0.86	0.73
1965-66	E	(values for 1964-65 cover two years)				–	41.8	–	37.3
	Eo					–	45.8	–	45.2
	E/Eo					–	0.92	–	0.82
1966-67	E	64.5	63.5	64.5	71.1	–	34.1	27.2	31.1
	Eo	52.1	48.3	52.1	59.1	–	44.2	26.2	43.9
	E/Eo	1.24	1.31	1.24	1.20	–	0.77	1.04	0.71
Mean	E/Eo	1.14	1.21	1.20	1.20	0.87	0.78	0.82	0.74

Source: D.F. Fourt and W.H. Hinson, "Water relations of tree crops: A comparison between Corsican pine and Douglas fir in southeast England," *Journal of Applied Ecology*, vol. 7 (1970), Blackwell Scientific Publications, Ltd.

gated and not found to account for the differences in evaporation.[17] Thus the apparent real differences in water use between these species may be related to wind movement through the distinctive canopy structures, leaf patterns, different rooting patterns, or the effects of different understory vegetation and humus layers beneath the trees. No mention was made of differences in albedo (reflectivity) of the two canopies, but it may be possible that absorbed energy differences could also account for some differences in evapotranspiration. The study suggests the need for real caution in generalization about the water use of different vegetation species whether the soil is at field capacity or suffering from a water deficit.

The Water Budget and Forest Fires

The National Fire-Danger Rating System of 1974 grew out of more than two decades of work by foresters directed toward achieving a nationally uniform fire-rating system based on those environmental factors that influence the day-to-day changes in the moisture content of fuels.[18] The system considers only the "initiating fire," defined as the fire that is not behaving erratically and that is spreading without spotting through fuels in contact with the ground (not through the crowns). It further attempts to evaluate the worst conditions that might exist in an area by utilizing observations at the time of day when fire danger is usually greatest and by measuring the fire danger on open westerly or southwesterly slopes. The system provides ratings that are relative rather than absolute, but that are capable of physical interpretation in terms of fire occurrence and behavior.

The rating of danger from fire is basically the prediction of how a potential fire will behave. The factors determining fire behavior are both variable and constant over time. The variable factors (functions of the weather) include wind, fuel moisture, and fuel temperature; the constant factors are topography and fuels. The National Fire Danger Rating System attempts to include all these factors, the variable factors on a daily basis.

Weather and climate condition in relation to seven important fires that occurred in the upper Midwest from 1870 to 1920 have been studied in some detail.[19] Three of the great fires occurred in 1871 (near Peshtigo and Sturgeon Bay, Wisconsin, Alpena and Thunder Bay, Michigan, and across south-central Michigan from Muskegon to Lansing and Port Huron) while the others were in the Michigan thumb area (north of Port Huron) in 1881; near Hinckley, Minnesota, in 1894; Baudette, Minnesota, in 1910; and Cloquet, Minnesota, in 1918.

Table 6-2 compares prefire precipitation conditions at stations located near the fire areas with conditions normally found during the same time periods. In every case, prefire precipitation was well below the normal precipitation for the area in question, and, at most stations, precipitation has only rarely been less than it was during those particular prefire situations.

Values of soil moisture storage in the upper three feet of the soil profile were obtained from water budget computations. In carrying out the computations, it was assumed that all soils in the fire regions had a 6-inch water-holding capacity and that the wilting point for the vegetation would be reached when soil moisture storage declined below 1.8 inches. Clearly such assumptions tend to generalize the different soil characteristics and rooting depths found in the different fire areas of the north-central states. Soil moisture storage profiles prepared for one station in each of the fire years (two for different areas in 1871) are included in figure 6-7. In every case, the normal summer soil moisture storage in the area always stayed above the wilting point.

However, in each of the fire years, soil moisture conditions were well below wilting at each station. The actual fire date, in all cases, came near the point of driest soil conditions and after the soil had been below the wilting point for more than one month and in most cases for more than two months. Although

Table 6-2

Comparison between Prefire Precipitation Conditions and Normal Precipitation

Year	Station	Months of drought preceding fire (1)	Total precipitation during months of drought (2)	Lowest precipitation amount ever recorded during same period of months (3)	Number of times total precipitation has been less than amounts given in column 2 (4)	Length of reliable station record[a] (5)	Normal precipitation amount during months in column 1 (6)
			Inches	Inches		Years	Inches
1871	Detroit	6 (April-Sept.)	12.35	10.89	6	96	17.75
	Grand Rapids	5 (May-Sept.)	11.08	7.46	11	96	15.18
	Lansing	5 (May-Sept.)	10.21	8.25	7	103	15.30
	Thunder Bay	5 (May-Sept.)	9.58	8,08	5	96	15.08
	Chicago	3 (July-Sept.)	5.27	4.01	3	96	9.26
	Embarrass	4 (June-Sept.)	12.54	10.98	1	28	18.86
	Sturgeon Bay	4 (June-Sept.)	4.75	4.75	0	80	12.12
1881	Port Huron	5 (April-Aug.)	9.15	7.29	8	92	15.38
	Thornville	5 (April-Aug.)	6.75	6.75	0	90	15.23
1894	Cambridge	3 (June-Aug.)	3.09	2.83	1	75	12.34
	Collegeville	3 (June-Aug.)	4.03	3.19	1	75	10.07
	Sandy Lake	4 (May-Aug.)	3.28	3.28	0	75	15.72
	St. Paul	3 (June-Aug.)	2.00	2.00	0	128	10.85
1910	Baudette	5 (May-Sept.)	6.60	6.36	1	58	14.86
1918	Cloquet	8+ (Feb.-Sept.)	14.20	13.52	1	96	23.19
	Duluth	8+ (Feb.-Sept.)	12.67	12.67	0	96	22.71

Source: D.A. Haines and R.W. Sando, "Climatic conditions preceding historically great fires in the North Central region," *Forest Service Research Paper NC-34*, North Central Forest Experiment Station, St. Paul, Minn., U.S. Department of Agriculture (1969).

[a]In some cases records at the indicated station were combined with those at a nearby station to fill in missing years and give the longest possible record. As an example, the St. Paul data have been combined with early Fort Snelling records and more recent Minneapolis observations to give the longest historical series of weather records west of the Mississippi River.

climate, especially both antecedent soil moisture conditions and prefire precipitation, appears to be an important contributor to the rapid spread of fires, other nonclimatic factors must contribute to the actual process of ignition and the later control of the fire.[20] Climate prepares the stage by readying the fuels for rapid burning but, in most cases, some other event, often involving human neglect, provides the actual trigger to initiate the outbreak.

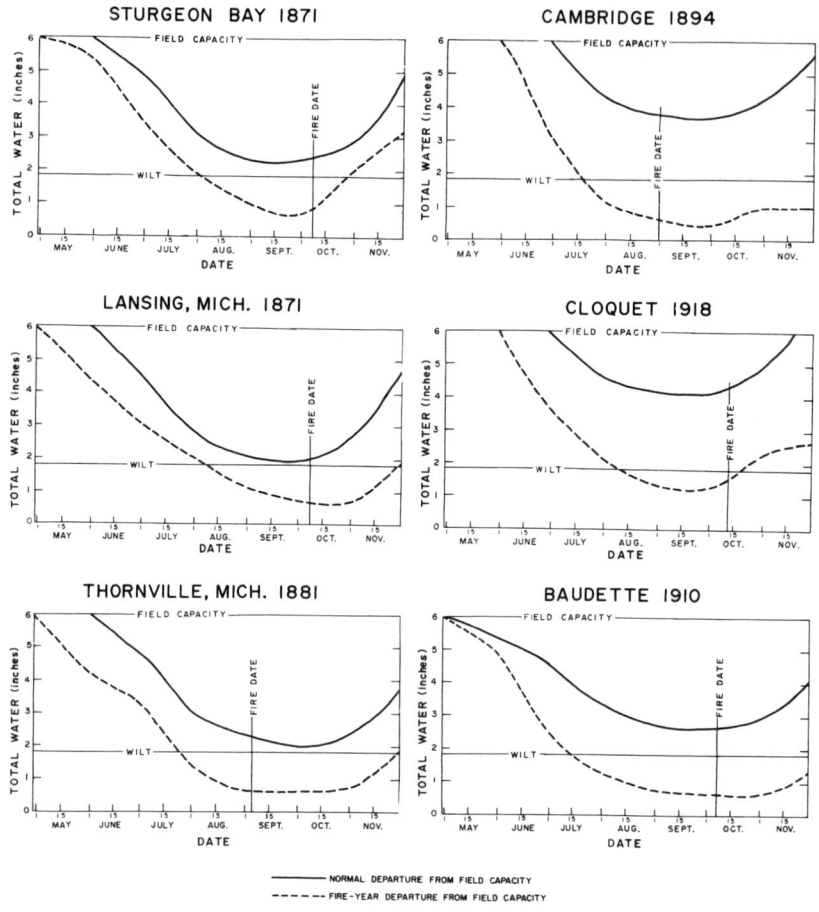

Source: D.A. Haines and R.W. Sando, "Climatic conditions preceding historically great fires in the North Central region," *Forest Service Research Paper NC-34*, North Central Forest Experiment Station, St. Paul, Minn., U.S. Department of Agriculture (1969).

Figure 6-7. March of Soil Moisture Storage During the Seasons of the Peshtigo, 1871 Michigan, 1881 Michigan Thumb, Hinckley, Cloquet, and Bandette Fires. Data were computed for a 3-foot soil depth assuming a 6-inch water-holding field capacity and a 1.8-inch wilt threshold value.

The new National Fire-Danger Rating System attempts to include all pertinent weather and fuel information related to fuel moisture. The system requires information on 24-hour maximum and minimum relative humidities, temperatures, rainfall amounts, and duration of rainfall. In addition, the so-called 10-hour time-lag fuel moisture value is included either as measured from fuel moisture sticks or as estimated from information on dry bulb temperature, cloudiness, and relative humidity. The 1-hour and 100-hour time-lag fuel moisture values are also needed in the relation, indicating the importance of some information on duff moisture in the overall fire-danger rating system.

Recognizing the place of fuel moisture in the whole problem of fire-danger indexing, a climatic water budget has been used in an attempt to develop a duff moisture model.[21] While duff holds very little water in relation to the storage capacity of the rooting zone, it can hold proportionately large amounts in relation to its own weight (over 200 percent of its oven-dry weight). Moisture removal from the duff is almost entirely by means of evaporation.

A useful formula is available for computing depth of capillary moisture (*DCM*) in the duff.[22]

$$DCM = \frac{\text{field moisture capacity}}{100} \text{ (volume weight)} \times \text{(depth of duff)}$$

where *DCM* is expressed as the equivalent volume of rainfall that could fill the capillary spaces of a duff that is as dry as possible. The available soil moisture capacity has been calculated as 0.25 inch in the duff in the Shawnee National Forest in southern Illinois.[23]

The duff can be assumed to dry because of the evaporative demand at the forest floor (*PEV*). This quantity can be stated as a percentage of the total potential evapotranspiration (*PE*) demands. Because of the influence of the leaf canopy on temperature, humidity, and wind conditions beneath the canopy, *PEV* is assumed to be 100 percent of *PE* in the dormant months, 70 percent of *PE* in the spring and fall months when leaf formation and fall occur, and 10 percent of *PE* during the growing season months.[24] Thus, two steps are needed to compute the actual moisture change in the duff. First, the potential evapotranspiration rate is determined from temperature conditions at a nearby weather station and the value is corrected on the basis of the evaporative demand (*PEV*) on the forest floor. Second, the rate of removal of water from the duff is adjusted by means of a simple exponential relationship of the form

$$\Delta ST_d = PEV_d \left(\frac{ST_{d-1}}{D \text{ Cap}} \right)$$

where ΔST_d is the change in the duff on the day in question, ST_{d-1} is the amount of duff storage on the previous day, and D Cap is the total storage capacity of the duff.

A simple daily bookkeeping procedure permits computing the actual duff moisture budget for each day. Relating values of duff storage to the number of fires occurring in the Shawnee National Forest in 1963, 1965, and 1966, a correlation coefficient of +0.86 was found between calculated duff moisture and average number of fires per day using Spearman's Rank Correlation.[25] This relation is significant at the 0.01 level. Some 74 percent of the variation in observed fire frequencies is accounted for by variation in calculated duff moisture. Figure 6-8 shows the results graphically. Though the variation in the number of fires per day is quite large with low values of duff storage, this can partly be explained on the basis of the limited record available for study. The approach would seem to be useful enough to warrant further testing and refinement. Inclusion of some such information on duff moisture in the National Fire-Danger Rating System might increase its prediction value by possibly improving the present estimations of fuel moisture.

Actual Evapotranspiration and Organic Decomposition

Information on the rate of breakdown of organic remains at the forest floor is not readily available or in a form that can be easily compared with other decomposition data. Two studies of litter decomposition, however, one in a

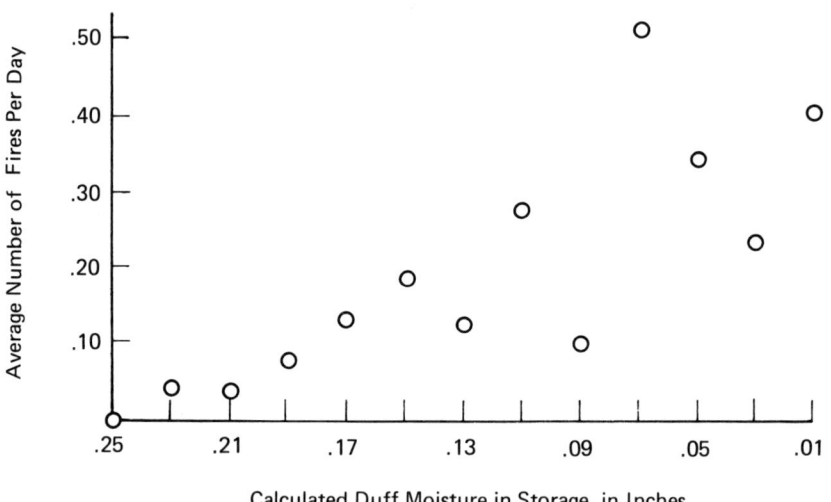

Source: V. Meentemeyer, "Climatic water budget approach to forest problems. I. The prediction of forest fire hazard through moisture budgeting," *Publications in Climatology*, Laboratory of Climatology, vol. 27, no. 1 (1974).

Figure 6-8. Relationship of Calculated Duff Moisture Storage to Number of Fire Occurrences, 1963, 1965, 1966, Shawnee National Forest in Southern Illinois

temperate forest in Holland from 1957 to 1962, and a second in four birch and conifer forests in both northern and southern Finland were reasonably comparable.[26] The study in Holland was of the actual accumulation and loss in dry weight of leaf litter in a mature deciduous forest, whereas the Finland study only included the loss in dry weight of litter placed in large bags with an intermediate mesh size. Combining the two studies, ten data points representing the annual percentage of decomposition of leaf litter in mid- to high-latitude forests are available for comparison with the annual actual evapotranspiration in those areas.[27] The results are given in figure 6-9. While the relation looks quite reasonable, the relation should only be used with caution in areas and in forest situations that are unlike those from which the relation was derived.

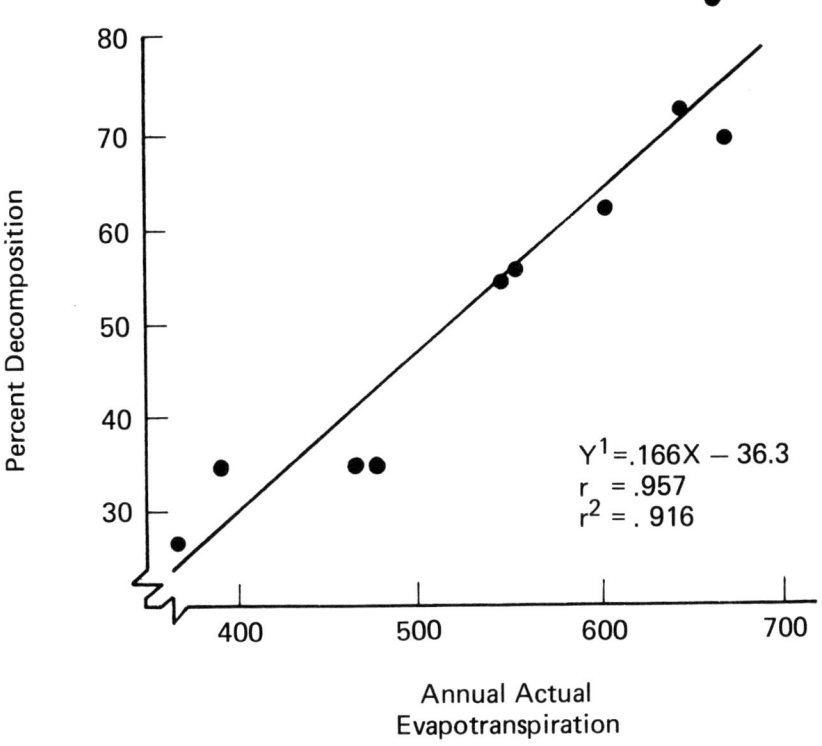

$$Y^1 = .166X - 36.3$$
$$r = .957$$
$$r^2 = .916$$

Annual Actual
Evapotranspiration

Source: V. Meentemeyer, "Climatic water budget approach to forest problems. II. The prediction of regional differences in decomposition rate of organic debris," *Publications in Climatology*, Laboratory of Climatology, vol. 27, no. 1 (1974).

Figure 6-9. Composite Regression Model of Decomposition Rate. Actual evapotranspiration (annual in mm) is plotted against annual percentage of material lost.

Figure 6-3 related net annual above-ground productivity to actual evapotranspiration, while figure 6-9 related plant decomposition and actual evapotranspiration. These two relationships have been combined to produce a diagram that expresses both annual production and destruction of organic matter in relation to annual actual evapotranspiration (figure 6-10).[28] Litter production and decomposition curves cross at an annual actual evapotranspiration of about 850 mm. The shaded area to the left of the cross-over point indicates more production of dry matter than decomposition and hence a holdover of organic material from one year to the next, whereas the area between curves 2 and 3 to the right of the cross-over point indicates an increasing tendency for organic production to be decomposed in time periods of less than one year. At a moist, tropical site with an AE of 1500 mm annually the organic dry matter production would be decomposed in a little less than six months.

Tree Vigor and Pine Beetle Infestation

Information from a climatic water budget model has also been correlated with the outbreak of southern pine beetle (*Dendroctonus frontalis* Zimm.) activity at two sites, one in eastern Texas and the other in southwestern Louisiana.[29] The southern pine beetle is a destructive pest whose economic impact on pine forests from New Jersey through the southeastern United States to Texas has increased markedly in the past several decades. Timber loss caused by the pine beetle was estimated at more than $100 million in 1973 throughout the southeastern United States.[30]

The beetle leads a generally secluded life, with the adult female beetle burrowing beneath the inner bark to deposit its eggs. The eggs hatch in three to nine days and the larvae construct tunnels in the cambium and inner bark in the process of feeding. The larval stage lasts from 25 to 38 days during which time the larvae enlarge their tunnels and may eventually girdle the tree. The beetle may also adversely affect the tree by introducing a blue staining fungus (*Ceratocystis minor* Hedgc.) in the tree phloem and xylem, which may limit conduction in the tree and dry the wood. In cooler regions, three to five beetle generations may develop in a year, whereas six or more generations may develop along the Gulf Coast. Temperature clearly affects the rate of maturation and development.

One of the major natural protective measures of the pine tree against beetle attack seems to be related to the oleoresin exudation pressure (*OEP*), the pressure at which resin is being transported through the phloem of the tree. The greater the *OEP* the less likely will be an attack of the southern pine beetle. Successful pine beetle attacks have been correlated with low values of resin production by the tree.[31] Resin production, in turn, seems to be related to the health and vigor of the tree. Healthy trees, not suffering from a moisture deficit

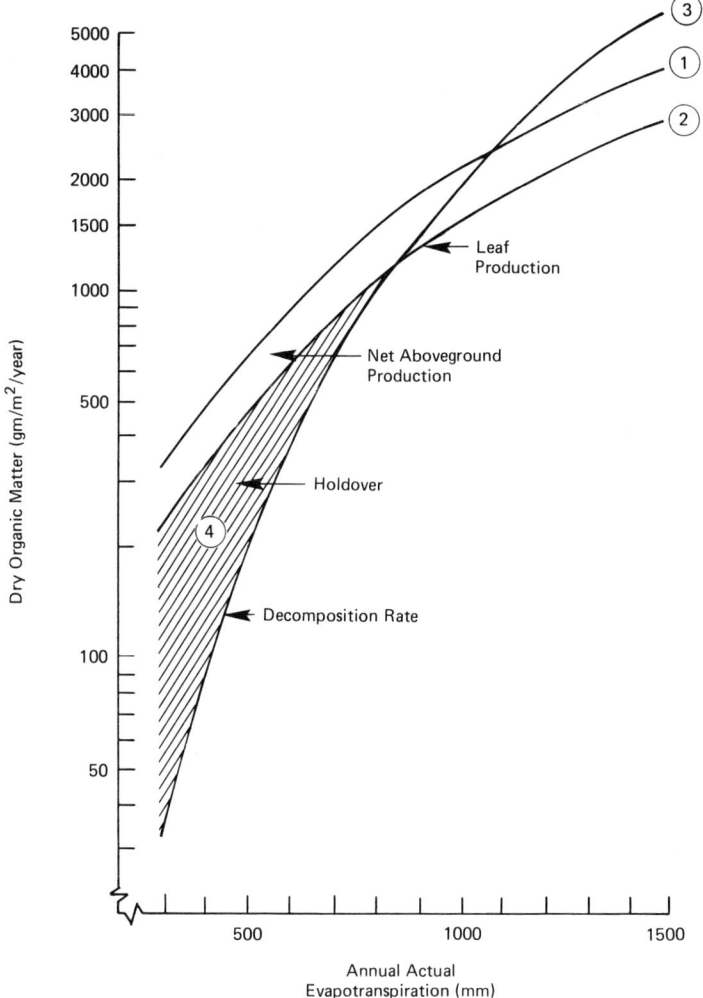

Source: V. Meentemeyer, "Climatic water budget approach to forest problems. II. The prediction of regional differences in decomposition rate of organic debris," *Publications in Climatology*, Laboratory of Climatology, vol. 27, no. 1 (1974).

Figure 6-10. Preliminary Semi-Log Plot of Annual *AE* Against (1) Net Production Above Ground (Annual); (2) Net Production of Leaf Litter; (3) Annual Decomposition of Current Leaf Litter. Net production and leaf production are derived from a modification of the relation shown in figure 6-3. Holdover (4) is the computed difference between annual leaf production and the decomposition of that production.

or from waterlogged soil conditions, produce a more abundant supply of resin, which evidently serves as a detractant to the southern pine beetle. Trees growing in well-drained areas in a season with adequate moisture are not as prone to attack as are trees in low-lying, poorly drained areas or trees suffering from severe droughts.[32]

In Texas and Louisiana, late spring and early summer is the principal period of beetle outbreak. Beetle activity is highly variable from year to year. Cold winters result in lowered infestations the following spring and summer whereas mild winters increase the likelihood of a serious beetle outbreak. Very high summer temperatures will also increase beetle mortality so that extremes of temperature put effective limits to the likelihood of serious beetle infestation.

Because precipitation distribution affects the vigor of the tree, this factor should be correlated with beetle infestation. For example, high precipitation in the winter period coupled with very low precipitation in the following summer can be shown to be related to much above normal beetle activity because both moisture extremes weaken tree vigor, reduce *OEP,* and make the tree more susceptible to attack.[33] Pine beetle activity follows a highly seasonal pattern with most intense outbreaks occurring in the early summer. Because of climatic variation there is a marked change within months from year to year. Thus, it might be desirable to consider *relative* intensity of beetle activity rather than *absolute* intensity. To do so, beetle activity can be expressed as the number of trees attacked as a departure from long-term normals.

Of the various climatic models available to relate to rate of beetle infestation, it was felt that a water budget model might prove most useful because it gives prominent place to two factors, precipitation distribution in relation to need and soil moisture storage, which have been found to be closely related to beetle activity.[34] Three factors from the climatic water budget were considered: potential evapotranspiration, moisture surplus, and moisture deficit. Because there might be some lag in the effect of any of these factors on beetle activity, that activity was correlated against each factor for the current month, for one month previous to the current month, for two months previous and so forth, up to six months previous to the current month.

A stepwise multiple regression analysis was employed to determine the climatic variable most closely related to either the number of trees attacked in the study area, as a departure from the long-term mean value for that particular month ($Y1$) or the actual number of trees attacked in the previous month ($Y2$). Significance of the relationship was determined.

Twelve predictive models were generated, six related to $Y1$, the departure in beetle activity from the monthly mean, and six related to $Y2$, the trend in relative activity from the previous month. Two of the twelve models were selected as most capable of predicting southern pine beetle activity based on variations in climate.[35] Expressed in a stepwise multiple regression form, they are:

*Y*2   Texas   1961-1972 data, May-August

$$Y2 = 12.493 - 220.760(PE3) - 371.804(PE0) - 37.914(S2)$$
$$+ 260.175(PE1) - 209.334(PE4) + 47.014(S1)$$
$$+ 173.535(D2) + 18.333(PE5)$$

Analysis of Variance

Regression   Deg. Freedom   8   F-Value 8.46 R^2 0.641

Error   Deg. Freedom 38

*Y*1   Louisiana   1964-1969 data, May-August

$$Y1 = 57.727 - 93.479(D1) - 66.450(D0) + 12.000(S3)$$
$$+ 138.562(PE6) + 11.250(PE5) + 166.780(D3)$$

Analysis of Variance

Regression   Deg. Freedom   6   F-Value 7.26 R^2 0.770

Error   Deg. Freedom 13

The letters in the parentheses indicate the climatic variable: *PE*, potential evapotranspiration; *S*, moisture surplus; *D*, moisture deficit. The number indicates the number of the month before the current one which is significant. Both *F* values were found to be significant at the 99 percent level. Use of the Texas model to predict monthly changes in beetle activity in Texas during 1973 (a year not included in the formulation of the model itself) gave only fair results (table 6-3).

Table 6-3
Predicted and Measured Values of Southern Pine Beetle Activity in Eastern Texas, 1973

Month	Measured Y2	Predicted Y2
May	−210	−113
June	−219	−256
July	+1440	+576
August	−781	−60

Source: L.S. Kalkstein, "The effect of climate upon outbreaks of southern pine beetles," *Publications in Climatology*, Laboratory of Climatology, vol. 27, no. 3 (1974).

The model correctly predicted trends but missed the magnitude of the changes in 1973. Though agreement was perhaps reasonable in May and June, it was appreciably off in July and August. The model would appear to have some value in being able to predict future trends in beetle activity and it does isolate at any time those climatic factors of greatest significance to beetle activity.

Obtaining reliable data on number of trees attacked may have been a problem because the Texas surveying was done by airplane observation of yellowing of trees. Yellowing was assumed to be caused by beetle activity. The Louisiana data were obtained from a much smaller sample area on the basis of ground observations. Individual trees were observed in the Louisiana program, whereas "active spots" or groups of trees were recorded in the Texas aerial survey and only later were the spots checked by ground observation. Some time could exist between aerial observation and ground check. Fifteen years of record were available from Texas but only five years of data were available from Louisiana. Thus, part of the weakness in any predictive model related to climate may result from inconsistancies in the input data of beetle infestation. Better data for $Y1$ and $Y2$ would greatly enhance the value of any predictive model that might be developed.

Summary

Water budget factors have been used in many aspects of forest management. Although it is intuitively known that such factors as evapotranspiration and soil moisture storage must be closely related to tree growth, tree vigor, leaf decomposition, and fire frequency, the attempt has been to express some of these relationships more quantitatively here. Many of the results are still quite imprecise but a start has been made and pathways for future, more definitive, studies have been suggested.

7 Urban Planning

For better or for worse, suburbanization of the rural environment has become a way of life during the past few decades. Changes in land use from woodlands or farms to residential suburbs, shopping centers or malls, industrial parks, or intensely settled housing developments all result in significant modification of the water budget. Planning for wisest development of the land and to minimize the adverse effects of such changes in land use on our water resources requires an understanding of the hydrologic effects of various land-use programs.

There are four interrelated but distinct effects of land-use changes on the hydrology of an area.[1] They include changes in (1) peak flow characteristics; (2) total quantity of runoff; (3) water quality; and (4) the hydrologic amenities, including the appearance of the river channel and the impression it leaves on an observer.

The two main factors that influence the flow characteristics of a stream are the actual percentage of land in an impervious condition in the basin and the rate of flow of water overland to the stream channel. Land use controls the first of these factors whereas density, size, and characteristics of tributaries or the extent of storm sewers control the second.[2]

Land-Use Changes with Urbanization

The change in land-use conditions in the Chester Creek basin in southeastern Pennsylvania from 1937 to 1965 has been determined by using random sampling of a large number of points from aerial photographs[3] (table 7-1). This is an urbanizing basin, part of the megalopolis corridor from Richmond to Boston.

The increase in the percentage of forest in table 7-1 is surprising but it evidently reflects an early stage of land-use change in an urbanizing area. As the pasture and cultivated land is taken out of farm use, some of it goes to suburban developments and some is allowed to regrow to natural woods until needed for housing or shopping center developments.

A more detailed determination of the change in land use in a small basin (7.46 square mile, Shellpot Creek watershed near Wilmington, Delaware) was achieved by actually scaling areas of buildings, parking lots, and roads from large-scale maps and aerial photographs.[4] Areas of forest and fields were determined by use of a dot grid on large-scale aerial photographs (scale: 1 inch equals 400 ft). Table 7-2 gives the actual areas of the various hydrologic surfaces found for three different time periods.

Table 7-1

Change in Land-Use Types, Chester Creek Basin, 1937-1965

Land Use	Percentage of Basin	
	1937	*1965*
Forest	19	28
Pasture	45	38
Cultivated	31	22
Impervious	5	12

Source: J.R. Mather, F.J. Swaye, and B.J. Hartmann, "The influence of the climatic water balance on conditions in the estuarine environment," *Publications in Climatology*, Laboratory of Climatology, vol. 25, no. 1 (1972).

Shellpot Creek basin, located just on the northern outskirts of Wilmington, was evidently undergoing more rapid urbanization with a greater rise in the percentage of impervious surfaces than was Chester Creek basin, a few miles farther north in southeastern Pennsylvania. A third study of the effect of urbanization on water yields has provided additional estimates of the percentage of land in each of ten generalized land-use categories in highly urbanized Middlesex County in north-central New Jersey.[5] Table 7-3 also includes estimates of the percentage of impervious surfaces associated with each land use type. It suggests that some 17.3 percent of the county was in impervious surfaces during the mid-1960s.

Changes in the Storm Hydrograph with Urbanization

The intensity and frequency of both flood peaks and low flows should increase in the streams draining urbanizing areas because there will be greater overland and storm sewer runoff as well as less available water for groundwater recharge. Figure 7-1 is a hypothetical storm hydrograph showing some of the changes in discharge that can result from urbanization.[6] Though the peakedness of the discharge curve increases greatly with urbanization, the duration (horizontal scale) of high discharges is markedly shorter. It is also possible that the flood-to-peak interval (the time interval between when the stream discharge is at flood stage until it reaches its peak discharge from a particular storm) might be a function of the size of the watershed as well.[7] Study of various sized basins within the Ohio River system showed a general relation between area of basin and duration of the flood-to-peak interval. One cannot conclude, however, that flood-to-peak duration is only a function of basin size, because such other factors as the source of water for flooding can also affect this time interval.

The increase in urbanization and in the percentage of an area served by

Table 7-2

Percentage of Land Area in Shellpot Creek Basin in Different Surface Covers in 1954, 1962, 1968

| Year | Area Under Different Surface Cover | | | |
	Impervious acre (%)	Building Lots acre (%)	Fields acre (%)	Forest acre (%)
1954	498 (11)	380 (09)	2116 (47)	1485 (33)
1962	824 (19)	711 (16)	1864 (42)	1020 (23)
1968	983 (22)	857 (19)	1694 (38)	945 (21)
Percentage Change 1954-1968	+97	+125	−20	−36

Source: J.C. Albrecht, "Alterations in the hydrologic cycle induced by urbanization in northern New Castle County, Delaware: Magnitudes and projections," *Final Report, OWRR Project No. A-017-DEL*, University of Delaware, Newark (1974).

storm sewers affects the total discharge from a storm.[8] For example, figure 7-2 shows the effect of urbanization on the mean annual flood for a one-square-mile drainage area with different percentages of the basin impervious and sewered. A basin 40 percent impervious and 20 percent sewered would have a discharge about twice as great as before any land-use changes had occurred.

The mean annual flood may be defined as the arithmetic mean of the peak flood each year for a number of years of record. Statistically, the recurrence interval of the mean annual flood is 2.3 years, regardless of the length of record used. This value of discharge can be expected to be equaled or exceeded 10 times in 23 years. The recurrence interval for the bankfull stage in most rivers is of the order of 1.5 to 2 years. Because urbanization increases flood potential, urbanization results in the recurrence of bankfull stages more often than 1.5 to 2 years. Using data from the Brandywine Creek basin in southeastern Pennsylvania, the discharge-frequency relation for a one-square-mile drainage basin can be developed. Such a relation indicates that a flow of 75 cfs would constitute the average annual flood for this basin. Mathematical manipulation of the discharge data and an understanding of the effect of sewering and impervious surfaces on runoff leads to the construction of the flood-frequency curves for a one-square-mile basin draining different degrees of urbanization in figure 7-3. The figure shows that with 20 percent of the area sewered and 20 percent impervious, the discharge would be expected to exceed flood stage (75 cfs) at least once a year. With 40 percent of the area sewered and 40 percent of the surface impervious, such flood stage conditions would be found at least twice a year on the average.[9]

Table 7-3

Land-Use Categories and Impervious Surfaces in Middlesex County, N.J., Mid-1960s

Land Use	Total Area[a] (%)	Impervious Surfaces[b] (%)	Total Area Impervious (%)
Undeveloped	60.3	0	0
Residential	16.4	20	3.3
Streets & roads	6.6	100	6.6
Public & quasi-public	4.2	60	2.5
Commercial	3.2	80	2.6
Industrial	3.2	40	1.3
Utilities, incl. RR	3.1	25	0.8
Recreation	1.6	5	0.1
Mining & construction	0.8	10	0.1
Cemeteries	0.6	5	0
			17.3

Source: R.A. Muller, "A water balance evaluation of the effects of urbanization on water yield in metropolitan northeastern New Jersey," Appendix H of "Benefits from Integrated Water Management in Urban Areas–The Case of the New York Metropolitan Region," L. Zobler and G.W. Cary, *Report to OWRR Under Grant No. 14-01-0001-1583*, Barnard College, Columbia University, New York (1969).

[a]Original data supplied by D. Rippey, Middlesex County Planning Board from field surveys by the planning board and by the Tri-State Transportation Commission.

[b]Estimated by Muller.

Effect of Urbanization on Water Quality

Water quality changes greatly with urbanization. Not only does the sediment content of rivers increase as runoff from construction areas increases but also pollution from city streets, industrial operations, domestic sewage treatment plants, as well as cesspools or septic tanks will all add to the pollution load of the stream. All land use, of course, affects water quality so that removing land from agricultural or grazing uses will merely change the nature and quantity of the pollutants. Nutrients in the stream from agricultural operations will decrease and pollutants resulting from residential, commercial, and industrial operations will replace them. Because of the more intensive use of the land by increased numbers of people, overall pollution loads should rise along with the quantity of sediments.

Study of the sediment discharge from two small streams near Washington, D.C. (Watts Branch in Rockville, draining a rural area, and Little Falls Branch near Bethesda, draining an urban area), shows that the sediment rating curves, a plot of the discharge versus the rate of sediment transport, tend to converge at

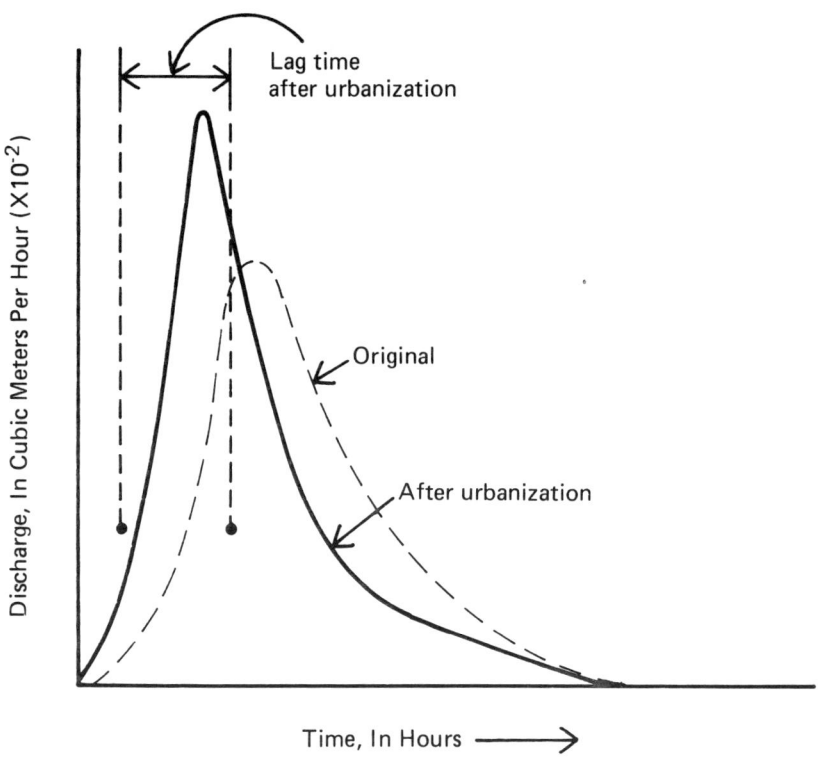

Source: L.B. Leopold, "Hydrology for urban land planning–a guidebook on the hydrologic effects of urban land use," *Geological Survey Circular 554,* U.S. Department of Interior, Washington, D.C. (1968).

Figure 7-1. Hypothetical Unit Hydrograph Showing Changes Involved with Process of Urbanization

high discharges.[10] Such a situation might lead one to suggest that at those discharges, the urban area contributes no more sediment to the stream than the rural area. However, it must be remembered that although sediment load may be nearly the same at these larger discharges, the effects of urbanization will cause such large discharges to occur much more frequently in the stream draining the urban area than in the stream draining the rural area. Total annual sediment load will be many times greater in the stream draining the urbanized area (table 7-4).

Study of rapid suburbanization in the Denver area has led to the suggestion that the large quantities of sediment produced by the widespread denudation of basins by bulldozers has resulted in rapid expansion of flood plains.[11] In one basin studied, the length of the trunk stream lined with floodplains increased from 22 percent to 50 percent in just five years. The stream was unable to carry

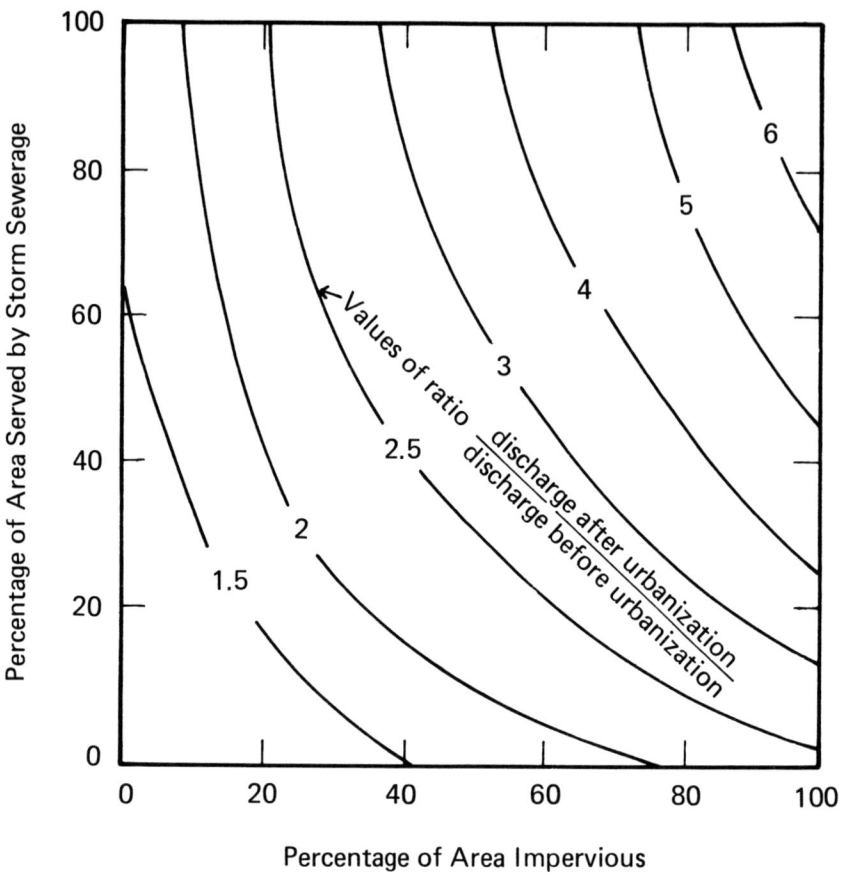

Source: L.B. Leopold, "Hydrology for urban land planning–a guidebook on the hydrologic effects of urban land use," *Geological Survey Circular 554*, U.S. Department of Interior, Washington, D.C. (1968).

Figure 7-2. Effect of Urbanization on Mean Annual Flood for a 1-Square-Mile Drainage Area

all the sediment load and so deposited it as floodplain alluvium. Later spread of paved surfaces and the resodding of the lawns greatly reduced sediment yield. At the same time the increased overland runoff that followed led to larger stream flows, which, in turn, began cutting through the newly developed floodplain materials.

Sedimentation rates of 2913 metric tons/km^2 per year for the whole basin studied or rates of 5457 metric tons/km^2 per year for the developed area alone were reported. This latter rate is some 30 times greater than the rate before suburban development started.[1,2]

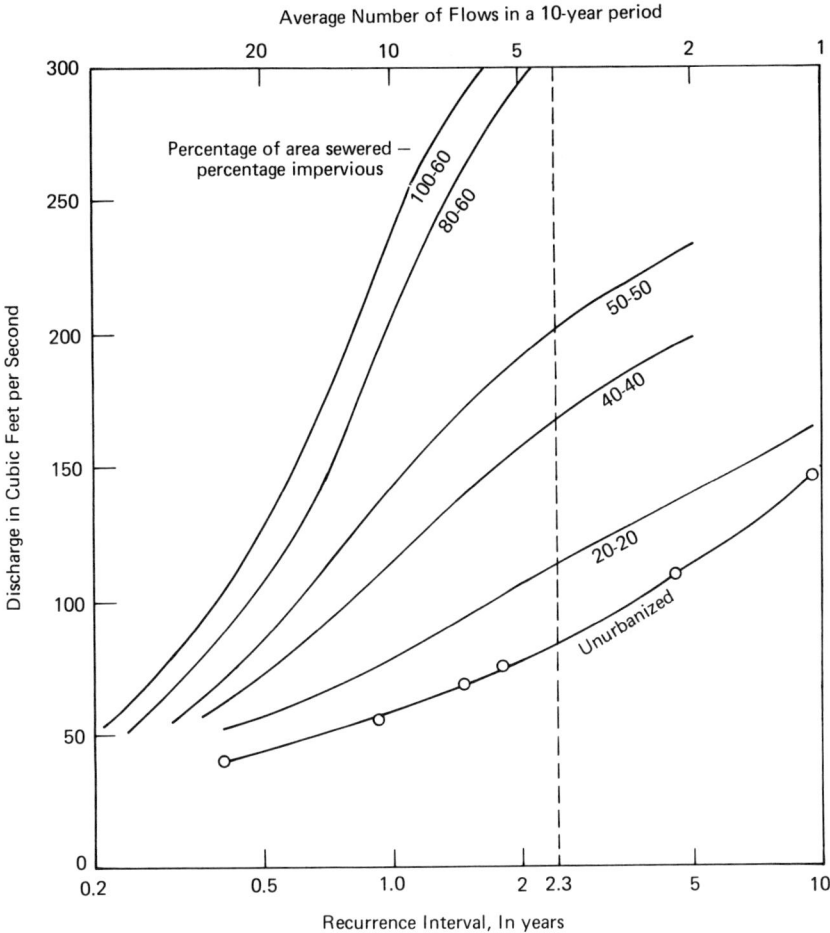

Source: L.B. Leopold, "Hydrology for urban land planning–a guidebook on the hydrologic effects of urban land use," *Geological Survey Circular 554*, U.S. Department of Interior, Washington, D.C. (1968).

Figure 7-3. Flood-Frequency Curves for a 1-Square-Mile Basin in Various States of Urbanization

Urbanization also affects water temperature in streams, primarily because of the ponding of water and the clear cutting of trees. Some heating effect from water running off warm city streets can also be found. Investigations of five streams on Long Island, showed that shallow streams had 10-15°F higher summer temperatures when draining urbanized areas than when draining rural areas.[13] These same urban streams were, however, 5-10°F cooler in winter than were streams in nonurban areas.

Table 7-4

Annual Sediment Load for Two Small Streams near Washington, D.C.

	Drainage Area (square miles)	Tons per Year	Tons per Year (per sq. mi.)
Watts Branch in Rockville, Md. (rural)	3.7	1,910	516
Little Falls Branch near Bethesda, Md. (urban)	4.1	9,530	3,220

Source: L.B. Leopold, "Hydrology for urban land planning–a guidebook on the hydrologic effects of urban land use," *Geological Survey Circular 554*, U.S. Department of Interior, Washington, D.C. (1968).

Examples of the Hydrologic Effect of Suburbanization

Streamflow

The climatic water budget can be used quite effectively to determine how increasing urbanization modifies streamflow. Both climate and changing land use influence streamflow. Use of the climatic water budget makes it possible to evaluate the role of climate separately so that the effect of changing land use becomes more clearly identified.

Let us simplify the approach to illustrate briefly how the climatic water budget can be utilized to determine the effects of changing land use. The water budget provides information on annual runoff of water from the land area around the station for which the data are being evaluated. Substituting different values for moisture storage capacity, one can estimate water surplus (and hence runoff) from different land uses. As water-holding capacities in the soil decrease, water surplus and runoff will increase. Even without measurements, it is possible to make some assumptions about quantities of water that can be stored in the soil at field capacity on the basis of type of ground cover. With a paved surface, storage will be essentially zero. In sandy loam, soil storage will increase to 50 mm or so under grass or shallow-rooted vegetation, to 150 mm under deeper-rooted shrubs, pastures, or low perennial vegetation, and possibly to 300 to 400 mm under mature forest vegetation.

Information on land-use conditions at some earlier time can be used to estimate values of moisture storage appropriate for those particular land-use conditions. Repeated evaluation of the water budget, month by month, will provide calculated values of streamflow under changing climatic conditions, holding land-use changes constant. Land use does, of course, change over time. If computed and measured runoff agree fairly well during the first few years of computations (indicating that our assumptions about moisture storage in the soil at that time were realistic) but diverge as time passes, we may reason that actual land use (and hence storage, evapotranspiration, and water runoff) is diverging from the originally assumed conditions. The effect of climatic conditions is always known because actual data are used in the water budget. The only unknown is the changing land-use situation. Comparing measured values of runoff over time with runoff computed on the basis of initial land-use conditions provides an estimate of the effect of changing land-use conditions on runoff.

This technique can be applied to the problem of determining the effect of land-use change in the Chester Creek basin located just north of Wilmington, Delaware. Land-use conditions in the Chester Creek basin in 1937 and again in 1965 were determined by means of aerial photographs (table 7-1). It can be estimated that the available moisture storage for impervious surfaces is 25 mm, whereas for cultivated areas it is 100 mm, for pastures 200 mm, and for forests 400 mm. Using 1937 climatic data, water budgets prepared for all stations in the basin using these water storage values show an annual computed runoff of 691 mm from the impervious surfaces, 636 mm from the cultivated areas, 596 mm from the pastures, and 549 mm from the forest areas. Multiplying these values of computed runoff by the percentage of land with each type of cover and summing the results provides an average computed streamflow from the basin for 1937 of 604 mm. Actual measured streamflow from the watershed for 1937 is found to be 542 mm. Agreement between measured and computed streamflow is only fair for the first year of the study.

The climatic water budgets are now recomputed using the same values of water-holding capacity as before but using 1965 climatic data. Multiplying the annual computed 1965 streamflow by the 1937 percentages of different land uses, as before, gives us the 1965 streamflow as if no change in land-use conditions had ever occurred. In other words, we will have taken into account any effect of changing climate so that any differences we notice between measured and computed values for 1965 will now result from changing land-use conditions. This has been done and the resulting computed streamflow from the basin using 1965 climatic data and 1937 land-use data is found to be 257 mm. Total measured streamflow for 1965 from Chester Creek basin is 271 mm as compared with 542 mm in 1937. Evidently 1965 was considerably drier than 1937 in addition to any possible influence of cultural conditions. Table 7-5 summarizes the results.

Computed streamflow decreased by 347 mm using the same land-use conditions—a decrease in streamflow caused just by changes in climatic conditions. Measured streamflow decreased 271 mm. Because streamflow should have decreased more from changes in climatic conditions, there must really have been an increase in streamflow between the two years because of land-use changes, which is superimposed on the measured values. Measured streamflow did not decrease as much as it should have because of climatic changes alone. The difference between these two decreases in streamflow represents the net increase in streamflow resulting from changed land-use conditions, a value of 76 mm in

Table 7-5

Summary of Computed (1937 Land-Use Data, 1937 and 1965 Climatic Data) and Measured Streamflow, Chester Creek Basin

	1937	1965	Decrease (1937 to 1965)
Computed streamflow based on 1937 land use (mm)	604	257	347 (caused by variation in climate)
Measured streamflow (mm)	542	271	271
Difference			76 (net increase in streamflow caused by land use)

30 years. This increase from land-use changes alone agrees well with figures from several other watersheds on the Eastern seaboard.[15]

As urbanization increases in coming years, this trend can be expected to continue and possibly even to accelerate. This could have important and farreaching hydrologic consequences. Such consequences may, however, be anticipated by means of climatic water budgeting techniques before they actually develop.

Groundwater Recharge

One problem currently facing many state and local planning agencies is the environmental impact of new housing subdivisions that are springing up around most of our city areas. Although many environmental changes will result from such subdivisions—small-scale urban heat islands, air and water pollution problems, traffic congestion, and the need for improved transportation networks—the impact of such developments on the water budget is of prime interest here. The foregoing sections have identified basic changes in the hydrology of the area that result from urbanization. A hypothetical example using a climatic water budget approach will make clear how the budget can be used to evaluate the possible choices available to regulatory groups as well as the magnitude of the hydrologic responses to different decisions.

For example, consider an 800-acre residential subdivision to be built on formerly agricultural land (with some areas of woodland) in northern Delaware. Using available data on the percentage of impervious surface area generally found with different sized residential lots (lot size below 560 sq meters, impervious area 80 percent; lot size 560 to 1400 sq meters, impervious area 40 percent; lot size above 1400 sq meters, impervious area 25 percent)[16] we will assume a figure of 25 percent of the area will be impervious and also served by storm sewers. This is not entirely correct; certainly some of the water falling on house roofs will flow in gutters and downspouts and emerge onto lawns. This loss to the storm sewers will, of course, be balanced by some overland runoff from grassed areas near roadways and drives onto the paved areas and to the storm sewers.

To begin our computation process we need to make several assumptions. These may be modified later allowing us to test the effect of different conditions on the hydrologic response of the overall development. Our concern in this study is with the effect of the development on the response of the water table. By taking this 800 acres out of cultivation and forests and putting it in a subdivision, we do not want to have any adverse effects on the water table in the area. Annual recharge should be maintained essentially the same as before the development. Assuming that annual evapotranspiration losses do not vary greatly, this would also ensure that annual streamflow from the area would be about the same after development as before (although peak flows would be greater and lag of peak flows behind rainfall would be less, as we have previously seen).

We will make the following assumptions in this hypothetical example:

1. Before development on the 800-acre plot:
   a. 400 acres shallow-rooted crops; 200 acres pasture and meadows; 200 acres wooded.
   b. Soil is sandy loam (storage capacity in the root zone as follows: cropped land 125 mm; pasture and meadows 200 mm; forests 400 mm). The area is gently rolling so that essentially all the rainfall in the area will infiltrate. Surface runoff of water from intense storms can be generally neglected. It might be pointed out that this is not such a questionable assumption as might appear at first glance. The technique to determine overland runoff from individual rainstorms developed by the Soil Conservation Service (described in chapter 4) was applied to the daily rainfall values at Seabrook, New Jersey (about 50 km from the area under study) for the years 1950-1952; it found that annual overland runoff varied from 50 to 150 mm of the total of 1060 to 1200 mm that fell in those three years. Largest amounts of overland runoff occurred during hurricanes or other heavy rainstorms in the fall of the year. Essentially no overland runoff occurred from gently sloping grass, meadowland, or forest (or even well-covered cropland) during the spring or summer.
2. After development of the 800-acre plot:
   a. Twenty-five percent of the area will be in impervious surfaces (roads, drives, roofs, sidewalks), whereas the remainder of the area will be in grass (lawns, golf course, scattered shrubs). Soil moisture storage in the root zone of the lawn areas will be 150 mm.
   b. Of the rain that falls on impervious surfaces, 1.25 mm per storm will evaporate directly and be lost from the area immediately. Assuming that there are 100 rains during the year, this means that 125 mm of the precipitation on impervious surfaces is lost immediately by evaporation.

c. Three different assumptions will be made concerning what happens to the water falling on the 200 acres of impervious surfaces that is not lost by evaporation.
   (1) All of the water flows to storm sewers and is lost from the area.
   (2) The water from half of the impervious area is trapped in lawns, ditches, and hollows and infiltrates into the soil while the rest runs off in storm sewers.
   (3) All the water from the impervious surfaces is trapped in retention basins, lawns, and hollows and recharges the water table.

d. The rain that falls on impervious surfaces and later is added to the grassed areas can be considered to be spread evenly over the remaining grassed area, thus essentially adding to the total monthly precipitation over the 600 acres of grassed area.

Evaluating the climatic water budget using average temperature and precipitation data for the area provides us with "before development" results:

Precipitation	1118 mm	
Water surplus	from cropped areas	392 mm
	from pasture areas	381 mm
	from wooded areas	369 mm

Multiplying each of these values of surplus (the water recharge to the water table or subsurface flow to the streams) by the percentage of land in each cover (50 percent cropped and 25 percent each pasture and woodland) gives us a weighted surplus from the whole area equal to 384 mm. This results in a "before development" recharge to the water table or flow to nearby surface streams of some 124×10^4 cubic meters from the tract—the water volume that must be approximated after development to result in no significant modification to the water table or to annual streamflow.

We can now repeat our computations of the water budget, modifying them for the conditions we have assumed will exist after development. Using a soil moisture storage capacity of 150 mm, we find water surplus from the 600 acres of lawn surface, assuming all water falling on the impervious surfaces runs off in storm sewers, will be 387 mm. Because this surplus results from just 600 acres, total annual recharge to the water table is 94×10^4 cubic meters. Assuming that 125 mm of the 1118 mm of precipitation falling on impervious surface evaporates, and that the remaining 993 mm precipitation falling on half the impervious area (100 acres) is distributed evenly over the surface of the 600 acres of lawn (and so can be considered to be additional precipitation to those areas), the water budget for the 600 acres of lawns can be recalculated. The new value of surplus from the lawn area, using an assumed annual precipitation of 1283 mm caused by the inflow of water from the 100 acres of impervious surface, is 528 mm. This surplus from 600 acres results in a recharge to the water table or flow to nearby surface streams of some 128×10^4 cubic meters, quite similar to the value obtained from the "before development" computations.

If we now assume that all the precipitation (except for the 125 mm evaporated) from the 200 acres of impervious surfaces is distributed to the lawn area through various retention basins and distribution laterals, we find that the total annual precipitation over the 600 acres of lawns approximates 1450 mm, resulting in an annual water surplus of some 687 mm. This value of surplus from 600 acres of lawn results in a recharge to the groundwater or flow to nearby surface streams of 167×10^4 cubic meters. If all the water from the impervious surfaces were held within the subdevelopment, there would be an appreciable net increase in recharge to the water table after development, water tables would rise, streamflow would ultimately increase, and other problems resulting from high water tables might develop. However, local reuse of about half the water running off from the impervious surfaces would seem to be desirable to keep groundwater recharge about the same before and after development.

The computations have allowed rapid evaluation of several different assumptions and provided an approximate answer to our question of what will be the impact on the water table of a new 800-acre residential subdivision in a formerly agricultural and wooded tract. Many other assumptions can be evaluated before final plans for the subdivision are approved. For example, it may be felt that the building of the subdivision will create a small urban heat island in this 800-acre tract so that the temperatures (and hence evapotranspiration) after development will be greater than before development.

This assumption can also be included in the climatic water budget computations by merely increasing the air temperature by one or two degrees each month and obtaining new values of potential evapotranspiration for use in the budget. This has been done in the case of our earlier assumption that the precipitation from half the impervious area is added to the lawn area as additional precipitation. A 0.8°C increase in temperature for each month of the year increases the annual potential evapotranspiration by just under 50 mm. This results in a new value of water surplus and recharge to the ground water of 489 mm or 119×10^4 cubic meters from the 600-acre lawn surface. Comparison of this value with the "before development" results shows that, with the assumed increase in air temperature in the area, it will be necessary to retain just slightly more than half the water from the impervious surfaces within the subdivision to eliminate any adverse impact on the groundwater table.

The computations have shown a diminished opportunity for groundwater recharge caused by suburbanization as long as the water falling on impervious surfaces is allowed to enter storm sewers. Actually, the groundwater table may even be higher after suburbanization depending on the particular potable water supply and waste water disposal situation of the suburb. If large volumes of potable water are transported into the subdivision, certainly some water will be added to the soil of the area through leaks in the water pipes as well as by use of this water for irrigation of lawns. It has been estimated that potable water imported to Harrisonborough, New Jersey, is equivalent to about 1830 mm of precipitation on an average annual basis.[17] Some of this water certainly recharges the soil moisture storage. If domestic sewage is not removed by a municipal sewerage system but rather enters individual cesspools or septic tanks, another large volume of water is available for groundwater recharge. Though these aspects were not considered in the previous example, it would be a simple matter to include them in the computations if they are considered to be significant factors.

Predicting Leachate from a Solid Waste Landfill

Solid waste landfills (or sanitary landfills) are widely used as a final repository for the majority of the solid waste products of our society. Areas devoted to solid waste storage are increasing rapidly because the burning of such wastes, except under controlled incinerator conditions, is not permitted. As a result, increasing volumes of solid wastes must be stored.

Possibly of greatest concern in the operation of any solid waste landfill is the matter of leaching of pollutants from the landfill with resulting contamination of the groundwater in the vicinity. Pollution of the water table by contaminants carried in the leachate from the landfill will continue for some time after dumping operations cease and the landfill is closed. Because of the nature of water movement underground, significant volumes of groundwater can become polluted and rendered unfit for human use as a result of the existence of the landfill. Thus, knowing the rate of percolation of water through a landfill and its subsequent movement to the groundwater table is important for managing such landfills. The climatic water budget lends itself to such an application.

Clearly, the precipitation that infiltrates the soil surface will be the major contributor to the leaching volume from the landfill. Some water may be lost by means of evapotranspiration from the soil layer covering the landfill (or the landfill itself if it is uncovered for a brief time) but because the area will often be bare of vegetation such water loss may be small. Also, because the surface of the landfill should be generally flat, overland runoff will be relatively minor. Precipitation in excess of that moisture lost by evapotranspiration will either be stored in the thin soil covering, in the landfill itself, or will percolate through the landfill to the water table.

The Environmental Protection Agency has recently issued a brief report illustrating how the water budget can be used to determine possible leachate generation from a landfill.[18] Based on a number of initial assumptions, some of which might be subject to question, the technique suggests annual volumes of leachate and possible time lags before the leachate reaches the groundwater table in different areas of the country. In undertaking the computations, it is first assumed that the landfill operation is already completed and that two feet of graded cover material are in place over the landfill. It is also assumed that the solid waste, and the cover are all put into place instantaneously so that no percolation will occur before the final cover is in place. The final cover is assumed to be moderately deep-rooted grass. Any lateral movement of water into or out of the area is neglected.

Computation of a monthly water budget for Cincinnati, Ohio, provides a value of annual surplus (or percolation to the top of the landfill) of 213 mm. The next step is to route the water through the landfill.[19] The water-holding capacity of the landfill materials may vary from 2.4 inches per foot (250 mm per meter) to 4.2 inches per foot (350 mm per meter). For the purposes of the example, a storage capacity of 3.6 inches per foot (300 mm per meter) is assumed. It is further assumed that the moisture content of the solid waste material is at 50 percent of its field capacity to start, and that moisture moves through the solid waste material as it does through a soil layer by bringing each successive layer of the material to field capacity before movement downward to the next portion of the landfill is possible. No cavities or cracks are assumed to exist in the landfill materials.

If the annual depth of surplus water at Cincinnati is considered to be 200 mm, this much water will bring 1.33 meters depth of the solid landfill to field capacity (material is originally holding 150 mm per m of water and can still hold another 150 mm per m depth). Thus, if the landfill is 15 m deep, it would take just over eleven years for the whole depth of the landfill to be brought to field capacity and for water to be ready to percolate from the bottom of the landfill, according to the Environmental Protection Agency report. A landfill only 7.5 m deep in Orlando, Florida would require some fifteen years for percolation to occur from the bottom of the landfill because annual water surplus is only 70 mm depth there. No percolation would ever occur from a landfill in Los Angeles, for example, because of the lack of any annual surplus water there. Figure 7-4 provides a graphic solution to the problem of determining time of first appearance of leachate for different values of percolate and depth of landfill. Volume of annual leachate can be determined from information on the area of the landfill because the depth of the percolate will equal the depth of annual surplus once the moisture content of the landfill is brought up to field capacity.

Though the use of the water budget approach in this example is quite appropriate, the assumptions are somewhat unrealistic and so suggest an answer that may not occur in nature. The landfill and cover cannot be created instantaneously but rather over a considerable period. As a result, in a humid climate, the water-holding capacity of the landfill may be brought up to field

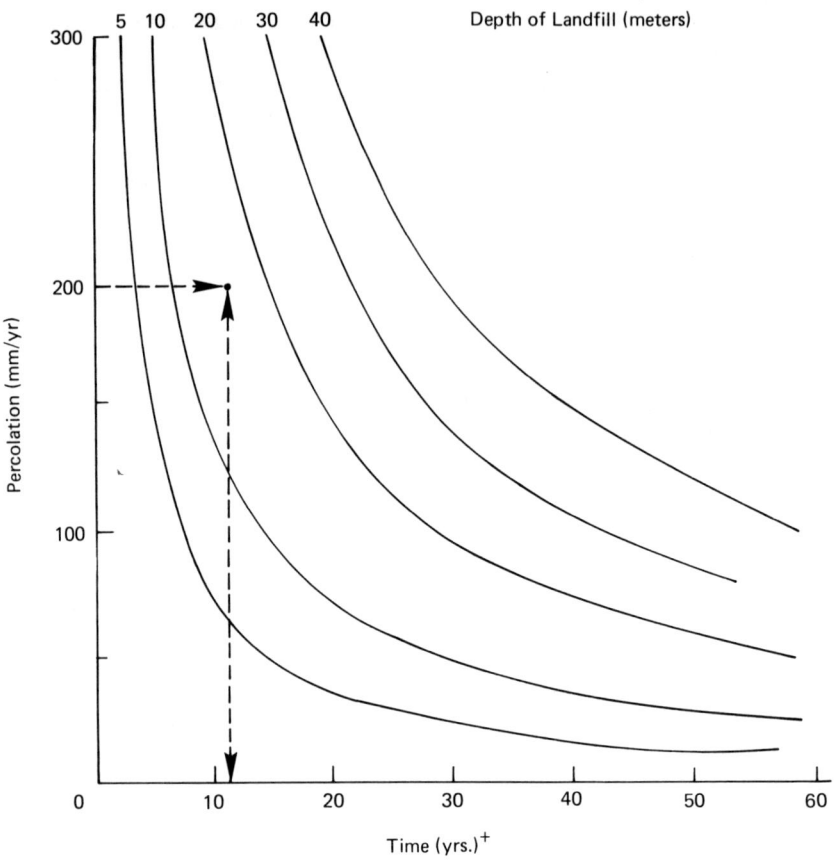

Source: D.G. Fenn, K.J. Hanley, and T.V. DeGeare, "Use of the water balance method for predicting leachate generation from solid waste disposal sites," *Solid Waste Management Program (SW-168)*, U.S. Environmental Protection Agency, Cincinnati, Ohio (1975).

Figure 7-4. Time of First Appearance of Leachate from Different Depths of Landfill and Different Percolation Rates. Water storage in landfill initially is 150 mm/m with field capacity 300 mm/m. Time zero is that time when the field capacity of the soil cover is first exceeded, producing the first amounts of percolation.

capacity before the landfill is completed. Percolation might begin from the base of the landfill while it is still being filled. If the annual depth of added landfill has a greater water storage capacity than the annual available water surplus, no percolation will occur until after the landfill is completed. If, however, the annual depth of landfill is less than the depth that can be filled by the available moisture surplus, percolation will start in the first year of landfill operations and continue each year thereafter. Many different assumptions can be tested by means of the water budget approach. It has great utility because it provides quantitative information on leaching volumes and time lags needed for better management control of the landfill operation.

Frequencies of Different Levels of Soil Moisture Storage

Knowledge of the expectancies or likelihoods of different values of soil moisture content through the year is also desirable for many purposes. For example, construction or road-building projects that are limited by high soil moisture conditions can be better planned if the contractor can estimate the risk of delays from climatic conditions by attempting construction at any particular time of the year. Values of soil moisture content that influence such activities are not the storage values from the water budget but rather those of total moisture detention. Moisture detention may vary from zero to well above field capacity depending on (1) the balance between precipitation and evapotranspiration; (2) the depth of snowfall (assumed to be the precipitation that occurs when temperatures are less than $-1°C$); and (3) the rapidity with which the surplus water (gravitational water) moves downward through upper soil layers.

To illustrate, monthly values of total detention have been obtained for Wilmington, Delaware, in the eastern United States for the seventy-year period from 1896 to 1965. Using Hazen's graphical method for determining probabilities, it is possible to determine the detention that can be expected to be equaled or exceeded different percentages of the time at the station in question.

The water budget computations used in this particular study are based on a value of 150 mm storage at field capacity. Values of 90, 75, 50, 25, and 10 percent likelihood of total detention are obtained from probability graphs and plotted on calendar paper. Connecting monthly points for the same probability values provides fairly smooth curves of the yearly course of total moisture detention (figure 7-5). The plotted lines indicate the percentage of time that total moisture detention is less than or equal to the indicated detention value. Thus on August 31 at Wilmington, Delaware, soil moisture detention will equal or be less than 155 mm 90 percent of the time, will equal or be less than 122 mm 75 percent of the time, and will equal or be less than 86 mm half of the time. Conversely, of course, detention will exceed 155 mm at Wilmington on August 31 no more than 10 percent of the time. Or one can conclude that on August 31, total moisture detention will exceed field capacity about one year in ten. In half the years, total moisture detention falls below field capacity on June 15 and stays below until November 28 at Wilmington.

If a road construction company in Wilmington is only able to operate successfully when moisture detention is below field capacity and they wish to

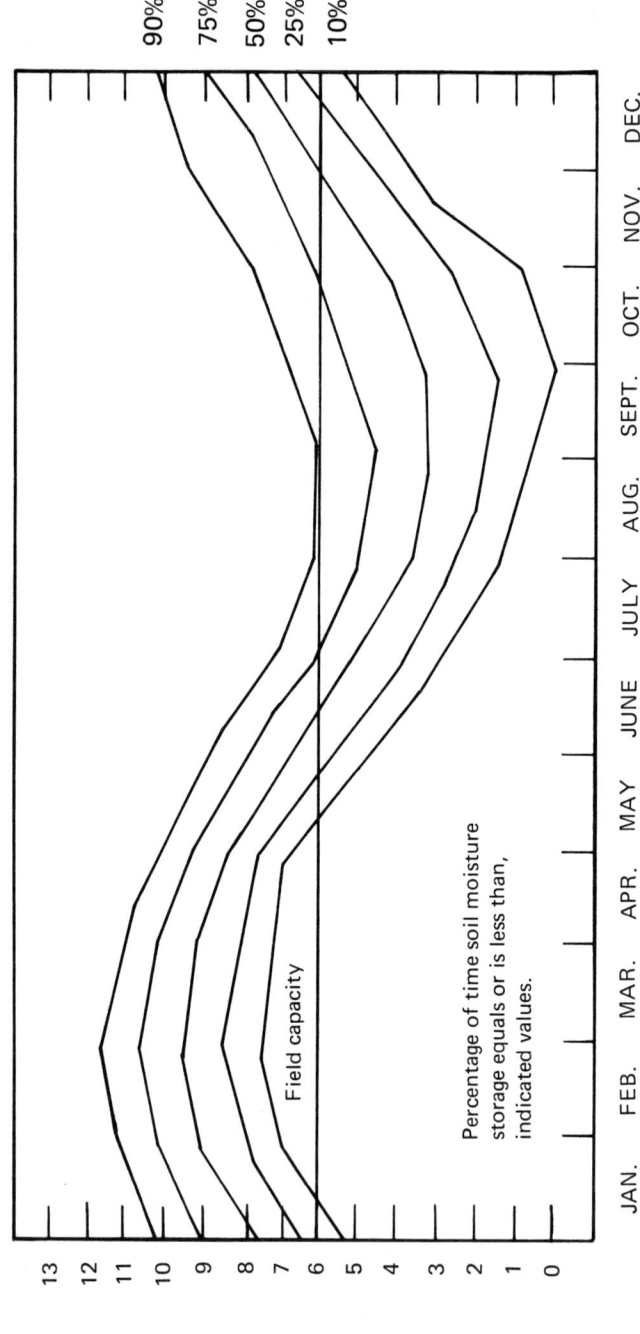

Source: J.R. Mather, "Factors of the climatic water balance over the Delmarva peninsula," *Publications in Climatology*, Laboratory of Climatology, vol. 22, no. 3 (1969).

Figure 7-5. Seasonal Course of the Probability of Total Soil Moisture Storage, Wilmington, Delaware

take only a 25 percent risk (one year in four) of having operations stopped by higher values of moisture detention, the diagram indicates that operations should not begin before July 10 and should be ended before October 20. If, however, the company is willing to take a 50 percent chance that higher values of moisture detention will interrupt construction, their operating season can extend from June 15 to November 28, nearly two months longer. Though figure 7-5 does not provide an actual forecast of conditions for a specific year, it permits the company to estimate its chances for continued operations, or to determine how many nonoperating days might exist under the level of risk they propose to take. Such information will result in more realistic estimates of costs resulting from weather delays for bidding purposes.

Suburbanization and Water Supply on Long Island

Without water importation, the ultimate source of essentially all fresh water on Long Island, New York, must be precipitation. A water budget approach can be used to delimit the various inputs, transfers, and outputs of water over the island. The hydrologic system of the island must respond to any water management program in a way that is predictable by the water budget because of the essential unity of water. If total outflow exceeds total inflow, fresh groundwater storage will be depleted to be replaced by salt water inflow. The amount of water that can be safely withdrawn from groundwater storage annually will vary widely depending on water management decisions concerning such things as the saving of natural discharge or the magnitude of artificial recharge.

From a water budget analysis of 760 square miles of Nassau and Suffolk counties, the following figures for the various inputs and outputs of water were obtained.[20] The 1600 million gallons per day (mgd) of precipitation is partitioned in the following manner: 795 mgd to evapotranspiration; 450 mgd to subsurface outflow of groundwater; 340 mgd to streamflow discharge; and 15 mgd to groundwater evapotranspiration. Although these figures are based on twenty-six years of observations (1940-1965), unknown factors can still result in the possibility of significant error in these estimations.

Humans have greatly modified the natural hydrologic system of Long Island through their actions influencing the groundwater reservoir. The groundwater development on Long Island may be divided into three major periods.[21] The first, beginning with the arrival of European settlers, involved withdrawing water from groundwater storage by means of shallow wells and its return by means of cesspools. The second period occurred when the shallow wells were generally replaced with deeper public supply wells tapping artesian aquifers. Because most effluent still returned to upper surficial deposits through cesspools and septic tanks, there was negligible withdrawal from the groundwater reservoir.

The third phase of groundwater development involved widespread introduction of sewage systems. Most effluent now was discharged to the ocean after treatment instead of being returned to the groundwater reservoir. This represented a new loss from the system, because water withdrawn from the groundwater was ultimately discharged from the area. The possibility of salt water encroachment into the groundwater reservoir increased markedly. These three major stages in groundwater development can still be found on Long Island as one travels eastward away from the industrialized New York City area to its rural eastern end. Figure 7-6 indicates the rough separation of the island into seven subareas, each with well-defined hydrologic characteristics.

A schematic flow diagram of the hydrologic system for the water budget area of Nassau and Suffolk counties is shown in figure 7-7.[22] It suggests the large number of ways that human activities can impinge on the natural system. These include the use of recharge basins, cesspools, recharge wells, storm and sewer drains as well as the transfer of water through pipes. It is estimated, for

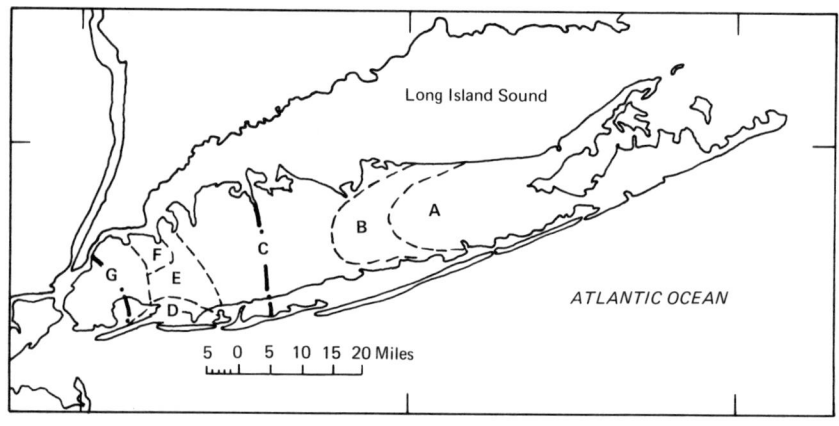

EXPLANATION

A Hydrologic system mainly is in a state of virtual quantitative equilibrium.
B Transitional in development between subareas A and C.
C Hydrologic system is locally out of balance; local salt-water intrusion.
D Hydrologic system is out of balance; widespread salt-water intrusion.
E Hydrologic system is out of balance; may be subject to salt-water intrusion in the future.
F Ground-water development is negligible, and the hydrologic system is in balance.
G Large parts of the subarea are contaminated with salty ground water owing to
    former intensive ground-water development and related salt-water intrusion.

Source: R.C. Heath, B.L. Foxworthy, and P. Cohen, "The changing pattern of ground-water development on Long Island, New York," *Geological Survey Circular 524*, U.S. Department of Interior, Washington, D.C. (1966).

Figure 7-6. Water Development Subareas, Long Island, New York, 1965

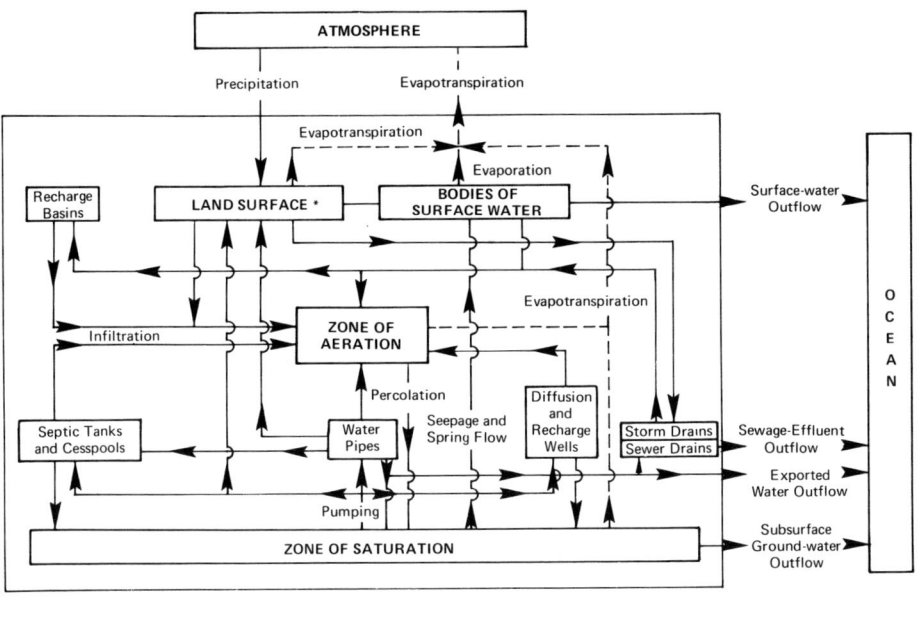

Source: O.L. Franke and N.E. McClymonds, "Summary of the hydrologic situation Long Island, New York, as a guide to water management alternatives," in *Hydrology and Some Effects of Urbanization on Long Island, New York*, Geological Survey Professional Paper 627F, U.S. Department of Interior, Washington, D.C. (1972).

Figure 7-7. Flow Diagram of the Hydrologic System, Nassau and Suffolk Counties, in the 1960s

example, that some 310 mgd of water was artificially recharged in Nassau and Suffolk counties in 1965-125 mgd from cesspools and septic tanks; 60 mgd from direct runoff in recharge basins; 25 mgd from waste water through recharge basins; 55 mgd from injection wells; and 45 mgd from leaking water and sewer pipes.[23]

Clearly this large amount of artificial groundwater recharge plays a significant role in the hydrologic regimen of Long Island. Additional modification of these numbers is certainly quite possible if legislation does away with the use of cesspools or septic tanks or improved water services eliminate leaks in buried water and sewer pipes. Reduction in artificial recharge can only lead to further decline in groundwater levels and the influx of additional salt water.

Those human activities which produce a loss of moisture from the hydrologic system in Nassau and Suffolk counties include evaporation of irrigation water (lawns, golf courses, and agricultural fields); runoff from urban areas to streams; disposal of sewage effluent into streams or the ocean; and transfer of fresh water to New York City.

In 1965, total losses caused by human actions were estimated to be about 125 mgd in the Nassau-Suffolk study area, about 60 percent (75 mgd) resulting from the disposal of sewage effluent into streams and to the ocean. Though total loss is less than 10 percent of water input through precipitation (1600 mgd), most of the loss is confined to a 70-square-mile area in southwestern Nassau county that is sewered. This loss had significant effect on local groundwater levels and streamflow.

Water management practices on Long Island include water withdrawal from both shallow and deep wells, artificial recharge of polluted effluent from cesspools and septic tanks, recharge of runoff water through shallow basins, discharge of treated effluent into the ocean, and injection of generally uncontaminated waste water through diffusion wells. These practices have resulted in total freshwater outflows exceeding total freshwater inflows so that the groundwater table is decreasing and salt water is encroaching landward.

One dilemma facing planners, therefore, is this: Should the present use of cesspools and septic tanks, which helps boost groundwater quantity at the expense of water quality, be maintained or eliminated in favor of sanitary sewers whose operation will help maintain groundwater quality at the expense of quantity? Other similar dilemmas exist. Planners must now begin to make hard decisions to guide development of the area for the next twenty-five, fifty, or one hundred years. These decisions must be based on a thorough understanding of the hydrologic system in all its aspects. Four suggested water management alternatives[24] that planners must consider in detail as they seek solutions to existing problems caused by the rapid development of Long Island are:

1. increase inflow to the hydrologic system.
2. salvage natural groundwater outflow.
3. allow a controlled decrease in fresh groundwater in storage.
4. seek to maintain an approximate balance between inflow and outflow by means of artificial recharge.

The first alternative can result from rainmaking, direct importation of water, reservoir construction, or desalination of sea water. Though the fourth alternative is a possibility, the second and third alternatives seem to be less feasible as current solutions. Making the second effective would involve a network of shallow wells (or skimming wells) and pumping galleries next to streams. This operation would decrease streamflow to the ocean and increase salinity of bays and estuaries, which might prove harmful. It should, however, result in a significant increase in available freshwater supplies with only a minimal decrease in groundwater storage. Suggestion 3 would permit a controlled inflow of salty groundwater through a planned imbalance in the hydrologic system. Some coastal wells would become contaminated with salt water. The suggestion is somewhat akin to the planned overpumping of wells in the southwest or to the continued use of nonrenewable resources. The time will come when other solutions to the problem will have to be found. Suggestion 4 is quite feasible but it could lead to increasing contamination of groundwater supplies. Additional water treatment is necessary before any effluent should be allowed to reenter the groundwater.

Summary

Some of the great changes in the factors of the water budget that can result from urbanization have been pointed out in this chapter. The climatic water budget can be used as a powerful tool, not only to provide quantitative information on the magnitude of the changes involved but also to allow rapid preliminary evaluations of many different possible alternatives. Knowing the magnitudes of responses to different possible planning decisions before actual developments are undertaken will result in greater protection for our valuable resources and their more rational development.

8 Society's Impact on the Water Budget

Nearly every action that society has undertaken at the surface of the earth has, in some way, resulted in a modification of the water or the energy budgets of that surface. Whereas, for most of human history, these actions have been taken with little regard for their consequences on the energy or water budgets, an increasing number of more recent activities have been willfully directed toward modifying these budgets for the welfare of mankind. Whether the actions have been planned or unplanned, it is certain that we live in a far different environmental situation now than did Pleistocene man or even our forefathers.

Human Alterations of Existing Moisture Relationships

We have been primarily concerned with the water budget or hydrologic cycle in this volume. As we have studied its component parts and seen how the various factors of the budget are related to agriculture, hydrology, forest ecosystems, or urban planning, we should have come to the clear realization that we have affected every part of that cycle by our actions on earth.

We have changed the nature of the surface of the earth through cutting of trees and building of cities. As a result we have rearranged the heat sources on the earth's surface, affected the roughness and, hence, the turbulent exchange, and modified the opportunities to exchange moisture with the atmosphere. We dam water in reservoirs and ponds; we drain lakes, marshes, and low-lying areas; we lower water tables through overpumping and raise water tables by artificial recharge. We change the course of rivers, modify the overland and subsurface flow of water to streams by remolding soils, leveling land, or installing storm sewers and tile drains, and thus destroy the classical relationships between precipitation, evaporation, soil moisture, and runoff. We change evaporation and transpiration losses from the surface of the earth to the atmosphere above by spreading thin films of long-chain alcohols (hexadecanol) on open water bodies, by draining wet areas, by replacing one vegetation species with another or one land-use type by another, or even by changing the temperature of the air or of the evaporating surface.

And finally, we have done many things to the atmosphere that may modify the precipitation phase of the hydrologic cycle. We add dust and smoke to the air and so may increase or decrease the possibilities of precipitation; we seed clouds both willfully or inadvertently to modify precipitation patterns, to suppress hail, and to eliminate fogs; we create artificial rain in dry areas through irrigation; and we attempt to modify hurricanes. A brief table of current or possible human alterations of various climatic elements on both a local and global scale (table 8-1) suggests the farreaching nature of our activities.[1]

In addition to all these activities, we have also helped nature by making additional fresh water with the desalination of salty or brackish water and by digging deeper wells to tap aquifers where the water had been almost lost in long-term storage. Without question, the hydrologic cycle has been tampered with, modified, and even forcibly changed by the various actions of people on this earth.

The water budget must be a fundamental area of concern in any examination of what happens as people modify both small- and large-scale environments. Modifying the factors of the water budget in either very humid or very arid areas

Table 8-1
Climatic Alterations by Man

Cause	Elements Affected	Space Scale
Deforestation	Temperature, Evaporation, Wind	Local
Aforestation	Runoff, Erosion	Local
Agriculture	Temperature, Wind, Evaporation, Soil Blowing	Local to Subcontinental
Drainage	Evaporation, Runoff	Local
Irrigation	Evaporation, (Rainfall?)	Local
Reservoirs	Evaporation, Temperature (Rainfall?)	Local to Regional
Urbanization	Temperature, Humidity, Runoff, Rainfall, Air Pollution	Local
Industrialization	Air Pollution, Rainwater, Composition	Regional
Power Production	Air Pollution, Thermal Pollution, Rainwater	Regional to Continental
CO_2 Production By Preceding Activities	Temperature	Global
NO_x From Stratospheric Aviation	(Temperature?), O_3 Reduction, Increased U.V. Radiation	Global
CL/F Compounds	O_3 Reduction, Increased U.V. Radiation (Temperature?)	Global

Source: H.E. Landsberg, "The definition and determination of climatic change, fluctuations and outlooks," in *Atmospheric Quality and Climatic Change*, R.J. Kopec (ed.), Second Carolina Geographical Symposium, Studies in Geography No. 9, Department of Geography, University of North Carolina at Chapel Hill (1976).

possibly has an impact on only a local scale. For example, bringing water to a desert area through an irrigation scheme results in significant changes but, because of the limited amounts of water available locally, the changes would be restricted to local oases with negligible effect beyond those isolated areas. In continuously moist areas, some local changes might result from improved drainage but there would be little possibility of bringing about significant climatic changes. It is rather in those extensive areas of the world where precipitation is excessive in one season and deficient in another that possibly more significant changes in climate can be achieved through widespread human manipulation of the factors of the water budget.

One of the more comprehensive reviews of human effects on all phases of climate resulted from a 1971 MIT-sponsored study on Inadvertent Climate Modification.[2] Though the effect of humans in modifying the water budget at the surface of the globe was only one of the many factors considered, the conference report emphasized that changes in factors of the heat and water budgets were interrelated. Any modification of surface or atmospheric environments could have farreaching effects on both heat and water budget factors both locally as well as over larger regional areas. It is not really possible to separate society's effect on the water budget from its effect on the heat budget. For example, evapotranspiration represents a flow of both moisture and latent heat. It results in water vapor in the atmosphere which will influence radiation exchanges not only through the presence of the vapor itself but also through the later formation of clouds.

Significant land surface changes have occurred over the centuries with the spread of people across the earth and with cultural changes from hunting to farming and to the domestication of grazing animals. The decline in certain tree pollens in western European peat bogs after 3500 B.C. have been related by some to the cutting of forests that accompanied the increase in the shepherd-farmer culture at that time. Vast amounts of land have been converted from steppe and forest areas into arable land and pasture.[3] Principal areas of such land conversion include large parts of Europe, eastern America, and the area of southwest Asia from Turkey to Afghanistan.

Some tropical and subtropical savannas may be manmade, the natural dry deciduous forest having been gradually destroyed by the inhabitants as a result of fires. Climatic and pedologic changes that occurred following the removal of the forest were often such that forests could not reestablish themselves in these areas. Overgrazing has resulted in a change in landscape in many dry areas from steppe to semidesert even though the amount of precipitation has remained essentially the same. Desert areas in some regions are manmade as a result of overgrazing; once started they can be self-perpetuating as a result of the conditions associated with the desert itself.[4]

In tropical rainforest areas, slash-and-burn agricultural practices have often resulted in nearly desertlike surfaces on lateritic materials after just a few seasons of agricultural use. Lush tropical forest vegetation often owes its existence to a continued supply of minerals and organic material from the decaying forest vegetation. When this is unavailable, the soil is quickly leached of most nutrients. After brief agricultural use, the impoverished soil will support little vegetation and much of the rainfall becomes surface runoff. The change in surface cover results in drier soil conditions because less rainfall infiltrates and more is lost by direct overland runoff. Partially balancing this increased water loss is, of course, the decreased evapotranspiration loss from the denuded area.

As much as 30×10^6 km^2 (about 20 percent of the total continental area of the globe) have been converted from one vegetation type to another (almost always to a drier climate species).[5] These changes cannot but have had a marked effect on both heat and water budgets of large regions of the globe. The changes have been gradual, however, involving time periods and areas without adequate meteorologic observations so that the magnitude of any attendant climatic changes can only be estimated.

Influence of Land-Use Change on Streamflow

Several different research methodologies can be used to determine the effect of changing land cover on streamflow or basin water yield. Two of the most common involve either the so-called physical approach or the hydrometric approach.[6] Both methods have been employed over the past half century with varying degrees of success.

The physical approach to basin analysis involves understanding the effects of changes in specific hydroclimatic elements on streamflow. The hydrometric method involves the measurement of water yield from entire watersheds. Two basic techniques have been used in this method. In one, two basins nearly identical in terms of size, climate, terrain, soil, and vegetation conditions are identified. One is used as a control and the other undergoes some particular change or treatment. Following a period of calibration (usually at least five years long) an equation is obtained that can be used to predict runoff from the "treated" watershed as a function of runoff from the control basin. After the basin is modified (usually through some form of vegetation change), the difference found between the observed and predicted water yield on the treated basin is accepted as the integrated effect of the land use change.

The foregoing method is known as the "paired-watershed" technique. A variation of it, called the "calibrated-watershed" method, involves observations on only one basin for a long number of years. During this period of calibration, a statistically valid relationship between precipitation and basin yield is obtained. After treatment, a new relationship is found and the nature of the changes from the before-treatment period can be inferred from the changed statistical relationship. The validity of the results depends, in large part, on the significance of the statistical relationship originally developed, which, in turn, is a function of the length of the calibration period.

To use the paired-watershed approach in evaluating the effect of land-use changes on a hydroclimatic factor such as evapotranspiration requires the solving of the following water budget equation for each basin:

$$E = P - Q - \Delta S$$

where E is the evapotranspiration; P is precipitation; Q is the basin streamflow; and ΔS is the change in basin water storage. Use of the technique requires many years of observations and is subject to various uncertainties, especially when there may be problems of leakage and underflow from the basin. Because of the need to make ΔS essentially zero unless quite reliable observations of water storage are available, it is not possible to obtain short-term estimates of a factor such as evapotranspiration from this technique.

One interesting example of the response of streamflow to clearcutting has been reported.[7] Two small forested watersheds near Coweeta were calibrated together for three years at the beginning of a period of study. In 1940, one of the basins was clearcut. In the first year after clearcutting, annual streamflow from the treated basin increased some 373 mm over the value expected from the regression equation with the control basin. As the hardwood forest regrew during the following twenty-three years, streamflow from the treated basin decreased logarithmically (figure 8-1) until at the end of this period the flow was only 75 mm greater than the value predicted for a full forest cover. Clearcutting again at that time resulted in a second marked increase in streamflow from the treated basin almost exactly equivalent to the response after the first cutting.

A fairly complete summary of published material on watershed experiments on land use modifications involving some thirty-nine experiments from North America, Asia, and Africa has been undertaken.[8] Most of the experiments were of the paired-watershed type. The streamflow response to vegetation modification in the first year varied significantly (figure 8-2) even in those experiments where complete clearcutting was practiced. Greater increases in streamflow were found to occur with cutting on north-facing slopes than on south-facing ones. The results do suggest, however, that in well-watered areas, streamflow response is somewhat proportional to the degree of reduction in forest cover.

In reviewing the paired-watershed work, one might conclude that information on basin water yields resulting from planned vegetation changes is still urgently needed. Existing studies permit prediction in only relative terms. There seems to be a growing recognition among experimenters that the period of paired-watershed or calibrated watershed studies is about over, to be replaced, according to some, by more detailed physical studies of the individual components of the water budget.[9]

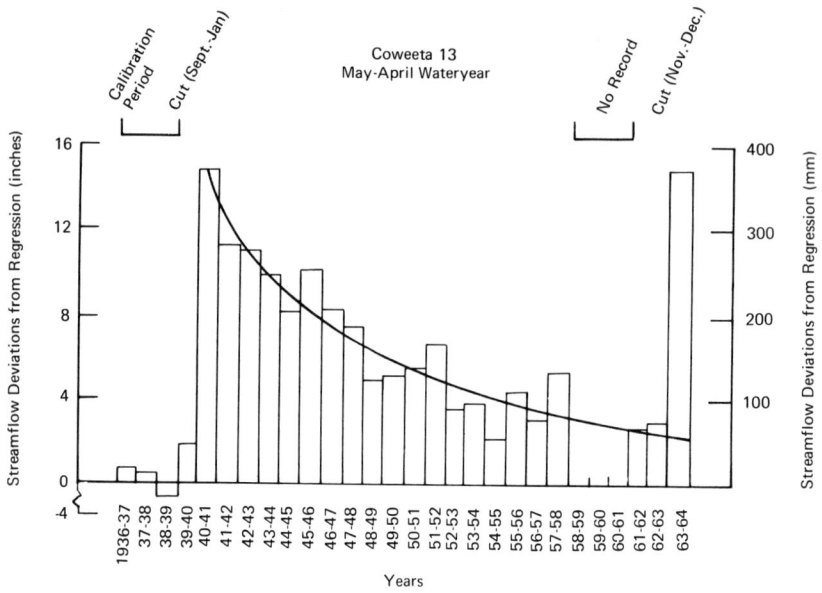

Source: A.R. Hibbert, "Forest treatment effects on water yield," *Forest Hydrology*, ed., W.E. Sopper and H.W. Lull, Proceedings of a NSF Advanced Science Seminar, Penn State Univ., August 29-September 10, 1965, Pergamon Press, Ltd. (1967).

Figure 8-1. Response of Water Yield to Clear-Cutting a Forest and Response to Cutting Again 23 Years Later, Coweeta Basin 13, May-April Water Year

The Climatic Water Budget in Studying the Effect of Land-Use Change

Using a climatic water budget model in land-use studies provides certain definite advantages not found with either the physical or hydrometric methods. There is no need for two identical basins or long periods of calibration before treatment begins because the climatic water budget approach utilizes computations from the water budget to provide the necessary control conditions. The technique involves using the climatic water budget to provide hydrologic data from a hypothetical watershed that can be compared with data obtained from an actual watershed. By computing annual streamflow from the hypothetical watershed for a long period without changing the initial conditions of land use, it is possible to evaluate the hydrologic effects of changes in only climatic conditions. Comparing these results with actual changes in basin discharge as measured on a real watershed in which both land use and climatic conditions have

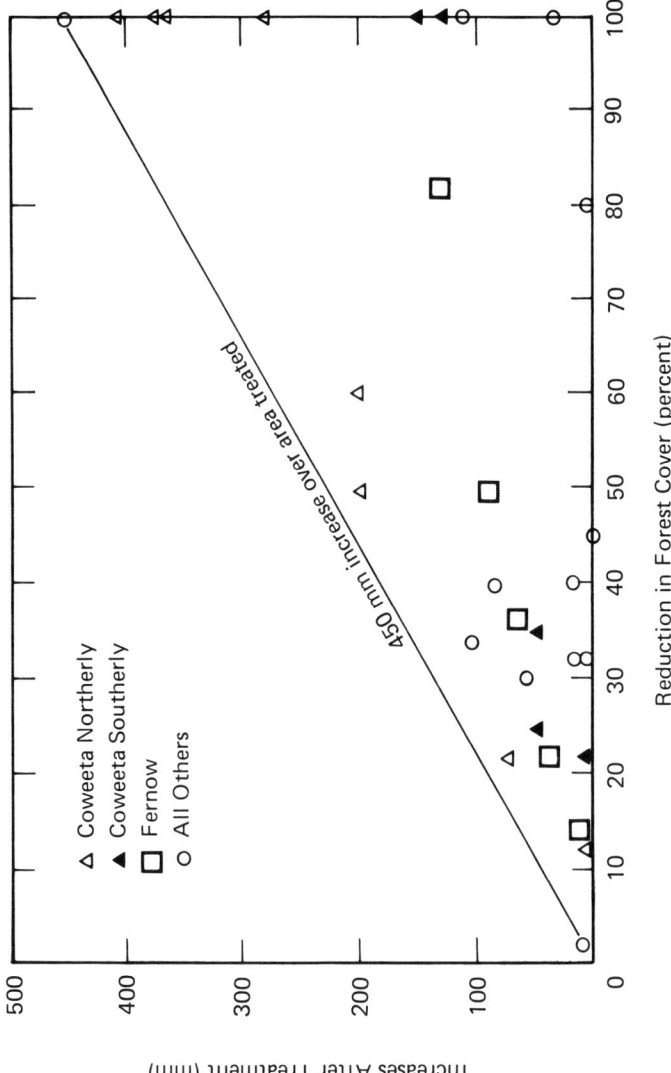

Source: A.R. Hibbert, "Forest treatment effects on water yield," *Forest Hydrology*, ed., W.E. Sopper and H.W. Lull, Proceedings of a NSF Advanced Science Seminar, Penn State Univ., August 29-September 10, 1965, Pergamon Press, Ltd. (1967).

Figure 8-2. Summary of Experiments To Study the Response of Forest Cutting on Water Yield

changed, it becomes possible to eliminate the effect of changing climate. This clearly identifies the hydrologic consequences of land use changes alone. The technique illustrated in chapter 7 in the example from the Chester Creek basin is most useful in identifying the relatively slow changes associated with gradual modification of a basin from one general cover type to another.

A similar approach has been used to study the effect of reforestation on annual streamflow from four small basins in the Allegheny plateau region of New York state from 1935 to 1957.[10] Keeping land-use conditions the same as they were in 1935, average annual streamflow can be calculated from the climatic data for each year of the study. When this is done, a progressively greater difference between annual measured streamflow and streamflow computed on the basis of land use conditions at the beginning of the study period (figure 8-3) is found. Measured streamflow approximates computed streamflow in the 1930s and early 1940s when forests covered 20 to 50 percent of the four basins, whereas computed streamflow was greater than measured streamflow in the late 1940s and 1950s when forests covered 80 to 90 percent of three of the four basins. Annual decreases in measured streamflow based on the calculated slopes of the regression lines vary from over 3 mm per year on Cold Spring Brook watershed to over 10 mm per year on Shackham Brook watershed (figure 8-3). Statistically significant differences between measured and computed streamflow were found on all basins but Cold Spring Brook.

The progressive decrease in measured streamflow is attributed to an increase in evapotranspiration losses from the developing and deeper-rooted tree cover.[11] During the study period, total measured streamflow decreased 74, 122, 163, and 234 mm respectively on the four basins. If similar changes were to occur on most of the basins throughout the area due to a regional emphasis on reforestation, the result could be a significant modification of the annual streamflow on the major rivers draining the area (the Susquehanna and Delaware Rivers, primarily).

The Effect of Mulches

Land management plays a significant role in retention or use of soil moisture. Farmers and gardeners alike have increasingly turned to the use of mulches to provide more optimal energy and moisture conditions for plant growth. The effect of different mulches on local microclimates has been studied in some detail by means of observations of incoming (R_i) and outgoing (R_o) radiation using hemispherical and net radiometers, energy losses by evapotranspiration (W) using small soil-filled aluminum cans, and soil heat flux (G) using heat flow transducers.[12] Energy exchange by conduction and convection with the air (A) was not determined but evaluated as a residual in the energy balance equation

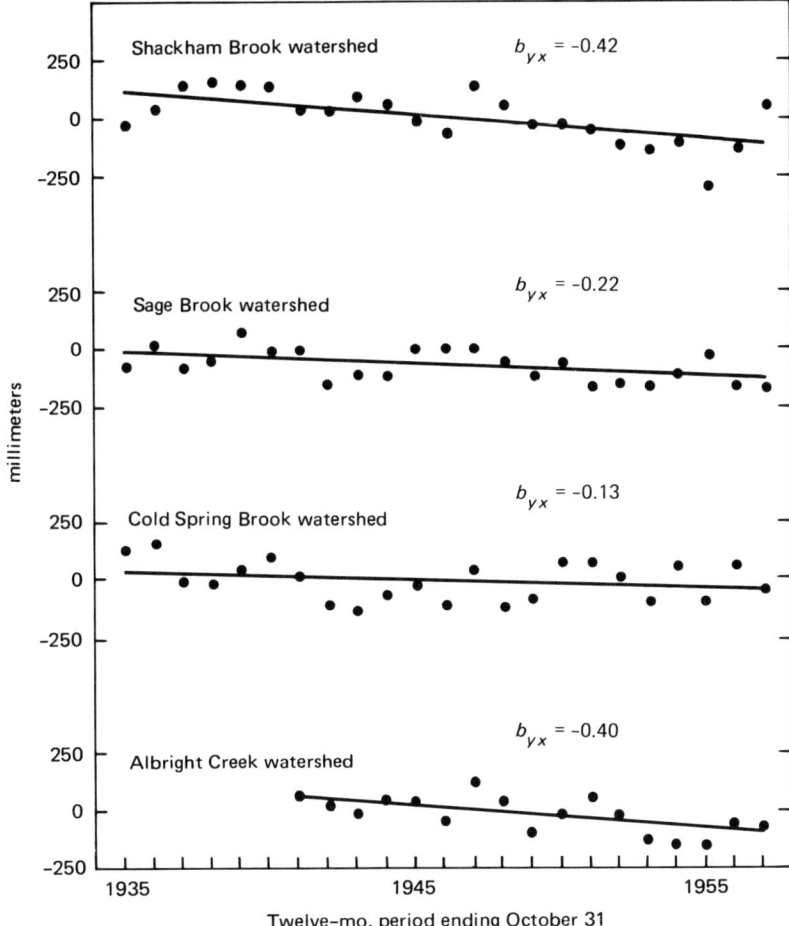

Source: R.A. Muller, "The effects of reforestation on water yield: A case study using energy and water balance models for the Allegheny plateau, New York, *Publications in Climatology,* Laboratory of Climatology, vol. 10, no. 3 (1966).

Figure 8-3. Differences Between Calculated and Measured Water Yield at Experimental Watersheds on the Allegheny Plateau, 1935-1957

$$R_i + R_o + W + A + G = 0.$$

The disposition of energy over several different surfaces including black and translucent plastic film (38 μm and 152 μm thick, respectively), aluminum film bonded to polyethylene film (each film 152 μm thick), as well as paper and straw surfaces was studied in this way. The results were compared with observations from a bare soil surface maintained as a control. It was found that the opaque black film resulted in little warming of the soil in the daytime although it did increase its temperature by several degrees at night. The translucent plastic film resulted in significant warming of the soil in the daytime and warming by several degrees at night. The reflective aluminum film kept the soil somewhat cooler in daytime and warmer at night. In all cases, the films reduced the evaporation of water from the surface, conserving heat in the soil and making additional water available for plant use. Paper and straw mulches were not as effective in conserving water as the film mulches because of the increased air movement through those mulches. The influences of the different mulches on both temperature and evaporation have been summed up in table 8-2 qualitatively. The plus sign stands for an increase (double plus, a marked increase), the minus for a decrease, and the 0 for no appreciable change in the tabulated quantity.

One widespread application of mulches in agriculture—the practice of summerfallowing—has been employed by farmers in dry or semiarid regions for many years. Summerfallowing received considerable study as well as publicity during the Dust Bowl years of the 1930s both in the United States and Canada. It was thought that good summerfallowing practice required the maintenance of a fine dry dust mulch on the surface. The surface should be reworked after rain to prevent the development of surface caking or clods and to reestablish the mulch. In theory, moisture was drawn to the surface by capillary action to be lost by evaporation. Cultivating the surface would break up the capillaries through which this water movement occurred and so reduce the evaporation loss of water. Summerfallowing would conserve water and allow the storage of some, at least, of the meager summer rains for later crop use.

Table 8-2
Summary of Temperature and Moisture Effects of Different Mulches
(+ for increase, − for decrease, 0 for no change)

	Black Film	Translucent Film	Aluminum Foil	Kraft Paper	Straw
Ground heat storage	−	+	− −	−	− −
Midday soil surf. temp.	0	++	−	−	− −
Night soil surf. temp.	+	+	+	0	+
Mean soil temp. (−3 cm depth)	0	+	0	−	−
Diurnal range temp. (−3 cm depth)	−	+	− − −	−	− −
Soil moisture conservation	++	++	++	+	+

Source: P.E. Waggoner, P.M. Miller, and H.C. DeRoo, "Plastic mulching, principles and benefits," *Bulletin 634*, The Connecticut Agricultural Experiment Station, New Haven (1960), 44 pp.

Summerfallowing did conserve moisture but at the same time it greatly increased the possibility of wind erosion and the blowing of great quantities of dust so common in the middle 1930s. Studies showed that weed growth, much more than capillary action, removed moisture from the soil. Instead of producing a fine dust mulch at the surface, farmers were advised not to work their summerfallow fields. Plowing, discing, and harrowing the soil should be done only to the extent necessary to control weeds. Plowing of dry soil should never be attempted because of the possibility of wind erosion.

During the 1930s the thinking about a dry dust summerfallow mulch changed markedly with the suggestion of a plowless fallow. But fields that had the stubble burned off to kill the weeds still were affected by wind erosion. Stubble fields left unburned did not suffer wind erosion but weeds would grow and vital moisture would be lost. Equipment was needed that would eliminate weed growth yet leave the stubble on the field. A blade-type cultivator that sliced through the soil just below the surface was developed. The idea of a dust mulch did not die easily, however. Farmers, accustomed to neat, cultivated fields, did not like to see rough, unplowed fields covered with stubble and dead weeds through the summerfallow period. New words such as "stubble mulch" and "trash cover" were coined to explain the new mulching technique. The success of the technique in reducing both moisture loss and wind erosion ultimately led to its widespread adoption by farmers throughout semiarid areas where farming with summerfallowing was necessary. Though plastic, paper, or hay mulches are also effective in reducing water loss and wind erosion, such techniques can hardly be applied over thousands of acres of farmlands. Stubble mulch, however, can. The result of this human interference with the natural operation of the water budget has been a real conservation of water without attendant problems of wind erosion in marginal moisture areas.

The Role of Antitranspirants

Research on antitranspirants or other techniques to reduce the water loss by vegetation without seriously influencing yield or health of the plant has the potential of significantly modifying the water relationship of an area. Reducing the total water need of a particular crop by only an inch or two would have the effect of expanding greatly current agricultural boundaries. With less water used in evapotranspiration, streamflow, groundwater recharge, and water available for reservoir storage might all increase, easing the competing demands for water in many areas of critical shortages. Three broad groups of antitranspirants have been considered: (1) those which will increase reflection and thus decrease heat load on the leaf; (2) those which form films to hinder the escape of water from the leaf; and (3) those which encourage stomatal closure to reduce transpiration from the leaf. It has been shown that antitranspirants are more effective in reducing transpiration losses (1) when the movement of water to the roots and through the plant to the leaves is not impaired in other ways, and (2) when there is a good coverage of leaf surfaces although new leaf development is minimal.[13]

Antitranspirants will not be effective under all conditions of vegetation and other environmental factors. The rapid growth of new leaves will, for example, quickly reduce the effectiveness of an earlier spraying. Whether the reduction in the soil moisture losses due to reduced evapotranspiration will be significant enough to influence stream runoff or groundwater recharge depends on many different hydrologic, climatic, and watershed factors. The many uncertainties in determining soil moisture content and water movement in soil make it difficult to estimate the real effectiveness of antitranspirants in the field.

The Effect of Urbanization on Factors of
the Water Budget

The growth of large urbanized areas has had a pronounced local effect on climatic factors. Two decades ago it was suggested that precipitation might be at least 10 percent greater in a city than in nearby rural areas.[14] Recent studies have confirmed this figure but have suggested that patterns of precipitation are not as simple as earlier inferred; significant changes have been found in suburban areas and even downwind from the city center itself.[15] Table 8-3 lists changes in precipitation and related conditions in five midwestern cities as compared with surrounding rural areas.

One place investigated was La Porte, Indiana, downwind of the Chicago-Gary industrial complex. The increase in precipitation appears so far out of line with increases noted at other stations that the results have led to considerable debate concerning their reliability. The suggestion has been made that particularly high concentrations of ice nuclei from the steel mills of Chicago and Gary as well as increased heat from nearby industrial sources contributed to the increased precipitation, hailstorms, and nocturnal thunderstorms found at La Porte.[16]

Cities, in general, might be expected to have increased precipitation because of increased water vapor content of the atmosphere due to presence of combustion sources; higher temperatures over cities both from thermal combustion and from absorption and retention of radiation resulting in stronger thermal convection; larger concentrations of both condensation and ice nuclei; and increased surface roughness leading to greater mechanical turbulence.

Cities will also produce changes in other factors of the water budget, as we have seen in the previous chapter. Evapotranspiration from urbanized areas will be less than from rural, vegetation-covered areas. The impervious surfaces in the city area provide little opportunity for water storage and vegetation will be largely confined to park and cemetery areas. Less water will be available for

Table 8-3

Summary of Urban Area Increases in Precipitation and Related Conditions

(Expressed as a percentage of rural values)

	Chicago	La Porte	St. Louis	Tulsa	Champaign-Urbana
Annual precipitation	5	31	7	8	5
Warmer half-year precipitation	4	30	a	5	4
Colder half-year precipitation	6	33	a	11	8
Rain days ⩾0.01 or 0.1 inch					
Annual	6	0	a	a	7
Warmer half-year	8	0	a	a	3
Colder half-year	4	0	a	a	10
Rain days ⩾0.25 or 0.5 inch					
Annual	5	34	a	a	5
Warmer half-year	7	54	a	a	9
Colder half-year	0	5	a	a	0
Annual number of thunder-storm days	6	38	11	a	7
Summer number of thunder-storm days	13	63	21	a	17

Source: S.A. Changnon, Jr., "Recent studies of urban effects on precipitation in the United States," *Bulletin of the American Meteorological Society*, vol. 50 (1969):411-421.

[a]Data not sufficient for comparison.

evapotranspiration from the whole city area. Because temperatures are higher within urban areas, potential evapotranspiration will be greater even though actual evapotranspiration will be less. Runoff from urban areas will be greater than from rural areas because water cannot infiltrate many urban surfaces. As a result, a water budget for an urban area would differ appreciably from that for a nearby rural area as the following comparisons indicate:

$$P_U > P_R \qquad ST_U < ST_R$$

$$AE_U < AE_R \qquad D_U > D_R$$

$$RO_U > RO_R \qquad S_U > S_R$$

subscripts U and R refer to urban and rural respectively; P is precipitation; AE is actual evapotranspiration; RO is runoff, ST is soil moisture storage; D is soil moisture deficit; and S is soil moisture surplus.

In 1971, a large-scale intensive study of the effects of a major city on weather and climate was begun in the St. Louis, Missouri, area. Entitled

METROMEX (*METRO*politan *M*eteorological *EX*periment), the project though still not completed, has provided a vast storehouse of information for future study. Its goals are to determine whether the urban area produced any precipitation or other severe weather anomalies and if so by what means; to develop ways to translate the findings to other urban areas; and to evalute the short- and long-term effects any such alteration might have on society.[17]

Preliminary results indicate that there is a fairly localized 20 to 30 percent increase in average summer precipitation associated with the presence of the city area along with evidence of an increase in hail and thunderstorms. No decrease in rainfall has been found within 160 km of St. Louis, so that the increased urban rainfall is not necessarily "borrowed" from some other area. The results suggest that urban thermal and moisture conditions along with the increased aerosol content in the air affect, in some way, clouds and rainfall distributions.

Modification of Surface Water Storage

Manipulating surface water supplies has had significant effects on factors of the water budget. Extensive irrigation enterprises, drainage of marshes and swamps, stream engineering works for flood control or other purposes, creation of vast lake and reservoir systems all influence evaporation, water runoff, and water storage factors. Though some might argue that such activities might also influence precipitation, changes in local evaporation often do not significantly influence local precipitation unless there is also some orographic feature to cause the more moist air to give up some of its moisture locally. Even that situation provides a significant increase only in a very restricted sense.

The total surface area of all manmade lakes and reservoirs in the world has been estimated to be about 300,000 km^2.[18] The evaporation from such water surfaces must be greater than from those same surfaces before lakes and reservoirs were established. This increased evaporation requires a significant amount of energy for the evaporation process and this energy is transferred to the air as latent heat. The albedo of the water will also be considerably lower than the albedo of the previous surface.

Drainage of swamps and marshes must produce water budget effects that are generally opposite to what happens when lakes and reservoirs are created. However, because drainage activities are most pronounced in humid areas where appreciable rainfall often occurs, the reduction in evapotranspiration will not be as evident as the increase in evaporation when lakes and reservoirs are created in fairly dry areas. If the drained swamp is used for industrial or urban purposes significant changes in the factors of the water budget can result, however. Aside from changes in albedo and energy storage as a result of the drainage process, direct water budget effects would include slightly lower evapotranspiration as a result of inadequate soil moisture conditions for potential evapotranspiration at all times, and, of course, reduced storage of water in or on the land surface. Once new equilibrium conditions were established, runoff from the area should be only slightly greater because of lower evapotranspiration losses. No significant changes in precipitation should occur.

Two general conclusions can be developed. First, these discussions have emphasized the essential unity of water in all phases of the hydrologic cycle. It is really impossible to talk about changes in storage or runoff without recognizing that any change in one aspect of the cycle must be balanced by corresponding changes in other aspects of the cycle either locally, in some more distant area, or on a global basis. Water, whether present as snow on some distant mountain, as water in a nearby lake, or as groundwater beneath the surface, is all part of a single system. Actions by individuals in one place must be balanced by nature's reaction either at the same place or someplace else.

Second, the sum of many small changes in factors of the water budget may result in more significant global effects than will be noticed locally. Increased evaporation from lake surfaces may produce hardly any local climatic changes but if such surfaces result in small changes in global albedo or cloud cover, the effect on the radiation budget might be sufficient to trigger considerably larger global responses. Although modification of about one fifth of our land area because of the development of agriculture and urbanization has modified our regional climates, such changes may have global consequences as well. Climates constantly vary and it requires many years of record to identify a climatic change because the record used may also include progressively changing data. When looked at from a future perspective, the actual global significance of the shift to agriculture and to urbanization over large parts of our globe in the nineteenth and twentieth centuries will become more clearly discernible.

The Role of Weather Modification Activities

Both willful or inadvertent weather modification activities can influence water budget factors over local areas and may result in some change in these factors over even larger areas. Possible weather modification activities in the vicinity of La Porte, Indiana, as a result of steel mills and other industrial activity upwind have already been discussed. Furthermore, seeding clouds with such nuclei as silver iodide can modify clouds. Whether such seeding activities can consistently result in increased precipitation so that a change in climate will develop over a period of time has yet to be demonstrated. Analyzed results include some accepted cases of increased precipitation of the order of 10 to 20 percent as well as some cases of no change or even possible decreased precipitation.[19]

Important problems must still be solved as we continue with our willful weather modification activities. For example, if seeding does result in increased rainfall in one place, will this be balanced by a decrease elsewhere or will there be a net global increase in precipitation? Is the increased precipitation largely evaporated or lost as increased runoff? If evaporation is increased, the result should be an intensification or speeding of the rate of exchange of water in the hydrologic cycle, whereas if runoff increases then the main consequence of seeding will be just a redistribution of moisture.

Weather modification activities to control or moderate the effect of hurricanes could have significant effects on the water budget as a result of changes in the large amounts of precipitation that accompany such tropical weathermakers. If hurricane rains of 8 to 10 inches were eliminated, water budget factors of storage and runoff would be significantly influenced. The effect of repeated hurricane control on long-term climate could also be very great. Hurricane rains are significant in long-term monthly and annual precipitation totals in many areas.

The effect of seeding on clouds themselves will depend in part on the number and type of nuclei present in the cloud. With many small cloud droplets, the addition of more small nuclei will result in decreased rainmaking efficiency. The presence of many small droplets will hinder the production of the larger droplets needed to produce rain. If, however, large ice nuclei are introduced into the cloud, they may effectively collect additional moisture and grow large enough to fall out of the cloud as rain. This process will ultimately lead to a reduction in cloud size.

The suggestion that, downwind from steel mills or paper mills, effective cloud seeding may be occurring by the nuclei introduced into the atmosphere through the processes of manufacture has already been mentioned. For example, an increase in cloud nuclei in the air as a result of burning sugar cane has been noted in Queensland.[20] Not only has there been a tenfold increase in cloud nuclei during burning but also there has been an increase in numbers of nuclei over the past fifty years. As nuclei concentration has increased, rainfall has decreased some 25 percent. The type of particles introduced into the atmosphere through burning evidently did not stimulate rainmaking.

Mechanisms, therefore, exist that can produce either increases or decreases in cloud cover and precipitation as a result of continued and increased pollution of the atmosphere. The ultimate effect on other aspects of the water budget is not clear because of the complex relationships between the heat and water budgets and because inadvertent seeding can result in either increases or decreases in cloud cover and precipitation amounts.

A Synergistic Example

A water budget approach has been used to determine whether the combined actions of rainmaking and evapotranspiration reduction through vegetation modification might produce larger streamflow response than is possible from summing streamflow responses to each action separately.[21] If so, a synergistic interaction results that might suggest new directions for environmental workers in their efforts to provide increased water resources.

The water yield of a basin is determined basically by precipitation and evapotranspiration. Increasing the former or reducing the latter can result in increased runoff but there is no guarantee of this because of the dependence of runoff on such factors as storage of moisture in the soil, timing of precipitation, and how nearly actual evapotranspiration satisfies potential climatic needs. Evapotranspiration reduction through vegetation control may be more successful in increasing runoff in humid climates where the increased runoff is not as important for human use. Similarly, in humid climates where soil is more often at field capacity, any increased precipitation may be more easily translated into increased runoff. For example, it has been shown that with a 10 percent increase in precipitation, 96 percent of that increase would appear as increased runoff in a humid area while only 22 percent of that increase would appear as runoff in subhumid areas.[22] Of a 10 percent decrease in potential evapotranspiration, 62 percent of that decrease would result in increased runoff in humid areas while only 1 percent of the decrease in evapotranspiration would find its way to increased runoff in subhumid areas.

Consider a hypothetical example where precipitation, P, initially equals AE and both are less than PE. It can be argued that if P is increased to equal PE or if PE is decreased to equal AE, there would be no increase in runoff. The reduction in potential evapotranspiration would produce no change in AE and result in no change in runoff. As a result of rainmaking, AE would be increased but since all the increased precipitation would be lost as PE there would again be no increase in runoff. Only when the two steps are combined will a decrease in PE to AE and the increase in P to PE then result in increased runoff.

To test this hypothesis three separate sets of climatic water budgets were evaluated at selected stations in different parts of the United States where woody vegetation occurred.[23] In the first set, potential evapotranspiration was decreased by 10 percent each month with no change in precipitation. The second set of budgets involved an increase in precipitation by 10 percent each month with no change in potential evapotranspiration. The third set of budgets considered a simultaneous decrease in PE and an increase in P by 10 percent each month. Later, other budgets were evaluated in which PE was decreased by 25 percent to simulate clear-cutting of a forest or converting woodland to grasses accompanied by cloud seeding. The results of these budget computations are summarized in table 8-4.

As expected, the so-called heavy vegetation treatment (25 percent reduction in PE) results in greater increases in runoff than the lighter, 10 percent reduction in PE. Also, the percentage of increased precipitation or decreased potential evapotranspiration appearing as streamflow is greater in more moist climates (Muscle Shoals, Lexington) than in drier climates (Levy).

Table 8-4

Annual Streamflow as a Result of Increasing Precipitation and Decreasing Evapotranspiration at Selected Stations in the United States

(In mm)

Station (normal RO)	Decrease PE by 10% (1)	Increase P by 10% (2)	Combine (1) and (2) (3)	Synergistic gain 3 − (1 + 2) (4)	Decrease PE by 25% (5)	Combine (2) and (4) (6)	Synergistic gain 6 − (2 + 4) (7)
Flagstaff, Ariz. (26 mm)	28	36	69	5	84	128	8
Muscle Shoals, Ala. (473 mm)	72	116	188	0	180	310	14
Mt. Palomar, Calif. (204 mm)	22	57	93	13	62	124	5
Potlatch, Ida. (126 mm)	28	47	77	2	76	125	2
Lexington, Ky. (367 mm)	53	92	149	4	147	250	11
Elsberry, Mo. (192 mm)	51	71	132	10	145	231	15
Levy, N.M. (0 mm)	0	0	0	0	2	45	43
Harrisburg. Pa. (259 mm)	55	83	142	4	152	246	11
Spearfish, S. Dak.	29	25	80	26	101	151	25

Source: D.R. Satterlund, "Combined weather and vegetation modification promises synergistic streamflow response," *Journal of Hydrology*, vol. 9 (1969), Elsevier Scientific Publishing Co., Amsterdam.

The combined effect of increasing precipitation and decreasing potential evapotranspiration resulted in more contribution to runoff at all listed stations except Muscle Shoals and Levy, the two listed stations with the extremes of moistness and aridity. Even these two stations showed a so-called synergistic gain when the heavier vegetation treatment was used. Possible synergistic gains resulting from combining 10 percent changes in both *PE* and *P* as opposed to summing the results of the individual changes (shown in column 4) range from 0 at Muscle Shoals and Levy to some 26 mm depth of increased runoff at Spearfish, South Dakota.

Conclusions

It is increasingly apparent that difficult water decisions need to be made throughout the world. In many areas, decisions have been made without adequate consideration of information readily available from the water budget. The result has been economic loss, contamination of water supplies, loss of other valuable resources as well as water, and unnecessary hardships for individuals and nations. Comprehensive plans are necessary if rational development of our environment and its resources is to occur.

Because water decisions in one area affect water supplies and quality in other areas, water budget analyses should play increasingly important roles in studies of resources development not only of local areas but also of larger, more complex areas. The present widespread use of water budgets in the solution of so many different types of problems emphasizes the utility of the water budget. Many major natural processes depend on the water and energy factors of the environment. It is possible to analyze many varied environmental processes by means of either water or energy budget techniques. From such understanding will come increased ability to plan rationally and to utilize available resources more wisely.

Appendixes

Appendix A
Computation of the
Monthly Climatic
Water Budget

To compute the climatic water budget, it is first necessary to obtain data of water supply (precipitation) and climatic water need (potential evapotranspiration).

The procedure may be illustrated by using data from San Francisco, California (table A-1). At San Francisco average monthly temperature varies from $9.2°C$ in January to $17.7°C$ in September. Unadjusted 30-day potential evapotranspiration has been closely related to air temperature by Thornthwaite through the expression $e = 1.6(^{10t}/I)^a$ where t is mean monthly temperature $°C$; I is the annual heat index, the sum of 12 monthly heat indices, i; and a is an expression that varies with I.

It is necessary to adjust the value of e by taking into account the actual number of daylight hours per day as well as the variation in number of days in the month from 28 to 31. Evaluation of the expression for unadjusted potential evapotranspiration is quite difficult and time-consuming without the use of tables to simplify the computational procedure. Table A-2 provides values of the monthly heat index i for different monthly temperatures. Summation of these 12 monthly values provides the annual heat index (I) for the station.

Table A-3 provides values of unadjusted daily potential evapotranspiration from information on the annual heat index, I, and mean monthly temperature in $°C$. Different I values are given along the top of the table (it is satisfactory to select the one closest to the particular I value for the station in question. This value would be 57.5 for San Francisco) while temperatures from 0 to $26.5°C$ are included on the vertical scale. Potential evapotranspiration is considered to be 0 whenever monthly temperatures are less than $0°C$. If average monthly temperatures exceed $26.5°C$, the relation between evapotranspiration and air temperature is independent of the heat index, I, so that only one relation is needed for all I values. (A few values for temperatures above $26.5°C$ are included at the end of table A-3.)

Table A-4 provides latitudinal values of the product of the number of days in the month times the mean daily duration of sunlight expressed in units of 12 hours. These are the correction factors by which the unadjusted daily potential evapotranspiration is multiplied to produce the adjusted monthly potential evapotranspiration or climatic water demand. Using the information in tables A-2, A-3, and A-4, the I values, the unadjusted potential evapotranspiration, and

Source for tables A-2 through A-8 is C.W. Thornthwaite and J.R. Mather, "Instructions and Tables for Computing Potential Evapotranspiration and the Water Balance." *Publications in Climatology*, Laboratory of Climatology, vol. 10, no. 3 (1957).

Table A-1

Average Climatic Water Budget for San Francisco, California

(All values but T(°C) and I (dimensionless) are in mm depth)

	J	F	M	A	M	J	J	A	S	O	N	D	Year
T°C	9.2	10.5	11.8	13.2	14.6	16.3	17.1	17.1	17.7	15.8	12.7	10.1	13.8
I	2.52	3.08	3.67	4.35	5.07	5.98	6.44	6.44	6.78	5.71	4.10	2.90	57.0
UnPE	1.0	1.2	1.4	1.7	1.9	2.2	2.4	2.4	2.6	2.2	1.6	1.2	
PE	26	30	43	56	70	82	90	84	81	63	40	30	695
P	102	88	68	33	12	3	0	1	5	19	40	104	475
P–PE	76	58	25	–23	–58	–79	–90	–83	–76	–44	0	74	
ST	150	150	150	128	86	51	28	16	9	7	7	81	
ΔST	+69	0	0	–22	–42	–35	–23	–12	–7	–2	0	+81	
AE	26	30	43	55	54	38	23	13	12	21	40	30	385
D	0	0	0	1	16	44	67	71	69	42	0	0	310
S	7	58	25	0	0	0	0	0	0	0	0	0	90
RO	4	31	28	14	7	3	2	1	0	0	0	0	90
DT	153	180	177	141	92	54	29	16	9	7	7	81	

Note: T is average air temperature in °C; I is the heat index, the annual heat index I equaling the sum of the twelve monthly values of heat index, i; $UnPE$ is daily unadjusted potential evapotranspiration; PE is monthly adjusted potential evapotranspiration; P is precipitation; ST is soil moisture storage in the root zone of the soil; ΔST is the change in storage from one month to the next; AE is the actual evapotranspiration; D is the water deficit; S is the water surplus; RO is the monthly runoff (on the assumption of a 50 percent hold over of total surplus water each month); DT is total monthly detention within and on the soil.

Table A-2
Monthly Values of *I* Corresponding to Monthly Mean Temperatures (°C)

$T°C$	.0	.1	.2	.3	.4	.5	.6	.7	.8	.9
0			.01	.01	.02	.03	.04	.05	.06	.07
1	.09	.10	.12	.13	.15	.16	.18	.20	.21	.23
2	.25	.27	.29	.31	.33	.35	.37	.39	.42	.44
3	.46	.48	.51	.53	.56	.58	.61	.63	.66	.69
4	.71	.74	.77	.80	.82	.85	.88	.91	.94	.97
5	1.00	1.03	1.06	1.09	1.12	1.16	1.19	1.22	1.25	1.29
6	1.32	1.35	1.39	1.42	1.45	1.49	1.52	1.56	1.59	1.63
7	1.66	1.70	1.74	1.77	1.81	1.85	1.89	1.92	1.96	2.00
8	2.04	2.08	2.12	2.15	2.19	2.23	2.27	2.31	2.35	2.39
9	2.44	2.48	2.52	2.56	2.60	2.64	2.69	2.73	2.77	2.81
10	2.86	2.90	2.94	2.99	3.03	3.08	3.12	3.16	3.21	3.25
11	3.30	3.34	3.39	3.44	3.48	3.53	3.58	3.62	3.67	3.72
12	3.76	3.81	3.86	3.91	3.96	4.00	4.05	4.10	4.15	4.20
13	4.25	4.30	4.35	4.40	4.45	4.50	4.55	4.60	4.65	4.70
14	4.75	4.81	4.86	4.91	4.96	5.01	5.07	5.12	5.17	5.22
15	5.28	5.33	5.38	5.44	5.49	5.55	5.60	5.65	5.71	5.76
16	5.82	5.87	5.93	5.98	6.04	6.10	6.15	6.21	6.26	6.32
17	6.38	6.44	6.49	6.55	6.61	6.66	6.72	6.78	6.84	6.90
18	6.95	7.01	7.07	7.13	7.19	7.25	7.31	7.37	7.43	7.49
19	7.55	7.61	7.67	7.73	7.79	7.85	7.91	7.97	8.03	8.10
20	8.16	8.22	8.28	8.34	8.41	8.47	8.53	8.59	8.66	8.72
21	8.78	8.85	8.91	8.97	9.04	9.10	9.17	9.23	9.29	9.36
22	9.42	9.49	9.55	9.62	9.68	9.75	9.82	9.88	9.95	10.01
23	10.08	10.15	10.21	10.28	10.35	10.41	10.48	10.55	10.62	10.68
24	10.75	10.82	10.89	10.95	11.02	11.09	11.16	11.23	11.30	11.37
25	11.44	11.50	11.57	11.64	11.71	11.78	11.85	11.92	11.99	12.06
26	12.13	12.21	12.28	12.35	12.42	12.49	12.56	12.63	12.70	12.78
27	12.85	12.92	12.99	13.07	13.14	13.21	13.28	13.36	13.43	13.50
28	13.58	13.65	13.72	13.80	13.87	13.94	14.02	14.09	14.17	14.24
29	14.32	14.39	14.47	14.54	14.62	14.69	14.77	14.84	14.92	14.99
30	15.07	15.15	15.22	15.30	15.38	15.45	15.53	15.61	15.68	15.76
31	15.84	15.92	15.99	16.07	16.15	16.23	16.30	16.38	16.46	16.54
32	16.62	16.70	16.78	16.85	16.93	17.01	17.09	17.17	17.25	17.33
33	17.41	17.49	17.57	17.65	17.73	17.81	17.89	17.97	18.05	18.13
34	18.22	18.30	18.38	18.46	18.54	18.62	18.70	18.79	18.87	18.95
35	19.03	19.11	19.20	19.28	19.36	19.45	19.53	19.61	19.69	19.78
36	19.86	19.95	20.03	20.11	20.20	20.28	20.36	20.45	20.53	20.62
37	20.70	20.79	20.87	20.96	21.04	21.13	21.21	21.30	21.38	21.47
38	21.56	21.64	21.73	21.81	21.90	21.99	22.07	22.16	22.25	22.33
39	22.42	22.51	22.59	22.68	22.77	22.86	22.95	23.03	23.12	23.21
40	23.30									

Table A-3

Values of Unadjusted Daily Potential Evapotranspiration (mm) for Different Mean Temperatures (°C) and I Values

T°C	I 25.0	27.5	30.0	32.5	35.0	37.5	40.0	42.5	45.0	47.5	50.0	52.5
0	0.0	0.0	0.0	0.0	0.0	0.0	0.0	0.0	0.0	0.0	0.0	0.0
.25	0.1	0.0	0.0	0.0	0.0	0.0	0.0	0.0	0.0	0.0	0.0	0.0
.50	0.1	0.1	0.1	0.1	0.1	0.1	0.1	0.0	0.0	0.0	0.0	0.0
.75	0.2	0.2	0.1	0.1	0.1	0.1	0.1	0.1	0.1	0.1	0.0	0.0
1.00	0.2	0.2	0.2	0.2	0.2	0.1	0.1	0.1	0.1	0.1	0.1	0.1
1.25	0.3	0.3	0.2	0.2	0.2	0.1	0.1	0.1	0.1	0.1	0.1	0.1
1.50	0.3	0.3	0.2	0.2	0.2	0.2	0.2	0.2	0.2	0.1	0.1	0.1
1.75	0.4	0.4	0.3	0.3	0.3	0.2	0.2	0.2	0.2	0.2	0.2	0.1
2.00	0.4	0.4	0.3	0.3	0.3	0.2	0.2	0.2	0.2	0.2	0.2	0.2
2.25	0.5	0.5	0.4	0.3	0.3	0.3	0.3	0.3	0.3	0.2	0.2	0.2
2.50	0.5	0.5	0.4	0.4	0.4	0.3	0.3	0.3	0.3	0.3	0.3	0.2
2.75	0.6	0.6	0.5	0.4	0.4	0.4	0.4	0.4	0.3	0.3	0.3	0.3
3.00	0.6	0.6	0.5	0.5	0.5	0.4	0.4	0.4	0.4	0.3	0.3	0.3
3.25	0.7	0.7	0.6	0.5	0.5	0.5	0.4	0.4	0.4	0.4	0.4	0.3
3.50	0.7	0.7	0.6	0.6	0.5	0.5	0.5	0.5	0.4	0.4	0.4	0.4
3.75	0.8	0.7	0.6	0.6	0.6	0.5	0.5	0.5	0.5	0.4	0.4	0.4
4.00	0.8	0.8	0.7	0.6	0.6	0.6	0.5	0.5	0.5	0.5	0.4	0.4
4.25	0.9	0.8	0.7	0.7	0.6	0.6	0.6	0.6	0.5	0.5	0.5	0.4
4.50	0.9	0.9	0.8	0.7	0.7	0.6	0.6	0.6	0.6	0.5	0.5	0.5
4.75	1.0	0.9	0.8	0.8	0.7	0.7	0.6	0.6	0.6	0.5	0.5	0.5
5.00	1.0	1.0	0.9	0.8	0.8	0.7	0.7	0.7	0.6	0.6	0.6	0.5
5.25	1.1	1.0	0.9	0.9	0.8	0.8	0.7	0.7	0.7	0.6	0.6	0.6
5.50	1.1	1.1	1.0	0.9	0.9	0.8	0.8	0.7	0.7	0.6	0.6	0.6
5.75	1.2	1.1	1.0	1.0	0.9	0.9	0.8	0.8	0.7	0.7	0.7	0.6
6.00	1.2	1.2	1.1	1.0	0.9	0.9	0.9	0.8	0.8	0.7	0.7	0.7
6.25	1.2	1.2	1.1	1.0	1.0	0.9	0.9	0.8	0.8	0.7	0.7	0.7
6.50	1.3	1.2	1.1	1.1	1.0	1.0	0.9	0.9	0.8	0.8	0.8	0.7
6.75	1.3	1.3	1.2	1.1	1.0	1.0	1.0	0.9	0.9	0.8	0.8	0.8
7.00	1.4	1.3	1.2	1.1	1.1	1.0	1.0	1.0	0.9	0.9	0.8	0.8
7.25	1.4	1.4	1.3	1.2	1.1	1.1	1.0	1.0	1.0	0.9	0.9	0.8
7.50	1.5	1.4	1.3	1.2	1.2	1.1	1.1	1.0	1.0	0.9	0.9	0.9
7.75	1.5	1.4	1.4	1.3	1.2	1.2	1.1	1.1	1.0	1.0	1.0	0.9
8.00	1.6	1.5	1.4	1.3	1.3	1.2	1.2	1.1	1.1	1.0	1.0	1.0
8.25	1.6	1.5	1.4	1.4	1.3	1.3	1.2	1.2	1.1	1.1	1.1	1.0
8.50	1.6	1.6	1.5	1.4	1.4	1.3	1.3	1.2	1.2	1.1	1.1	1.0
8.75	1.7	1.6	1.5	1.5	1.4	1.3	1.3	1.2	1.2	1.1	1.1	1.1
9.00	1.7	1.6	1.5	1.5	1.4	1.4	1.3	1.3	1.2	1.2	1.2	1.1
9.25	1.7	1.7	1.6	1.5	1.5	1.4	1.4	1.3	1.3	1.2	1.2	1.1
9.50	1.8	1.7	1.6	1.6	1.5	1.5	1.4	1.4	1.3	1.3	1.2	1.2
9.75	1.8	1.8	1.7	1.6	1.6	1.5	1.5	1.4	1.4	1.3	1.3	1.2
10.00	1.9	1.8	1.7	1.7	1.6	1.6	1.5	1.4	1.4	1.4	1.3	1.3
10.25	1.9	1.9	1.8	1.7	1.7	1.6	1.5	1.5	1.4	1.4	1.4	1.3

Table A-3 (cont.)

T°C	I 25.0	27.5	30.0	32.5	35.0	37.5	40.0	42.5	45.0	47.5	50.0	52.5
10.50	2.0	1.9	1.8	1.8	1.7	1.7	1.6	1.5	1.5	1.4	1.4	1.4
10.75	2.0	2.0	1.9	1.8	1.8	1.7	1.6	1.6	1.5	1.5	1.5	1.4
11.00	2.1	2.0	1.9	1.8	1.8	1.7	1.7	1.6	1.6	1.5	1.5	1.4
11.25	2.1	2.0	1.9	1.9	1.8	1.8	1.7	1.6	1.6	1.5	1.5	1.5
11.50	2.1	2.1	2.0	1.9	1.9	1.8	1.7	1.7	1.6	1.6	1.6	1.5
11.75	2.2	2.1	2.0	1.9	1.9	1.8	1.8	1.7	1.7	1.6	1.6	1.5
12.00	2.2	2.2	2.1	2.0	1.9	1.9	1.8	1.8	1.7	1.7	1.7	1.6
12.25	2.3	2.2	2.1	2.0	2.0	1.9	1.9	1.8	1.8	1.7	1.7	1.6
12.50	2.3	2.3	2.2	2.1	2.0	2.0	1.9	1.9	1.8	1.8	1.8	1.7
12.75	2.3	2.3	2.2	2.1	2.1	2.0	2.0	1.9	1.9	1.8	1.8	1.7
13.00	2.4	2.3	2.3	2.2	2.1	2.1	2.0	2.0	1.9	1.9	1.9	1.8
13.25	2.4	2.4	2.3	2.2	2.2	2.1	2.1	2.0	2.0	1.9	1.9	1.8
13.50	2.5	2.4	2.3	2.3	2.2	2.2	2.1	2.1	2.0	2.0	2.0	1.9
13.75	2.5	2.4	2.4	2.3	2.3	2.2	2.1	2.1	2.0	2.0	2.0	1.9
14.00	2.5	2.5	2.4	2.3	2.3	2.2	2.2	2.2	2.1	2.0	2.0	1.9
14.25	2.6	2.5	2.4	2.4	2.3	2.3	2.2	2.2	2.1	2.1	2.1	2.0
14.50	2.6	2.5	2.5	2.4	2.4	2.3	2.3	2.3	2.2	2.1	2.1	2.0
14.75	2.7	2.6	2.5	2.5	2.4	2.4	2.3	2.3	2.2	2.2	2.2	2.1
15.00	2.7	2.6	2.6	2.5	2.5	2.4	2.4	2.3	2.3	2.2	2.2	2.1
15.25	2.8	2.7	2.6	2.6	2.5	2.5	2.4	2.4	2.3	2.3	2.3	2.2
15.50	2.8	2.7	2.7	2.6	2.6	2.5	2.5	2.4	2.4	2.3	2.3	2.2
15.75	2.9	2.8	2.7	2.7	2.6	2.6	2.5	2.5	2.4	2.4	2.4	2.3
16.00	2.9	2.8	2.8	2.7	2.7	2.6	2.6	2.5	2.5	2.4	2.4	2.3
16.25	2.9	2.8	2.8	2.7	2.7	2.6	2.6	2.5	2.5	2.4	2.4	2.4
16.50	3.0	2.9	2.8	2.8	2.7	2.7	2.6	2.6	2.5	2.5	2.5	2.4
16.75	3.0	2.9	2.9	2.8	2.8	2.7	2.7	2.6	2.6	2.5	2.5	2.5
17.00	3.0	3.0	2.9	2.9	2.8	2.8	2.7	2.7	2.6	2.6	2.6	2.5
17.25	3.1	3.0	2.9	2.9	2.9	2.8	2.8	2.7	2.7	2.6	2.6	2.6
17.50	3.1	3.0	3.0	3.0	2.9	2.9	2.8	2.8	2.7	2.7	2.7	2.6
17.75	3.2	3.1	3.0	3.0	3.0	2.9	2.9	2.8	2.8	2.8	2.7	2.7
18.00	3.2	3.1	3.1	3.1	3.0	3.0	2.9	2.9	2.9	2.8	2.8	2.7
18.25	3.2	3.2	3.1	3.1	3.1	3.0	3.0	2.9	2.9	2.9	2.8	2.8
18.50	3.3	3.2	3.2	3.1	3.1	3.1	3.0	3.0	3.0	2.9	2.9	2.8
18.75	3.3	3.2	3.2	3.2	3.1	3.1	3.0	3.0	3.0	2.9	2.9	2.9
19.00	3.3	3.3	3.2	3.2	3.2	3.1	3.1	3.0	3.0	3.0	3.0	2.9
19.25	3.4	3.3	3.3	3.2	3.2	3.2	3.1	3.1	3.1	3.0	3.0	3.0
19.50	3.4	3.4	3.3	3.3	3.3	3.2	3.2	3.1	3.1	3.1	3.1	3.0
19.75	3.5	3.4	3.4	3.3	3.3	3.3	3.2	3.2	3.2	3.1	3.1	3.1
20.00	3.5	3.5	3.4	3.4	3.4	3.3	3.3	3.2	3.2	3.2	3.2	3.1
20.25	3.6	3.5	3.5	3.4	3.4	3.4	3.3	3.3	3.3	3.2	3.2	3.2
20.50	3.6	3.5	3.5	3.5	3.5	3.4	3.4	3.3	3.3	3.3	3.3	3.2
20.75	3.7	3.6	3.5	3.5	3.5	3.5	3.4	3.4	3.4	3.3	3.3	3.3

Table A-3 (cont.)

T°C	I 25.0	27.5	30.0	32.5	35.0	37.5	40.0	42.5	45.0	47.5	50.0	52.5
21.00	3.7	3.6	3.6	3.6	3.5	3.5	3.5	3.4	3.4	3.4	3.4	3.3
21.25	3.7	3.6	3.6	3.6	3.6	3.5	3.5	3.4	3.4	3.4	3.4	3.4
21.50	3.8	3.7	3.6	3.6	3.6	3.6	3.5	3.5	3.5	3.5	3.5	3.4
21.75	3.8	3.7	3.7	3.7	3.6	3.6	3.6	3.5	3.5	3.5	3.5	3.5
22.00	3.8	3.8	3.7	3.7	3.7	3.7	3.6	3.6	3.6	3.6	3.6	3.5
22.25	3.9	3.8	3.8	3.8	3.7	3.7	3.7	3.7	3.6	3.6	3.6	3.6
22.50	3.9	3.8	3.8	3.8	3.8	3.8	3.7	3.7	3.7	3.7	3.7	3.6
22.75	4.0	3.9	3.9	3.8	3.8	3.8	3.8	3.8	2.7	2.7	2.7	2.7
23.00	4.0	3.9	3.9	3.9	3.9	3.9	3.8	3.8	3.8	3.8	3.8	3.8
23.25	4.1	4.0	4.0	3.9	3.9	3.9	3.9	3.9	3.8	3.8	3.8	3.8
23.50	4.1	4.0	4.0	4.0	4.0	4.0	3.9	3.9	3.9	3.9	3.9	3.9
23.75	4.1	4.0	4.0	4.0	4.0	4.0	4.0	3.9	3.9	3.9	3.9	3.9
24.00	4.2	4.1	4.1	4.0	4.0	4.0	4.0	4.0	4.0	4.0	4.0	3.9
24.25	4.2	4.1	4.1	4.1	4.1	4.1	4.1	4.0	4.0	4.0	4.0	4.0
24.50	4.2	4.1	4.1	4.1	4.1	4.1	4.1	4.1	4.1	4.1	4.1	4.1
24.75	4.3	4.2	4.2	4.2	4.2	4.2	4.2	4.1	4.1	4.1	4.1	4.1
25.00	4.3	4.2	4.2	4.2	4.2	4.2	4.2	4.2	4.2	4.2	4.2	4.2
25.25	4.3	4.3	4.3	4.3	4.3	4.3	4.3	4.2	4.2	4.2	4.2	4.2
25.50	4.4	4.3	4.3	4.3	4.3	4.3	4.3	4.3	4.3	4.3	4.3	4.3
25.75	4.4	4.4	4.4	4.4	4.4	4.4	4.4	4.4	4.4	4.4	4.4	4.4
26.00	4.5	4.4	4.4	4.4	4.4	4.4	4.4	4.4	4.4	4.4	4.4	4.4
26.25	4.5	4.5	4.5	4.5	4.5	4.5	4.5	4.5	4.5	4.5	4.5	4.5
26.50	4.5	4.5	4.5	4.5	4.5	4.5	4.5	4.5	4.5	4.5	4.5	4.5

T°C	I 55.0	57.5	60.0	62.5	65.0	67.5	70.0	72.5	75.0	77.5	80.0	82.5
0	0.0	0.0	0.0	0.0	0.0	0.0	0.0	0.0	0.0	0.0	0.0	0.0
.25	0.0	0.0	0.0	0.0	0.0	0.0	0.0	0.0	0.0	0.0	0.0	0.0
.50	0.0	0.0	0.0	0.0	0.0	0.0	0.0	0.0	0.0	0.0	0.0	0.0
.75	0.0	0.0	0.0	0.0	0.0	0.0	0.0	0.0	0.0	0.0	0.0	0.0
1.00	0.1	0.1	0.0	0.0	0.0	0.0	0.0	0.0	0.0	0.0	0.0	0.0
1.25	0.1	0.1	0.0	0.0	0.0	0.0	0.0	0.0	0.0	0.0	0.0	0.0
1.50	0.1	0.1	0.1	0.0	0.0	0.0	0.0	0.0	0.0	0.0	0.0	0.0
1.75	0.1	0.1	0.1	0.0	0.0	0.0	0.0	0.0	0.0	0.0	0.0	0.0
2.00	0.1	0.1	0.1	0.1	0.1	0.1	0.0	0.0	0.0	0.0	0.0	0.0
2.25	0.2	0.1	0.1	0.1	0.1	0.1	0.1	0.1	0.1	0.1	0.1	0.0
2.50	0.2	0.2	0.2	0.1	0.1	0.1	0.1	0.1	0.1	0.1	0.1	0.1
2.75	0.2	0.2	0.2	0.1	0.1	0.1	0.1	0.1	0.1	0.1	0.1	0.1
3.00	0.3	0.2	0.2	0.2	0.1	0.1	0.1	0.1	0.1	0.1	0.1	0.1
3.25	0.3	0.3	0.2	0.2	0.2	0.1	0.1	0.1	0.1	0.1	0.1	0.1
3.50	0.3	0.3	0.3	0.2	0.2	0.2	0.1	0.1	0.1	0.1	0.1	0.1
3.75	0.3	0.3	0.3	0.2	0.2	0.2	0.2	0.1	0.1	0.1	0.1	0.1
4.00	0.4	0.3	0.3	0.3	0.2	0.2	0.2	0.2	0.2	0.2	0.1	0.1
4.25	0.4	0.4	0.3	0.3	0.3	0.2	0.2	0.2	0.2	0.2	0.2	0.1

Table A-3 (cont.)

T°C	I 55.0	57.5	60.0	62.5	65.0	67.5	70.0	72.5	75.0	77.5	80.0	82.5
4.50	0.4	0.4	0.4	0.3	0.3	0.3	0.2	0.2	0.2	0.2	0.2	0.2
4.75	0.4	0.4	0.4	0.3	0.3	0.3	0.3	0.2	0.2	0.2	0.2	0.2
5.00	0.5	0.4	0.4	0.4	0.3	0.3	0.3	0.3	0.3	0.3	0.2	0.2
5.25	0.5	0.5	0.4	0.4	0.4	0.3	0.3	0.3	0.3	0.3	0.2	0.2
5.50	0.5	0.5	0.5	0.4	0.4	0.4	0.3	0.3	0.3	0.3	0.3	0.3
5.75	0.6	0.5	0.5	0.5	0.4	0.4	0.4	0.3	0.3	0.3	0.3	0.3
6.00	0.6	0.6	0.5	0.5	0.5	0.4	0.4	0.4	0.4	0.3	0.3	0.3
6.25	0.6	0.6	0.6	0.5	0.5	0.4	0.4	0.4	0.4	0.4	0.3	0.3
6.50	0.7	0.6	0.6	0.6	0.5	0.5	0.4	0.4	0.4	0.4	0.4	0.4
6.75	0.7	0.7	0.6	0.6	0.6	0.5	0.5	0.4	0.4	0.4	0.4	0.4
7.00	0.7	0.7	0.7	0.6	0.6	0.5	0.5	0.5	0.5	0.4	0.4	0.4
7.25	0.8	0.7	0.7	0.7	0.6	0.6	0.5	0.5	0.5	0.5	0.5	0.4
7.50	0.8	0.8	0.7	0.7	0.7	0.6	0.6	0.5	0.5	0.5	0.5	0.4
7.75	0.9	0.8	0.8	0.7	0.7	0.6	0.6	0.6	0.6	0.5	0.5	0.5
8.00	0.9	0.9	0.8	0.8	0.7	0.7	0.6	0.6	0.6	0.6	0.5	0.5
8.25	0.9	0.9	0.8	0.8	0.8	0.7	0.7	0.6	0.6	0.6	0.6	0.5
8.50	1.0	0.9	0.9	0.8	0.8	0.8	0.7	0.7	0.7	0.6	0.6	0.6
8.75	1.0	1.0	0.9	0.9	0.8	0.8	0.7	0.7	0.7	0.7	0.6	0.6
9.00	1.0	1.0	0.9	0.9	0.9	0.8	0.8	0.7	0.7	0.7	0.7	0.6
9.25	1.1	1.0	1.0	0.9	0.9	0.9	0.8	0.8	0.8	0.7	0.7	0.7
9.50	1.1	1.1	1.0	1.0	0.9	0.9	0.9	0.8	0.8	0.8	0.7	0.7
9.75	1.2	1.1	1.1	1.0	1.0	0.9	0.9	0.8	0.8	0.8	0.8	0.7
10.00	1.2	1.2	1.1	1.1	1.0	1.0	0.9	0.9	0.9	0.8	0.8	0.8
10.25	1.3	1.2	1.2	1.1	1.1	1.0	1.0	0.9	0.9	0.9	0.8	0.8
10.50	1.3	1.2	1.2	1.2	1.1	1.1	1.0	1.0	1.0	0.9	0.9	0.8
10.75	1.3	1.3	1.2	1.2	1.2	1.1	1.1	1.0	1.0	0.9	0.9	0.9
11.00	1.4	1.3	1.3	1.3	1.2	1.1	1.1	1.0	1.0	1.0	1.0	0.9
11.25	1.4	1.3	1.3	1.3	1.2	1.2	1.1	1.1	1.1	1.0	1.0	0.9
11.50	1.4	1.4	1.3	1.3	1.3	1.2	1.2	1.1	1.1	1.0	1.0	1.0
11.75	1.5	1.4	1.4	1.4	1.3	1.3	1.2	1.1	1.1	1.1	1.1	1.0
12.00	1.5	1.5	1.4	1.4	1.4	1.3	1.3	1.2	1.2	1.1	1.1	1.0
12.25	1.6	1.5	1.5	1.5	1.4	1.4	1.3	1.2	1.2	1.2	1.2	1.1
12.50	1.6	1.6	1.5	1.5	1.5	1.4	1.4	1.3	1.3	1.2	1.2	1.2
12.75	1.7	1.6	1.6	1.5	1.5	1.5	1.4	1.4	1.3	1.3	1.2	1.2
13.00	1.7	1.7	1.6	1.6	1.5	1.5	1.5	1.5	1.3	1.3	1.3	1.2
13.25	1.8	1.7	1.7	1.6	1.6	1.6	1.5	1.5	1.4	1.4	1.3	1.3
13.50	1.8	1.8	1.7	1.7	1.6	1.6	1.6	1.5	1.4	1.4	1.4	1.3
13.75	1.9	1.8	1.8	1.7	1.7	1.7	1.6	1.6	1.5	1.5	1.4	1.4
14.00	1.9	1.8	1.8	1.7	1.7	1.7	1.6	1.6	1.5	1.5	1.5	1.4
14.25	2.0	1.9	1.9	1.8	1.7	1.7	1.7	1.7	1.6	1.5	1.5	1.5
14.50	2.0	1.9	1.9	1.8	1.8	1.8	1.7	1.7	1.6	1.6	1.6	1.5
14.75	2.1	2.0	2.0	1.9	1.8	1.8	1.8	1.7	1.7	1.6	1.6	1.6

Table A-3 (cont.)

T°C	I 55.0	57.5	60.0	62.5	65.0	67.5	70.0	72.5	75.0	77.5	80.0	82.5
15.00	2.1	2.0	2.0	1.9	1.9	1.9	1.8	1.8	1.7	1.7	1.7	1.6
15.25	2.2	2.1	2.1	2.0	1.9	1.9	1.9	1.8	1.8	1.7	1.7	1.7
15.50	2.2	2.1	2.1	2.0	2.0	1.9	1.9	1.9	1.8	1.8	1.8	1.7
15.75	2.3	2.2	2.2	2.1	2.0	2.0	2.0	1.9	1.9	1.8	1.8	1.8
16.00	2.3	2.2	2.2	2.1	2.1	2.0	2.0	2.0	2.0	1.9	1.9	1.8
16.25	2.3	2.2	2.2	2.1	2.1	2.0	2.0	2.0	2.0	1.9	1.9	1.9
16.50	2.4	2.3	2.3	2.2	2.1	2.1	2.1	2.0	2.0	1.9	1.9	1.9
16.75	2.4	2.3	2.3	2.2	2.2	2.1	2.1	2.1	2.1	2.0	2.0	2.0
17.00	2.5	2.4	2.4	2.3	2.3	2.2	2.2	2.1	2.1	2.0	2.0	2.0
17.25	2.5	2.5	2.4	2.4	2.3	2.3	2.2	2.2	2.2	2.1	2.1	2.1
17.50	2.6	2.5	2.5	2.4	2.4	2.3	2.3	2.3	2.2	2.2	2.2	2.1
17.75	2.6	2.6	2.5	2.5	2.4	2.4	2.4	2.3	2.3	2.3	2.2	2.2
18.00	2.7	2.6	2.6	2.5	2.5	2.4	2.4	2.4	2.3	2.3	2.3	2.3
18.25	2.7	2.7	2.6	2.6	2.5	2.5	2.5	2.4	2.4	2.4	2.4	2.4
18.50	2.8	2.7	2.7	2.6	2.6	2.5	2.5	2.5	2.4	2.4	2.4	2.4
18.75	2.8	2.8	2.7	2.7	2.6	2.6	2.6	2.5	2.5	2.5	2.5	2.5
19.00	2.9	2.8	2.8	2.7	2.7	2.6	2.6	2.6	2.5	2.5	2.5	2.5
19.25	2.9	2.9	2.8	2.8	2.7	2.7	2.7	2.6	2.6	2.6	2.6	2.6
19.50	3.0	2.9	2.9	2.8	2.8	2.7	2.7	2.7	2.7	2.6	2.6	2.6
19.75	3.0	3.0	2.9	2.9	2.9	2.8	2.8	2.7	2.7	2.7	2.7	2.7
20.00	3.1	3.0	3.0	3.0	2.9	2.9	2.8	2.8	2.8	2.8	2.8	2.8
20.25	3.2	3.1	3.1	3.0	3.0	3.0	2.9	2.9	2.9	2.8	2.8	2.8
20.50	3.2	3.2	3.2	3.1	3.1	3.0	3.0	3.0	2.9	2.9	2.9	2.9
20.75	3.3	3.2	3.2	3.1	3.1	3.1	3.0	3.0	3.0	3.0	3.0	3.0
21.00	3.3	3.3	3.3	3.2	3.2	3.1	3.1	3.1	3.0	3.0	3.0	3.0
21.25	3.4	3.3	3.3	3.2	3.2	3.2	3.1	3.1	3.1	3.1	3.1	3.1
21.50	3.4	3.4	3.4	3.3	3.3	3.2	3.2	3.2	3.2	3.1	3.1	3.1
21.75	3.5	3.4	3.4	3.3	3.3	3.3	3.2	3.2	3.2	3.2	3.2	3.2
22.00	3.5	3.5	3.4	3.4	3.4	3.3	3.3	3.3	3.3	3.3	3.3	3.3
22.25	3.6	3.5	3.5	3.4	3.4	3.4	3.3	3.3	3.3	3.3	3.3	3.3
22.50	3.6	3.6	3.6	3.5	3.5	35.	3.4	3.4	3.4	3.4	3.4	3.4
22.75	3.7	3.7	3.6	3.6	3.6	3.6	3.5	3.5	3.5	3.5	3.5	3.5
23.00	3.7	3.7	3.7	3.6	3.6	3.6	3.6	3.6	3.6	3.6	3.6	3.6
23.25	3.8	3.8	3.8	3.7	3.7	3.7	3.7	3.7	3.7	3.7	3.7	3.7
23.50	3.8	3.8	3.8	3.8	3.8	3.8	3.8	3.7	3.7	3.7	3.7	3.7
23.75	3.9	3.9	3.9	3.8	3.8	3.8	3.8	3.8	3.8	3.8	3.8	3.8
24.00	3.9	3.9	3.9	3.9	3.9	3.9	3.9	3.8	3.8	3.8	3.8	3.8
24.25	4.0	4.0	4.0	3.9	3.9	3.9	3.9	3.9	3.9	3.9	3.9	3.9
24.50	4.0	4.0	4.0	4.0	4.0	4.0	4.0	3.9	3.9	3.9	3.9	3.9
24.75	4.1	4.1	4.0	4.0	4.0	4.0	4.0	4.0	4.0	4.0	4.0	4.0
25.00	4.2	4.1	4.1	4.1	4.1	4.1	4.1	4.1	4.1	4.0	4.0	4.0
25.25	4.2	4.2	4.2	4.2	4.2	4.2	4.1	4.1	4.1	4.1	4.1	4.1

Table A-3 (cont.)

	I											
	55.0	57.5	60.0	62.5	65.0	67.5	70.0	72.5	75.0	77.5	80.0	82.5
T°C												
25.50	4.3	4.3	4.3	4.3	4.3	4.2	4.2	4.2	4.2	4.2	4.2	4.2
25.75	4.3	4.3	4.3	4.3	4.3	4.3	4.3	4.3	4.3	4.3	4.2	4.2
26.00	4.4	4.4	4.4	4.4	4.4	4.4	4.4	4.4	4.4	4.4	4.3	4.3
26.25	4.5	4.5	4.5	4.5	4.5	4.5	4.5	4.5	4.5	4.5	4.4	4.4
26.50	4.5	4.5	4.5	4.5	4.5	4.5	4.5	4.5	4.5	4.5	4.5	4.5

	I											
	85.0	87.5	90.0	92.5	95.0	97.5	100.0	102.5	105.0	107.5	110.0	112.5
T°C												
0	0.0	0.0	0.0	0.0	0.0	0.0	0.0	0.0	0.0	0.0	0.0	0.0
.25	0.0	0.0	0.0	0.0	0.0	0.0	0.0	0.0	0.0	0.0	0.0	0.0
.50	0.0	0.0	0.0	0.0	0.0	0.0	0.0	0.0	0.0	0.0	0.0	0.0
.75	0.0	0.0	0.0	0.0	0.0	0.0	0.0	0.0	0.0	0.0	0.0	0.0
1.00	0.0	0.0	0.0	0.0	0.0	0.0	0.0	0.0	0.0	0.0	0.0	0.0
1.25	0.0	0.0	0.0	0.0	0.0	0.0	0.0	0.0	0.0	0.0	0.0	0.0
1.50	0.0	0.0	0.0	0.0	0.0	0.0	0.0	0.0	0.0	0.0	0.0	0.0
1.75	0.0	0.0	0.0	0.0	0.0	0.0	0.0	0.0	0.0	0.0	0.0	0.0
2.00	0.0	0.0	0.0	0.0	0.0	0.0	0.0	0.0	0.0	0.0	0.0	0.0
2.25	0.0	0.0	0.0	0.0	0.0	0.0	0.0	0.0	0.0	0.0	0.0	0.0
2.50	0.1	0.1	0.0	0.0	0.0	0.0	0.0	0.0	0.0	0.0	0.0	0.0
2.75	0.1	0.1	0.1	0.0	0.0	0.0	0.0	0.0	0.0	0.0	0.0	0.0
3.00	0.1	0.1	0.1	0.1	0.0	0.0	0.0	0.0	0.0	0.0	0.0	0.0
3.25	0.1	0.1	0.1	0.1	0.1	0.1	0.0	0.0	0.0	0.0	0.0	0.0
3.50	0.1	0.1	0.1	0.1	0.1	0.1	0.1	0.0	0.0	0.0	0.0	0.0
3.75	0.1	0.1	0.1	0.1	0.1	0.1	0.1	0.0	0.0	0.0	0.0	0.0
4.00	0.1	0.1	0.1	0.1	0.1	0.1	0.1	0.0	0.0	0.0	0.0	0.0
4.25	0.1	0.1	0.1	0.1	0.1	0.1	0.1	0.0	0.0	0.0	0.0	0.0
4.50	0.2	0.1	0.1	0.1	0.1	0.1	0.1	0.1	0.1	0.1	0.1	0.1
4.75	0.2	0.2	0.1	0.1	0.1	0.1	0.1	0.1	0.1	0.1	0.1	0.1
5.00	0.2	0.2	0.2	0.1	0.1	0.1	0.1	0.1	0.1	0.1	0.1	0.1
5.25	0.2	0.2	0.2	0.2	0.2	0.1	0.1	0.1	0.1	0.1	0.1	0.1
5.50	0.2	0.2	0.2	0.2	0.2	0.2	0.1	0.1	0.1	0.1	0.1	0.1
5.75	0.3	0.2	0.2	0.2	0.2	0.2	0.2	0.1	0.1	0.1	0.1	0.1
6.00	0.3	0.3	0.2	0.2	0.2	0.2	0.2	0.1	0.1	0.1	0.1	0.1
6.25	0.3	0.3	0.2	0.2	0.2	0.2	0.2	0.1	0.1	0.1	0.1	0.1
6.50	0.3	0.3	0.3	0.3	0.2	0.2	0.2	0.1	0.1	0.1	0.1	0.1
6.75	0.3	0.3	0.3	0.3	0.3	0.3	0.2	0.2	0.2	0.2	0.2	0.1
7.00	0.4	0.3	0.3	0.3	0.3	0.3	0.2	0.2	0.2	0.2	0.2	0.2
7.25	0.4	0.4	0.3	0.3	0.3	0.3	0.3	0.2	0.2	0.2	0.2	0.2
7.50	0.4	0.4	0.4	0.4	0.3	0.3	0.3	0.3	0.2	0.2	0.2	0.2
7.75	0.5	0.4	0.4	0.4	0.3	0.3	0.3	0.3	0.3	0.2	0.2	0.2
8.00	0.5	0.5	0.4	0.4	0.4	0.3	0.3	0.3	0.3	0.3	0.3	0.2
8.25	0.5	0.5	0.5	0.4	0.4	0.4	0.4	0.3	0.3	0.3	0.3	0.3
8.50	0.6	0.5	0.5	0.5	0.4	0.4	0.4	0.3	0.3	0.3	0.3	0.3
8.75	0.6	0.5	0.5	0.5	0.4	0.4	0.4	0.4	0.4	0.3	0.3	0.3

Table A-3 (cont.)

T°C	*I* 85.0	87.5	90.0	92.5	95.0	97.5	100.0	102.5	105.0	107.5	110.0	112.5
9.00	0.6	0.6	0.5	0.5	0.5	0.4	0.4	0.4	0.4	0.4	0.3	0.3
9.25	0.6	0.6	0.6	0.5	0.5	0.5	0.5	0.4	0.4	0.4	0.4	0.3
9.50	0.7	0.6	0.6	0.6	0.5	0.5	0.5	0.4	0.4	0.4	0.4	0.4
9.75	0.7	0.7	0.6	0.6	0.6	0.5	0.5	0.5	0.5	0.4	0.4	0.4
10.00	0.7	0.7	0.7	0.6	0.6	0.6	0.5	0.5	0.5	0.4	0.4	0.4
10.25	0.8	0.7	0.7	0.7	0.6	0.6	0.6	0.5	0.5	0.5	0.5	0.4
10.50	0.8	0.8	0.7	0.7	0.7	0.7	0.6	0.6	0.5	0.5	0.5	0.5
10.75	0.8	0.8	0.8	0.8	0.7	0.7	0.6	0.6	0.6	0.5	0.5	0.5
11.00	0.9	0.8	0.8	0.8	0.7	0.7	0.7	0.6	0.6	0.6	0.6	0.5
11.25	0.9	0.9	0.8	0.8	0.8	0.7	0.7	0.6	0.6	0.6	0.6	0.5
11.50	0.9	0.9	0.9	0.9	0.8	0.8	0.7	0.7	0.7	0.6	0.6	0.6
11.75	1.0	0.9	0.9	0.9	0.8	0.8	0.8	0.7	0.7	0.7	0.6	0.6
12.00	1.0	1.0	0.9	0.9	0.9	0.8	0.8	0.7	0.7	0.7	0.7	0.6
12.25	1.1	1.0	1.0	1.0	0.9	0.9	0.8	0.8	0.8	0.8	0.7	0.7
12.50	1.1	1.1	1.0	1.0	0.9	0.9	0.9	0.8	0.8	0.8	0.7	0.7
12.75	1.2	1.1	1.1	1.1	1.0	1.0	0.9	0.9	0.8	0.8	0.8	0.7
13.00	1.2	1.2	1.1	1.1	1.0	1.0	1.0	0.9	0.9	0.9	0.8	0.8
13.25	1.2	1.2	1.2	1.1	1.1	1.0	1.0	1.0	0.9	0.9	0.9	0.8
13.50	1.3	1.2	1.2	1.2	1.1	1.1	1.0	1.0	1.0	0.9	0.9	0.9
13.75	1.3	1.3	1.2	1.2	1.1	1.1	1.1	1.1	1.0	1.0	0.9	0.9
14.00	1.4	1.3	1.3	1.2	1.2	1.1	1.1	1.1	1.0	1.0	1.0	0.9
14.25	1.4	1.3	1.3	1.3	1.2	1.2	1.2	1.1	1.1	1.0	1.0	1.0
14.50	1.5	1.4	1.4	1.3	1.3	1.2	1.2	1.2	1.1	1.1	1.0	1.0
14.75	1.5	1.4	1.4	1.3	1.3	1.3	1.3	1.2	1.1	1.1	1.1	1.1
15.00	1.6	1.5	1.5	1.4	1.4	1.3	1.3	1.3	1.2	1.1	1.1	1.1
15.25	1.6	1.6	1.5	1.5	1.5	1.4	1.4	1.3	1.2	1.2	1.2	1.2
15.50	1.7	1.6	1.6	1.6	1.5	1.5	1.4	1.4	1.3	1.3	1.3	1.2
15.75	1.7	1.7	1.7	1.6	1.6	1.5	1.5	1.4	1.3	1.3	1.3	1.3
16.00	1.8	1.7	1.7	1.7	1.6	1.6	1.5	1.5	1.4	1.4	1.4	1.3
16.25	1.8	1.8	1.8	1.7	1.7	1.6	1.6	1.5	1.4	1.4	1.4	1.4
16.50	1.9	1.8	1.8	1.7	1.7	1.7	1.6	1.6	1.5	1.5	1.5	1.4
16.75	1.9	1.9	1.9	1.8	1.8	1.7	1.7	1.6	1.6	1.5	1.5	1.5
17.00	2.0	1.9	1.9	1.8	1.8	1.8	1.7	1.7	1.7	1.6	1.6	1.5
17.25	2.1	2.0	2.0	1.9	1.9	1.8	1.8	1.7	1.7	1.6	1.6	1.6
17.50	2.1	2.0	2.0	2.0	1.9	1.9	1.8	1.8	1.7	1.7	1.7	1.6
17.75	2.2	2.1	2.1	2.0	2.0	1.9	1.9	1.8	1.8	1.8	1.8	1.7
18.00	2.3	2.2	2.1	2.1	2.1	2.0	2.0	1.9	1.9	1.8	1.8	1.8
18.25	2.3	2.2	2.2	2.2	2.2	2.1	2.1	2.0	1.9	1.9	1.9	1.8
18.50	2.4	2.3	2.2	2.2	2.2	2.2	2.2	2.0	2.0	1.9	1.9	1.9
18.75	2.4	2.3	2.3	2.3	2.3	2.2	2.2	2.1	2.0	2.0	2.0	2.0
19.00	2.5	2.4	2.4	2.3	2.3	2.3	2.3	2.1	2.1	2.0	2.0	2.0
19.25	2.5	2.4	2.4	2.4	2.4	2.3	2.3	2.2	2.1	2.1	2.1	2.1

Table A-3 (cont.)

T°C	I 85.0	87.5	90.0	92.5	95.0	97.5	100.0	102.5	105.0	107.5	110.0	112.5
19.50	2.6	2.5	2.5	2.4	2.4	2.4	2.4	2.2	2.2	2.2	2.2	2.1
19.75	2.6	2.5	2.5	2.5	2.5	2.4	2.4	2.3	2.2	2.2	2.2	2.2
20.00	2.7	2.6	2.6	2.6	2.5	2.5	2.5	2.4	2.3	2.3	2.3	2.3
20.25	2.8	2.7	2.7	2.6	2.6	2.6	2.6	2.5	2.4	2.4	2.4	2.4
20.50	2.8	2.8	2.8	2.7	2.7	2.7	2.6	2.5	2.5	2.5	2.5	2.5
20.75	2.9	2.8	2.8	2.8	2.8	2.7	2.7	2.6	2.6	2.6	2.6	2.6
21.00	3.0	2.9	2.9	2.9	2.8	2.8	2.8	2.7	2.7	2.7	2.7	2.6
21.25	3.0	2.9	2.9	2.9	2.9	2.9	2.8	2.8	2.7	2.7	2.7	2.7
21.50	3.1	3.0	3.0	2.9	2.9	2.9	2.9	2.8	2.8	2.8	2.8	2.7
21.75	3.2	3.1	3.1	3.0	3.0	3.0	3.0	2.9	2.9	2.9	2.9	2.8
22.00	3.2	3.1	3.1	3.1	3.1	3.1	3.1	3.0	3.0	3.0	3.0	2.9
22.25	3.3	3.2	3.2	3.2	3.2	3.2	3.2	3.1	3.0	3.0	3.0	3.0
22.50	3.4	3.3	3.3	3.2	3.2	3.2	3.2	3.1	3.1	3.1	3.1	3.1
22.75	3.5	3.4	3.4	3.3	3.3	3.3	3.3	3.2	3.2	3.2	3.2	3.2
23.00	3.6	3.5	3.5	3.4	3.4	3.4	3.4	3.3	3.3	3.3	3.3	3.3
23.25	3.6	3.5	3.5	3.5	3.5	3.5	3.5	3.4	3.3	3.3	3.3	3.3
23.50	3.7	3.6	3.6	3.6	3.6	3.6	3.5	3.5	3.4	3.4	3.4	3.4
23.75	3.7	3.7	3.7	3.6	3.6	3.6	3.6	3.6	3.5	3.5	3.5	3.4
24.00	3.8	3.7	3.7	3.7	3.7	3.7	3.6	3.6	3.5	3.5	3.5	3.5
24.25	3.9	3.8	3.8	3.8	3.8	3.8	3.7	3.7	3.6	3.6	3.6	3.6
24.50	3.9	3.8	3.8	3.8	3.8	3.8	3.8	3.8	3.7	3.7	3.7	3.7
24.75	4.0	3.9	3.9	3.9	3.9	3.9	3.9	3.9	3.8	3.8	3.8	3.8
25.00	4.0	4.0	4.0	4.0	4.0	4.0	4.0	4.0	3.9	3.9	3.9	3.9
25.25	4.1	4.1	4.1	4.1	4.1	4.1	4.1	4.1	4.0	4.0	4.0	4.0
25.50	4.2	4.2	4.2	4.2	4.2	4.2	4.2	4.2	4.1	4.1	4.1	4.1
25.75	4.3	4.3	4.3	4.3	4.3	4.3	4.3	4.3	4.2	4.2	4.2	4.2
26.00	4.4	4.4	4.4	4.4	4.4	4.4	4.4	4.4	4.3	4.3	4.3	4.3
26.25	4.5	4.5	4.5	4.5	4.5	4.5	4.5	4.5	4.4	4.4	4.4	4.4
26.50	4.5	4.5	4.5	4.5	4.5	4.5	4.5	4.5	4.5	4.5	4.5	4.5

T°C	I 115.0	117.5	120.0	122.5	125.0	127.5	130.0	132.5	135.0	137.5	140.0
0	0.0	0.0	0.0	0.0	0.0	0.0	0.0	0.0	0.0	0.0	0.0
.25	0.0	0.0	0.0	0.0	0.0	0.0	0.0	0.0	0.0	0.0	0.0
.50	0.0	0.0	0.0	0.0	0.0	0.0	0.0	0.0	0.0	0.0	0.0
.75	0.0	0.0	0.0	0.0	0.0	0.0	0.0	0.0	0.0	0.0	0.0
1.00	0.0	0.0	0.0	0.0	0.0	0.0	0.0	0.0	0.0	0.0	0.0
1.25	0.0	0.0	0.0	0.0	0.0	0.0	0.0	0.0	0.0	0.0	0.0
1.50	0.0	0.0	0.0	0.0	0.0	0.0	0.0	0.0	0.0	0.0	0.0
1.75	0.0	0.0	0.0	0.0	0.0	0.0	0.0	0.0	0.0	0.0	0.0
2.00	0.0	0.0	0.0	0.0	0.0	0.0	0.0	0.0	0.0	0.0	0.0
2.25	0.0	0.0	0.0	0.0	0.0	0.0	0.0	0.0	0.0	0.0	0.0
2.50	0.0	0.0	0.0	0.0	0.0	0.0	0.0	0.0	0.0	0.0	0.0
2.75	0.0	0.0	0.0	0.0	0.0	0.0	0.0	0.0	0.0	0.0	0.0

Table A-3 (cont.)

T°C	*I* 115.0	117.5	120.0	122.5	125.0	127.5	130.0	132.5	135.0	137.5	140.0
3.00	0.0	0.0	0.0	0.0	0.0	0.0	0.0	0.0	0.0	0.0	0.0
3.25	0.0	0.0	0.0	0.0	0.0	0.0	0.0	0.0	0.0	0.0	0.0
3.50	0.0	0.0	0.0	0.0	0.0	0.0	0.0	0.0	0.0	0.0	0.0
3.75	0.0	0.0	0.0	0.0	0.0	0.0	0.0	0.0	0.0	0.0	0.0
4.00	0.0	0.0	0.0	0.0	0.0	0.0	0.0	0.0	0.0	0.0	0.0
4.25	0.0	0.0	0.0	0.0	0.0	0.0	0.0	0.0	0.0	0.0	0.0
4.50	0.0	0.0	0.0	0.0	0.0	0.0	0.0	0.0	0.0	0.0	0.0
4.75	0.1	0.0	0.0	0.0	0.0	0.0	0.0	0.0	0.0	0.0	0.0
5.00	0.1	0.1	0.0	0.0	0.0	0.0	0.0	0.0	0.0	0.0	0.0
5.25	0.1	0.1	0.0	0.0	0.0	0.0	0.0	0.0	0.0	0.0	0.0
5.50	0.1	0.1	0.1	0.1	0.1	0.0	0.0	0.0	0.0	0.0	0.0
5.75	0.1	0.1	0.1	0.1	0.1	0.1	0.0	0.0	0.0	0.0	0.0
6.00	0.1	0.1	0.1	0.1	0.1	0.1	0.1	0.0	0.0	0.0	0.0
6.25	0.1	0.1	0.1	0.1	0.1	0.1	0.1	0.1	0.0	0.0	0.0
6.50	0.1	0.1	0.1	0.1	0.1	0.1	0.1	0.1	0.0	0.0	0.0
6.75	0.1	0.1	0.1	0.1	0.1	0.1	0.1	0.1	0.1	0.1	0.0
7.00	0.1	0.1	0.1	0.1	0.1	0.1	0.1	0.1	0.1	0.1	0.0
7.25	0.2	0.1	0.1	0.1	0.1	0.1	0.1	0.1	0.1	0.1	0.1
7.50	0.2	0.1	0.1	0.1	0.1	0.1	0.1	0.1	0.1	0.1	0.1
7.75	0.2	0.2	0.2	0.1	0.1	0.1	0.1	0.1	0.1	0.1	0.1
8.00	0.2	0.2	0.2	0.2	0.1	0.1	0.1	0.1	0.1	0.1	0.1
8.25	0.2	0.2	0.2	0.2	0.2	0.2	0.1	0.1	0.1	0.1	0.1
8.50	0.3	0.2	0.2	0.2	0.2	0.2	0.2	0.1	0.1	0.1	0.1
8.75	0.3	0.2	0.2	0.2	0.2	0.2	0.2	0.2	0.1	0.1	0.1
9.00	0.3	0.3	0.2	0.2	0.2	0.2	0.2	0.2	0.1	0.1	0.1
9.25	0.3	0.3	0.3	0.2	0.2	0.2	0.2	0.2	0.1	0.1	0.1
9.50	0.3	0.3	0.3	0.2	0.2	0.2	0.2	0.2	0.2	0.2	0.1
9.75	0.4	0.3	0.3	0.3	0.3	0.2	0.2	0.2	0.2	0.2	0.2
10.00	0.4	0.3	0.3	0.3	0.3	0.3	0.2	0.2	0.2	0.2	0.2
10.25	0.4	0.4	0.3	0.3	0.3	0.3	0.3	0.2	0.2	0.2	0.2
10.50	0.4	0.4	0.4	0.3	0.3	0.3	0.3	0.3	0.2	0.2	0.2
10.75	0.5	0.4	0.4	0.4	0.4	0.3	0.3	0.3	0.2	0.2	0.2
11.00	0.5	0.5	0.4	0.4	0.4	0.4	0.3	0.3	0.3	0.2	0.2
11.25	0.5	0.5	0.4	0.4	0.4	0.4	0.4	0.3	0.3	0.3	0.3
11.50	0.5	0.5	0.5	0.4	0.4	0.4	0.4	0.3	0.3	0.3	0.3
11.75	0.6	0.5	0.5	0.4	0.4	0.4	0.4	0.4	0.3	0.3	0.3
12.00	0.6	0.5	0.5	0.5	0.5	0.4	0.4	0.4	0.3	0.3	0.3
12.25	0.6	0.6	0.6	0.5	0.5	0.5	0.5	0.4	0.4	0.3	0.3
12.50	0.7	0.6	0.6	0.5	0.5	0.5	0.5	0.5	0.4	0.4	0.4
12.75	0.7	0.6	0.6	0.6	0.6	0.6	0.5	0.5	0.4	0.4	0.4
13.00	0.7	0.7	0.7	0.6	0.6	0.6	0.6	0.5	0.5	0.4	0.4
13.25	0.7	0.7	0.7	0.6	0.6	0.6	0.6	0.6	0.5	0.5	0.5

Table A-3 (cont.)

T°C	115.0	117.5	120.0	122.5	125.0	127.5	130.0	132.5	135.0	137.5	140.0
13.50	0.8	0.8	0.7	0.7	0.7	0.6	0.6	0.6	0.5	0.5	0.5
13.75	0.8	0.8	0.8	0.7	0.7	0.7	0.6	0.6	0.6	0.5	0.5
14.00	0.8	0.8	0.8	0.7	0.7	0.7	0.7	0.6	0.6	0.5	0.5
14.25	0.9	0.9	0.8	0.8	0.8	0.7	0.7	0.7	0.6	0.5	0.5
14.50	0.9	0.9	0.9	0.8	0.8	0.8	0.7	0.7	0.6	0.6	0.6
14.75	1.0	1.0	0.9	0.9	0.8	0.8	0.8	0.7	0.7	0.6	0.6
15.00	1.0	1.0	1.0	0.9	0.9	0.9	0.8	0.8	0.7	0.7	0.7
15.25	1.1	1.1	1.0	1.0	0.9	0.9	0.9	0.8	0.8	0.7	0.7
15.50	1.2	1.1	1.1	1.0	1.0	1.0	0.9	0.9	0.8	0.8	0.8
15.75	1.2	1.1	1.1	1.1	1.1	1.0	1.0	0.9	0.9	0.8	0.8
16.00	1.3	1.2	1.2	1.1	1.1	1.1	1.0	1.0	0.9	0.9	0.9
16.25	1.3	1.2	1.2	1.2	1.1	1.1	1.1	1.0	1.0	0.9	0.9
16.50	1.4	1.3	1.2	1.2	1.2	1.1	1.1	1.1	1.0	0.9	0.9
16.75	1.4	1.3	1.3	1.2	1.2	1.2	1.2	1.1	1.0	1.0	1.0
17.00	1.5	1.4	1.3	1.3	1.3	1.3	1.2	1.2	1.1	1.0	1.0
17.25	1.6	1.5	1.4	1.3	1.3	1.3	1.3	1.2	1.2	1.1	1.1
17.50	1.6	1.5	1.5	1.4	1.4	1.4	1.3	1.3	1.2	1.2	12.
17.75	1.7	1.6	1.5	1.5	1.5	1.4	1.4	1.4	1.3	1.2	1.2
18.00	1.8	1.7	1.6	1.5	1.5	1.5	1.5	1.5	1.4	1.3	1.3
18.25	1.8	1.7	1.6	1.6	1.6	1.6	1.5	1.5	1.4	1.4	1.4
18.50	1.9	1.8	1.7	1.6	1.6	1.6	1.6	1.6	1.5	1.4	1.4
18.75	1.9	1.8	1.8	1.7	1.7	1.7	1.6	1.6	1.5	1.5	1.5
19.00	1.9	1.8	1.8	1.7	1.7	1.7	1.7	1.7	1.6	1.5	1.5
19.25	2.0	1.9	1.9	1.8	1.8	1.8	1.7	1.7	1.7	1.6	1.6
19.50	2.1	2.0	1.9	1.9	1.9	1.9	1.8	1.8	1.7	1.7	1.6
19.75	2.2	2.0	2.0	1.9	1.9	1.9	1.9	1.9	1.8	1.8	1.7
20.00	2.2	2.1	2.1	2.0	2.0	2.0	2.0	2.0	1.9	1.9	1.8
20.25	2.3	2.2	2.2	2.1	2.1	2.1	2.1	2.1	2.0	2.0	1.9
20.50	2.4	2.3	2.3	2.2	2.2	2.2	2.2	2.2	2.1	2.1	2.0
20.75	2.5	2.4	2.3	2.3	2.3	2.3	2.3	2.2	2.2	2.1	2.1
21.00	2.6	2.5	2.4	2.4	2.3	2.3	2.3	2.3	2.2	2.2	2.2
21.25	2.7	2.6	2.5	2.4	2.4	2.4	2.4	2.3	2.3	2.3	2.3
21.50	2.7	2.6	2.5	2.5	2.4	2.4	2.4	2.4	2.3	2.3	2.3
21.75	2.8	2.7	2.6	2.5	2.5	2.5	2.5	2.5	2.4	2.4	2.4
22.00	2.9	2.8	2.7	2.6	2.6	2.6	2.6	2.6	2.6	2.5	2.5
22.25	3.0	2.9	2.8	2.7	2.7	2.7	2.7	2.7	2.7	2.6	2.6
22.50	3.1	3.0	2.9	2.8	2.8	2.8	2.8	2.8	2.8	2.7	2.7
22.75	3.2	3.1	3.0	2.9	2.9	2.9	2.9	2.9	2.9	2.8	2.8
23.00	3.3	3.2	3.1	3.0	3.0	3.0	3.0	3.0	3.0	2.9	2.9
23.25	3.3	3.3	3.2	3.1	3.1	3.1	3.1	3.1	3.1	3.0	3.0
23.50	3.4	3.4	3.3	3.2	3.2	3.2	3.2	3.2	3.2	3.1	3.1
23.75	3.5	3.5	3.4	3.3	3.2	3.2	3.2	3.2	3.2	3.2	3.1

Table A-3 (cont.)

	I										
	115.0	117.5	120.0	122.5	125.0	127.5	130.0	132.5	135.0	137.5	140.0
T°C											
24.00	3.5	3.5	3.4	3.3	3.3	3.3	3.3	3.3	3.3	3.3	3.2
24.25	3.6	3.6	3.5	3.4	3.4	3.4	3.4	3.4	3.4	3.4	3.3
24.50	3.7	3.7	3.6	3.5	3.5	3.5	3.5	3.5	3.5	3.5	3.4
24.75	3.8	3.8	3.7	3.6	3.6	3.6	3.6	3.6	3.6	3.6	3.5
25.00	3.9	3.9	3.8	3.8	3.8	3.8	3.8	3.8	3.8	3.8	3.7
25.25	4.0	4.0	3.9	3.9	3.9	3.9	3.9	3.9	3.9	3.9	3.8
25.50	4.1	4.1	4.0	4.0	4.0	4.0	4.0	4.0	4.0	4.0	3.9
25.75	4.2	4.2	4.2	4.2	4.2	4.2	4.2	4.2	4.2	4.2	4.1
26.00	4.3	4.3	4.3	4.3	4.3	4.3	4.3	4.3	4.3	4.3	4.2
26.25	4.4	4.4	4.4	4.4	4.4	4.4	4.4	4.4	4.4	4.4	4.3
26.50	4.5	4.5	4.5	4.5	4.5	4.5	4.5	4.5	4.5	4.5	4.4

*Values of Unadjusted Daily Potential Evapotranspiration
for Mean Temperatures Above 26.5° C*

(Unadjusted Potential Evapotranspiration in mm)

T°C	0.0	0.1	0.2	0.3	0.4	0.5	0.6	0.7	0.8	0.9
26						4.5	4.5	4.6	4.6	4.6
27	4.6	4.7	4.7	4.7	4.8	4.8	4.8	4.8	4.9	4.9
28	4.9	5.0	5.0	5.0	5.0	5.1	5.1	5.1	5.1	5.2
29	5.2	5.2	5.2	5.2	5.3	5.3	5.3	5.3	5.4	5.4
30	5.4	5.4	5.4	5.5	5.5	5.5	5.5	5.5	5.6	5.6
31	5.6	5.6	5.6	5.6	5.7	5.7	5.7	5.7	5.7	5.8
32	5.8	5.8	5.8	5.8	5.8	5.8	5.9	5.9	5.9	5.9
33	5.9	5.9	5.9	5.9	6.0	6.0	6.0	6.0	6.0	6.0
34	6.0	6.0	6.0	6.0	6.1	6.1	6.1	6.1	6.1	6.1
35	6.1	6.1	6.1	6.1	6.1	6.1	6.1	6.1	6.1	6.1
36	6.1	6.1	6.2	6.2	6.2	6.2	6.2	6.2	6.2	6.2
37	6.2	6.2	6.2	6.2	6.2	6.2	6.2	6.2	6.2	6.2
38	6.2									

the monthly adjusted potential evapotranspiration have been obtained for San Francisco in table A-1. San Francisco is located at 38°N latitude.

The annual variation in potential evapotranspiration at San Francisco ranges from a low value of 26 mm in January to a high value of 90 mm in July. Total potential evapotranspiration for the year is 695 mm.

Monthly precipitation or climatic water supply at San Francisco is more variable than potential evapotranspiration ranging from essentially 0 mm in the dry summer months of July and August to a high value of 104 mm in December. Annual precipitation equals 475 mm. Precipitation and potential evapotranspiration appear to be about six months out of phase at San Francisco, California.

The next step in the evaluation of the climatic water budget is to compare precipitation (supply) with potential evapotranspiration (need) on a monthly basis. Monthly precipitation and potential evapotranspiration never coincide at San Francisco. There is too much precipitation in fall, winter, and spring and not enough in summer. Subtracting potential evapotranspiration from precipitation results in a series of positive and negative values clearly identifying periods when supply is greater or less than need.

Next, the water storage capacity in the root zone of the soil must be determined. Possible variations in this factor have been discussed in some detail in chapter 2. We will assume a root zone water-holding capacity of 150 mm at San Francisco. This is an average value for moderate-rooted vegetation on a sandy loam soil. We must now determine if, and in what month, the moisture in the soil fills the available root zone storage capacity. Even if storage were zero at the end of November in San Francisco, the last month with a negative value of *P–PE*, it can be seen that the accumulated positive *P–PE* values from December to March will bring the storage back to more than 150 mm. If there is some question whether the excess *P–PE* will fill the available storage capacity by the end of the series of months with positive *P–PE* values, it is possible to make that assumption and to test it. Substitute the water storage capacity value for storage in the last month of a series of positive *P–PE* values and actually determine the storage for the succeeding months. If, following the water budget computation for the next 12 months, the soil storage actually does not return to its capacity, continue the computations for another 12 months starting with the newly determined value of storage. Repeat the computations until the value of storage for that first month no longer changes as you go through 12 months of computation.

To simplify the monthly computations of soil moisture storage, tables A-5 through A-8 provide actual values of storage remaining in the soil after vegetation has tried to remove different amounts of water (*P–PE*) from storage for soils holding 50, 100, 150, and 300 mm of water in the root zone. We have assumed a root zone storage capacity of 150 mm at San Francisco and so make use of table A-7 in the following computations.

Total *P–PE* for San Francisco in April is −23 mm. Locate this value on the margins of table A-7 (the twenty is found on the vertical scale and the three is found across the top). Read in the body of the table the depth of water still remaining in the soil after the vegetation has tried to remove 23 mm of water (*P–PE*). In May, *P–PE* equals −58 mm. Again the plants need more water than they can obtain from precipitation alone and so they try to remove additional water from the soil.

Two techniques can be used to determine the remaining storage at the end of May. In the first method, the value of *P–PE* for May may be added to the value of *P–PE* for April making a total of −81 mm and this value is found on the borders of the table. The storage value for the end of May, 86 mm, is found in the body of the table for this value of potential removal. In the second

Table A-4
Mean Possible Monthly Duration of Sunlight in the Northern Hemisphere
(Expressed in units of 12 hours)

	J	F	M	A	M	J	J	A	S	O	N	D
Northern Latitudes												
0°	31.2	28.2	31.2	30.3	31.2	30.3	31.2	31.2	30.3	31.2	30.3	31.2
1	31.2	28.2	31.2	30.3	31.2	30.3	31.2	31.2	30.3	31.2	30.3	31.2
2	31.2	28.2	31.2	30.3	31.5	30.6	31.2	31.2	30.3	31.2	30.0	30.9
3	30.9	28.2	30.9	30.3	31.5	30.6	31.5	31.2	30.3	31.2	30.0	30.9
4	30.9	27.9	30.9	30.6	31.8	30.9	31.5	31.5	30.3	30.9	30.0	30.6
5	30.6	27.9	30.9	30.6	31.8	30.9	31.8	31.5	30.3	30.9	29.7	30.6
6	30.6	27.9	30.9	30.6	31.8	31.2	31.8	31.5	30.3	30.9	29.7	30.3
7	30.3	27.6	30.9	30.6	32.1	31.2	32.1	31.8	30.3	30.9	29.7	30.3
8	30.3	27.6	30.9	30.9	32.1	31.5	32.1	31.8	30.6	30.6	29.4	30.0
9	30.0	27.6	30.9	30.9	32.4	31.5	32.4	31.8	30.6	30.6	29.4	30.0
10	30.0	27.3	30.9	30.9	32.4	31.8	32.4	32.1	30.6	30.6	29.4	29.7
11	29.7	27.3	30.9	30.9	32.7	31.8	32.7	32.1	30.6	30.6	29.1	29.7
12	29.4	27.3	30.9	31.2	32.7	32.1	33.0	32.1	30.6	30.3	29.1	29.4
13	29.4	27.3	30.9	31.2	33.0	32.1	33.0	32.4	30.6	30.3	28.8	29.4
14	29.4	27.3	30.9	31.2	33.0	32.4	33.3	32.4	30.6	30.3	28.8	29.1
15	29.1	27.3	30.9	31.2	33.3	32.4	33.6	32.4	30.6	30.3	28.5	29.1
16	29.1	27.3	30.9	31.2	33.3	32.7	33.6	32.7	30.6	30.3	28.5	28.8
17	28.8	27.3	30.9	31.5	33.6	32.7	33.9	32.7	30.6	30.0	28.2	28.8
18	28.8	27.0	30.9	31.5	33.6	33.0	33.9	33.0	30.6	30.0	28.2	28.5
19	28.5	27.0	30.9	31.5	33.9	33.0	34.2	33.0	30.6	30.0	27.9	28.5
20	28.5	27.0	30.9	31.5	33.9	33.3	34.2	33.3	30.6	30.0	27.9	28.2
21	28.2	27.0	30.9	31.5	33.9	33.3	34.5	33.3	30.6	30.0	27.6	28.2
22	28.2	26.7	30.9	31.8	34.2	33.6	34.5	33.3	30.6	29.7	27.6	27.9
23	27.9	26.7	30.9	31.8	34.2	33.9	34.8	33.6	30.6	29.7	27.6	27.6
24	27.9	26.7	30.9	31.8	34.5	34.2	34.8	33.6	30.6	29.7	27.3	27.6
25	27.9	26.7	30.9	31.8	34.5	34.2	35.1	33.6	30.6	29.7	27.3	27.3
26	27.6	26.4	30.9	32.1	34.8	34.5	35.1	33.6	30.6	29.7	27.3	27.3
27	27.6	26.4	30.9	32.1	34.8	34.5	35.4	33.9	30.6	29.7	27.0	27.0
28	27.3	26.4	30.9	32.1	35.1	34.8	35.4	33.9	30.9	29.4	27.0	27.0
29	27.3	26.1	30.9	32.1	35.1	34.8	35.7	33.9	30.9	29.4	26.7	26.7
30	27.0	26.1	30.9	32.4	35.4	35.1	36.0	34.2	30.9	29.4	26.7	26.4
31	27.0	26.1	30.9	32.4	35.4	35.1	36.0	34.2	30.9	29.4	26.4	26.4
32	26.7	25.8	30.9	32.4	35.7	35.4	36.3	34.5	30.9	29.4	26.4	26.1
33	26.4	25.8	30.9	32.7	35.7	35.7	36.3	34.5	30.9	29.1	26.1	25.8
34	26.4	25.8	30.9	32.7	36.0	36.0	36.6	34.8	30.9	29.1	26.1	25.8
35	26.1	25.5	30.9	32.7	36.3	36.3	36.9	34.8	30.9	29.1	25.8	25.5
36	26.1	25.5	30.9	33.0	36.3	36.6	37.2	34.8	30.9	29.1	25.8	25.2
37	25.8	25.5	30.9	33.0	36.6	36.9	37.5	35.1	30.9	29.1	25.5	24.9
38	25.5	25.2	30.9	33.0	36.9	37.2	37.5	35.1	31.2	28.8	25.2	24.9
39	25.5	25.2	30.9	33.3	36.9	37.2	37.8	35.4	31.2	28.8	25.2	24.6

Table A-4 (cont.)

	J	F	M	A	M	J	J	A	S	O	N	D
Northern Latitudes												
40	25.2	24.9	30.9	33.3	37.2	37.5	38.1	35.4	31.2	28.8	24.9	24.3
41	24.9	24.9	30.9	33.3	37.5	37.8	38.1	35.7	31.2	28.8	24.6	24.0
42	24.6	24.6	30.9	33.6	37.8	38.1	38.4	35.7	31.2	28.5	24.6	23.7
43	24.3	24.6	30.6	33.6	37.8	38.4	38.7	36.0	31.2	28.5	24.3	23.1
44	24.3	24.3	30.6	33.6	38.1	38.7	39.0	36.0	31.2	28.5	24.0	22.8
45	24.0	24.3	30.6	33.9	38.4	38.7	39.3	36.3	31.2	28.2	23.7	22.5
46	23.7	24.0	30.6	33.9	38.7	39.0	39.6	36.6	31.2	28.2	23.7	22.2
47	23.1	24.0	30.6	34.2	39.0	39.6	39.9	36.6	31.5	27.9	23.4	21.9
48	22.8	23.7	30.6	34.2	39.3	39.9	40.2	36.9	31.5	27.9	23.1	21.6
49	22.5	23.7	30.6	34.5	39.6	40.2	40.5	37.2	31.5	27.6	22.8	21.3
50	22.2	23.4	30.6	34.5	39.9	40.8	41.1	37.5	31.8	27.6	22.8	21.0

method, one starts with the value of storage found in the body of the table at the end of April, 128 mm, and counts ahead in the body of the table a total of 58 numbers, equivalent to the *P–PE* for May. On counting ahead (and onto following lines, if necessary), one is not concerned with the actual numbers appearing in the table but rather with moving forward the proper number of entries in the table, one entry for each mm of *P–PE* for May. Both methods should arrive at the same value of storage in the soil at the end of May. This process is repeated as long as *P–PE* for the month remains negative.

When *P–PE* becomes positive (in December at San Francisco), add these values directly to the storage value of the previous month until the total storage again reaches the water-holding capacity of the soil (150 mm in our example). Storage cannot go above the water-holding capacity unless air temperature drops below $-1°C$. With monthly temperatures lower than this, it is assumed that precipitation falls as snow and is stored on the surface; storage can exceed field capacity by the amount of the snow accumulation.

The following line, ΔST, or change is soil moisture storage merely indicates the month-to-month change in value of storage either positive or negative. This value is used in later portions of the computations.

Actual evapotranspiration (*AE*) represents the actual transfer of moisture from the soil and vegetation to the atmosphere. When the soil storage is at capacity, it is assumed that there is sufficient moisture to meet the climatic demands and so *AE* will equal *PE*. Similarly, even if the soil is not at its storage capacity but if $P > PE$ it is assumed that current precipitation will be sufficient to satisfy climatic moisture requirements. When $P < PE$ (and storage change is negative), it is assumed that the actual evapotranspiration will consist of all of the precipitation plus that water that the vegetation can remove from the soil

Table A-5
Soil Moisture Retention Table—50 mm

(Soil Moisture Retained After Different Amounts of Potential Evapotranspiration Have Occurred. Water-Holding Capacity of Soil Is 50 mm)

Accum. P–PE	0	1	2	3	4	5	6	7	8	9
					Water Retained in Soil					
0	50	49	48	47	46	45	44	43	42	41
10	41	40	39	38	37	36	36	35	34	33
20	33	32	32	31	30	30	29	28	28	27
30	27	26	25	25	24	24	23	23	22	22
40	21	21	20	20	19	19	19	18	18	18
50	17	17	17	16	16	16	15	15	15	14
60	14	14	13	13	13	13	12	12	11	11
70	11	11	11	10	10	10	10	9	9	9
80	9	9	9	8	8	8	8	8	8	8
90	7	7	7	7	7	7	7	6	6	6
100	6	6	6	6	6	6	5	5	5	5
110	5	5	5	5	4	4	4	4	4	4
120	4	4	4	4	4	4	4	4	3	3
130	3	3	3	3	3	3	3	3	3	3
140	3	3	3	3	2	2	2	2	2	2
150	2	2	2	2	2	2	2	2	2	2
160	2	2	2	2	2	2	2	2	1	1
170	1	1	1	1	1	1	1	1	1	1
180	1	1	1	1	1	1	1	1	1	1
190	1	1	1	1	1	1	1	1	1	1
200	1	1	1	1	1	1	1	1	1	1
210	1	1	1	1	1	1	1	1	1	1
220	1	1	1	1	1					

(storage change without regard to the negative sign). This assumption might seem questionable because it can be argued that not all the precipitation can be used for evapotranspiration. This seems to be more normally the case in the late fall through early spring periods of the year in most stations where soils are often full of water and climatic demands for water are well satisfied. During summer dry periods, little overland flow occurs from most well-vegetated areas so that the assumption that all precipitation is available for evapotranspiration works out more reasonably in practice than might be originally anticipated.

Actual evapotranspiration at San Francisco in April is 55 mm. It consists of 33 mm of precipitation plus 22 mm of water removed from storage. In May, *AE* is 54 mm. derived from 12 mm of precipitation and 42 mm of water removed from storage in the soil (−42 mm storage change without regard to the sign).

Water deficit (D) is merely $PE-AE$, the difference between the climatic demands for water and the actual evapotranspiration losses. Deficits can only exist in those months in which $P-PE$ is negative, the soil is drying out, and there is not enough water to satisfy the vegetation needs.

Water surplus (S) is the excess water available to percolate through the soil both as recharge to the groundwater table or as throughflow. When storage reaches its capacity, surplus is equal to the amount that P exceeds PE $(P-PE)$. When the soil storage is not at its capacity, no surplus can exist. In that month in which the soil moisture storage capacity is just satisfied, surplus will equal the difference between $P-PE$ and ΔST since the amount of water needed to bring the soil storage to its capacity (ΔST) must first be taken out of the available excess water $(P-PE)$ before surplus can occur. In San Francisco, January is the month in which soil moisture storage reaches 150 mm. In that month, $P-PE$ equals 76 mm. It requires 69 mm of this excess water to bring storage from 81 mm in December to 150 mm; only the remaining $P-PE$ ($76 - 69 = 7$ mm) is available as surplus. This value is entered as the January surplus.

Annual runoff is, by definition, equal to the available annual surplus. However, because of the lag between the time of precipitation and the time the water actually passes the gaging station, it is clear that monthly computed surplus is not the same as monthly runoff. Though Thornthwaite has suggested a lag factor of 50 percent (50 percent of the surplus in any month will runoff while the remainder will be held over and added to the surplus of the following month) for watersheds whose drainage areas exceed 10,000 square miles or so, the actual lag factor must be determined on the basis of detailed knowledge of each particular basin.

Using a 50 percent lag factor, one starts the computation of runoff with the first month after a long dry spell. This would be January in San Francisco. Of the surplus of 7 mm, 50 percent or 4 mm will runoff and 3 mm will be held over and added to the 58 mm of surplus in February. Fifty percent of 61 mm is 31 mm of runoff for February with 30 mm being held over and added to the 25 mm of surplus in March.

The process is repeated until July. In this case, with a surplus of only 1 in August it is all considered to run off in that month. If, in the computations, there is still some holdover of surplus in December that must be added to the January surplus it would then have been necessary to continue the month-by-month computations using the new values of surplus carryover until the value of monthly runoff did not change from one year to the next.

Total moisture detention (DT) consists of three factors: (1) soil moisture storage; (2) snow stored on the ground (all precipitation that occurs at monthly mean temperatures below $-1°C$ is considered to be snow and stored on the soil surface); and (3) that portion of the surplus which has not run off but is being held over to be added to the surplus of the following month. Thus for January at San Francisco, DT consists of 150 mm soil moisture storage + 0 snow storage + 3

Table A-6
Soil Moisture Retention Table—100 mm

(Soil Moisture Retained after Different Amounts of Potential Evapotranspiration Have Occurred. Water-Holding Capacity of Soil Is 100 mm)

Accum. P−PE	0	1	2	3	4	5	6	7	8	9
					Water Retained in Soil					
0	100	99	98	97	96	95	94	93	92	91
10	90	89	88	88	87	86	85	84	83	82
20	81	81	80	79	78	77	77	76	75	74
30	74	73	72	71	70	70	69	68	68	67
40	66	66	65	64	64	63	62	62	61	60
50	60	59	59	58	58	57	56	56	55	54
60	54	53	53	52	52	51	51	50	50	49
70	49	48	48	47	47	46	46	45	45	44
80	44	44	43	43	42	42	41	41	40	40
90	40	39	39	38	38	38	37	37	36	36
100	36	35	35	35	34	34	34	33	33	33
110	32	32	32	31	31	31	30	30	30	30
120	29	29	29	28	28	28	27	27	27	27
130	26	26	26	26	25	25	25	24	24	24
140	24	24	23	23	23	23	22	22	22	22
150	22	21	21	21	21	20	20	20	20	20
160	19	19	19	19	19	18	18	18	18	18
170	18	17	17	17	17	17	16	16	16	16
180	16	16	15	15	15	15	15	15	14	14
190	14	14	14	14	14	14	13	13	13	13
200	13	13	12	12	12	12	12	12	12	12
210	12	11	11	11	11	11	11	11	11	11
220	10	10	10	10	10	10	10	10	10	10
230	9	9	9	9	9	9	9	9	9	9
240	8	8	8	8	8	8	8	8	8	8
250	8	8	8	7	7	7	7	7	7	7
260	7	7	7	7	7	7	6	6	6	6
270	6	6	6	6	6	6	6	6	6	6
280	6	6	6	6	6	5	5	5	5	5
290	5	5	5	5	5	5	5	5	5	5
300	5	5	4	4	4	4	4	4	4	4
310	4	4	4	4	4	4	4	4	4	4
320	4	4	4	4	4	4	4	4	4	4
330	3	3	3	3	3	3	3	3	3	3
340	3	3	3	3	3	3	3	3	3	3
350	3	3	3	3	3	3	3	3	3	2
360	2	2	2	2	2	2	2	2	2	2
370	2	2	2	2	2	2	2	2	2	2
380	2	2	2	2	2	2	2	2	2	2
390	2	2	2	2	2	2	2	2	2	2

Table A-6 (cont.)

Accum. P–PE	0	1	2	3	4	5	6	7	8	9
					Water Retained in Soil					
400	2	2	2	2	2	2	2	2	2	2
410	2	2	2	2	2	1	1	1	1	1
420	1	1	1	1	1	1	1	1	1	1
430	1	1	1	1	1	1	1	1	1	1
440	1	1	1	1	1	1	1	1	1	1
450	1	1	1	1	1	1	1	1	1	1
460	1	1	1	1	1	1	1	1	1	1
470	1	1	1	1	1	1	1	1	1	1
480	1	1	1	1	1	1	1	1	1	1
490	1	1	1	1	1	1	1	1	1	1
500	1	1	1	1	1	1	1	1	1	1

mm of surplus holdover for a total of 153 mm. For February, DT is 150 mm soil moisture storage + 0 snow storage, + 30 mm of surplus hold over, for a total detention of 180 mm depth.

Snow accumulation and snowmelt runoff are extremely complex problems to deal with in a water budget approach. The reader would be well advised to consult the comprehensive volume, *Snow Hydrology,* prepared by the U.S. Army Corps of Engineers in 1956, in which several techniques for handling the problem of snowmelt runoff are suggested. It is difficult to make a single series of rules that can be followed in every case. Rather, each situation must be looked at as a special case and runoff determined on the basis of careful consideration of all available facts.

Water budget computations can easily be checked to see that mathematical steps have been completed correctly. On an average annual basis, potential evapotranspiration must equal the sum of actual evapotranspiration and deficit. At the same time, precipitation must equal the sum of actual evapotranspiration, the surplus, and any net change in storage from the beginning to the end of the year. These checks must work out exactly. If they do not, some arithmetic error exists in the steps between $P–PE$ and S.

Table A-7
Soil Moisture Retention Table—150 mm

(Soil Moisture Retained after Different Amounts of Potential Evapotranspiration Have Occurred. Water-Holding Capacity of Soil Is 150 mm)

Accum. P–PE	0	1	2	3	4	5	6	7	8	9
					Water Retained in Soil					
0	150	149	148	147	146	145	144	143	142	141
10	140	139	138	137	136	135	134	133	132	131
20	131	130	129	128	127	127	126	125	124	123
30	122	122	121	120	119	118	117	116	115	114
40	114	113	113	112	111	111	110	109	108	107
50	107	106	106	105	104	103	103	102	101	100
60	100	99	98	97	97	97	96	95	94	93
70	93	92	92	91	90	90	89	89	88	87
80	87	86	86	85	84	84	84	83	83	82
90	82	81	81	80	79	79	78	77	77	76
100	76	76	75	75	74	74	73	72	72	71
110	71	71	70	70	69	69	68	68	67	67
120	66	66	66	65	65	64	64	63	63	62
130	62	62	61	61	60	60	60	59	59	58
140	58	58	57	57	56	56	55	55	54	54
150	54	53	53	53	52	52	52	52	51	51
160	51	51	50	50	50	49	49	48	48	47
170	47	47	47	46	46	46	45	45	45	44
180	44	44	44	43	43	43	42	42	42	41
190	41	41	41	40	40	40	40	39	39	39
200	39	38	38	38	37	37	37	37	36	36
210	36	36	35	35	35	35	35	34	34	34
220	34	34	33	33	33	33	33	32	32	32
230	32	31	31	31	31	31	30	30	30	30
240	30	29	29	29	29	29	28	28	28	28
250	28	27	27	27	27	27	26	26	26	26
260	26	26	25	25	25	25	25	24	24	24
270	24	24	24	23	23	23	23	23	23	23
280	22	22	22	22	22	22	22	22	21	21
290	21	21	21	20	20	20	20	20	20	20
300	20	19	19	19	19	19	19	19	18	18
310	18	18	18	18	18	18	18	17	17	17
320	17	17	17	17	17	17	17	16	16	16
330	16	16	16	16	16	16	16	15	15	15
340	15	15	15	15	15	15	14	14	14	14
350	14	14	14	14	14	14	14	13	13	13
360	13	13	13	13	13	13	13	12	12	12
370	12	12	12	12	12	12	12	12	11	11
380	11	11	11	11	11	11	11	11	11	11
390	11	11	11	10	10	10	10	10	10	10

Table A-7 (cont.)

Accum. P–PE	0	1	2	3	4	5	6	7	8	9
					Water Retained in Soil					
400	10	10	10	10	10	10	10	10	9	9
410	9	9	9	9	9	9	9	9	9	9
420	9	9	9	8	8	8	8	8	8	8
430	8	8	8	8	8	8	8	8	8	8
440	8	8	8	7	7	7	7	7	7	7
450	7	7	7	7	7	7	7	7	7	7
460	7	7	7	7	6	6	6	6	6	6
470	6	6	6	6	6	6	6	6	6	6
480	6	6	6	6	6	6	6	6	5	5
490	5	5	5	5	5	5	5	5	5	5
500	5	5	5	5	5	5	5	5	5	5
510	5	5	5	5	5	5	5	5	4	4
520	4	4	4	4	4	4	4	4	4	4
530	4	4	4	4	4	4	4	4	4	4
540	4	4	4	4	4	4	4	4	4	4
550	4	4	4	4	4	4	4	3	3	3
560	3	3	3	3	3	3	3	3	3	3
570	3	3	3	3	3	3	3	3	3	3
580	3	3	3	3	3	3	3	3	3	3
590	3	3	3	3	3	3	3	3	3	3
600	3	3	3	3	3	2	2	2	2	2
610	2	2	2	2	2	2	2	2	2	2
620	2	2	2	2	2	2	2	2	2	2
630	2	2	2	2	2	2	2	2	2	2
640	2	2	2	2	2	2	2	2	2	2
650	2	2	2	2	2	2	2	2	2	2
660	2	2	2	2	2	2	2	2	2	2
670	2	2	2	2	2	2	2	2	2	2
680	2	2	1	1	1	1	1	1	1	1
690	1	1	1	1	1	1	1	1	1	1
700	1	1	1	1	1	1	1	1	1	1
710	1	1	1	1	1	1	1	1	1	1
720	1	1	1	1	1	1	1	1	1	1
730	1	1	1	1	1	1	1	1	1	1
740	1	1	1	1	1	1	1	1	1	1

* * * * * * * * * * *

	0	5			0	5			0	5
750	1	1		790	1	1		830	1	1
760	1	1		800	1	1		840	1	1
770	1	1		810	1	1				
780	1	1		820	1	1				

Table A-8
Soil Moisture Retention Table—300 mm

(Soil Moisture Retained after Different Amounts of Potential Evapotranspiration Have Occurred. Water-Holding Capacity of Soil Is 300 mm)

Accum. P–PE	0	1	2	3	4	5	6	7	8	9
					Water Retained in Soil					
0	300	299	298	297	296	295	294	293	292	291
10	290	289	288	287	286	285	284	283	282	281
20	280	279	278	278	277	276	275	274	273	272
30	271	270	269	268	268	267	266	265	264	263
40	262	261	260	260	259	258	257	256	255	254
50	254	253	252	251	250	249	248	248	247	246
60	245	244	244	243	242	241	240	240	239	238
70	237	236	236	235	234	233	232	232	231	230
80	229	228	228	227	226	225	225	224	223	222
90	222	221	220	219	219	218	217	216	215	215
100	214	214	213	212	212	211	210	209	209	208
110	207	207	206	205	204	204	203	202	202	201
120	200	200	199	198	198	197	196	196	195	194
130	194	193	192	192	191	191	190	189	189	188
140	187	187	186	186	185	184	184	183	182	182
150	181	181	180	179	179	178	178	177	176	176
160	175	175	174	173	173	172	172	171	171	170
170	170	169	168	168	167	167	166	166	165	164
180	164	163	163	162	162	161	160	160	159	159
190	158	158	157	157	156	156	155	155	154	154
200	153	153	152	152	151	151	150	150	149	149
210	148	148	147	147	146	146	145	145	144	144
220	143	143	142	142	141	141	140	140	139	139
230	138	138	138	137	137	136	136	135	135	134
240	134	133	133	132	132	132	131	131	130	130
250	130	129	128	128	128	127	127	126	126	126
260	125	125	124	124	124	123	123	122	122	121
270	121	121	120	120	119	119	119	118	118	117
280	117	117	116	116	115	115	115	114	114	114
290	113	113	112	112	112	111	111	110	110	110
300	109	109	109	108	108	108	107	107	106	106
310	106	105	105	105	104	104	104	103	103	103
320	102	102	102	101	101	101	100	100	100	99
330	99	98	98	98	98	97	97	97	96	96
340	96	95	95	95	94	94	94	93	93	93
350	92	92	92	92	91	91	91	90	90	90
360	89	89	89	88	88	88	88	87	87	87
370	86	86	86	86	85	85	85	84	84	84
380	84	83	83	83	82	82	82	82	81	81
390	81	80	80	80	80	80	79	79	79	78

Table A-8 (cont.)

Accum. P–PE	0	1	2	3	4	5	6	7	8	9
				Water Retained in Soil						
400	78	78	78	77	77	77	77	76	76	76
410	76	75	75	75	74	74	74	74	74	73
420	73	73	72	72	72	72	72	71	71	71
430	71	70	70	70	70	70	69	69	69	68
440	68	68	68	68	67	67	67	67	66	66
450	66	66	66	65	65	65	65	64	64	64
460	64	64	63	63	63	63	63	62	62	62
470	62	62	61	61	61	61	61	60	60	60
480	60	60	59	59	59	59	59	58	58	58
490	58	58	57	57	57	57	57	56	56	56
500	56	56	55	55	55	55	55	54	54	54
510	54	54	54	53	53	53	53	53	52	52
520	52	52	52	52	51	51	51	51	51	50
530	50	50	50	50	50	50	49	49	49	49
540	49	49	48	48	48	48	48	48	47	47
550	47	47	47	47	46	46	46	46	46	46
560	46	45	45	45	45	45	45	44	44	44
570	44	44	44	44	44	43	43	43	43	43
580	43	42	42	42	42	42	42	42	42	41
590	41	41	41	41	41	41	40	40	40	40
600	40	40	40	39	39	39	39	39	39	39
610	38	38	38	38	38	38	38	38	38	37
620	37	37	37	37	37	37	36	36	36	36
630	36	36	36	36	36	36	35	35	35	35
640	35	35	35	34	34	34	34	34	34	34
650	34	34	33	33	33	33	33	33	33	33
660	32	32	32	32	32	32	32	32	32	32
670	32	31	31	31	31	31	31	31	31	31
680	30	30	30	30	30	30	30	30	30	30
690	30	29	29	29	29	29	29	29	29	29
700	28	28	28	28	28	28	28	28	28	28
710	28	27	27	27	27	27	27	27	27	27
720	27	26	26	26	26	26	26	26	26	26
730	26	26	26	26	25	25	25	25	25	25
740	25	25	25	25	25	24	24	24	24	24
750	24	24	24	24	24	24	24	24	23	23
760	23	23	23	23	23	23	23	23	23	23
770	22	22	22	22	22	22	22	22	22	22
780	22	22	22	22	22	21	21	21	21	21
790	21	21	21	21	21	21	21	21	20	20

Table A-8 (cont.)

Accum. P–PE	0	1	2	3	4	5	6	7	8	9
				Water Retained in Soil						
800	20	20	20	20	20	20	20	20	20	20
810	20	20	20	20	20	19	19	19	19	19
820	19	19	19	19	19	19	19	19	19	18
830	18	18	18	18	18	18	18	18	18	18
840	18	18	18	18	18	18	18	17	17	17
850	17	17	17	17	17	17	17	17	17	17
860	17	17	17	17	16	16	16	16	16	16
870	16	16	16	16	16	16	16	16	16	16
880	16	16	16	16	15	15	15	15	15	15
890	15	15	15	15	15	15	15	15	15	15
900	15	15	14	14	14	14	14	14	14	14
910	14	14	14	14	14	14	14	14	14	14
920	14	14	14	14	13	13	13	13	13	13
930	13	13	13	13	13	13	13	13	13	13
940	13	13	13	13	12	12	12	12	12	12
950	12	12	12	12	12	12	12	12	12	12
960	12	12	12	12	12	12	12	12	12	12
970	12	12	11	11	11	11	11	11	11	11
980	11	11	11	11	11	11	11	11	11	11
990	11	11	11	11	11	11	11	10	10	10
1000	10	10	10	10	10	10	10	10	10	10
1010	10	10	10	10	10	10	10	10	10	10
1020	10	10	10	10	10	10	10	10	10	10
1030	9	9	9	9	9	9	9	9	9	9
1040	9	9	9	9	9	9	9	9	9	9
1050	9	9	9	9	9	9	9	9	9	9
1060	8	8	8	8	8	8	8	8	8	8
1070	8	8	8	8	8	8	8	8	8	8
1080	8	8	8	8	8	8	8	8	8	8
1090	8	8	8	8	8	8	8	8	8	8
1100	7	7	7	7	7	7	7	7	7	7
1110	7	7	7	7	7	7	7	7	7	7
1120	7	7	7	7	7	7	7	7	7	7
1130	7	7	7	7	7	7	7	7	7	7
1140	6	6	6	6	6	6	6	6	6	6
1150	6	6	6	6	6	6	6	6	6	6
1160	6	6	6	6	6	6	6	6	6	6
1170	6	6	6	6	6	6	6	6	6	6
1180	6	6	6	6	6	6	6	6	6	6
1190	6	6	6	6	6	5	5	5	5	5

* * * * * * * * * * * *

Table A-8 (cont.)

Accum. P–PE	0	5		0	5		0	5
			Water Retained in Soil					
1200	5	5	1300	4	4	1400	3	3
1210	5	5	1310	4	4	1410	3	3
1220	5	5	1320	4	4	1420	2	2
1230	5	5	1330	3	3	1430	2	2
1240	5	5	1340	3	3	1440	2	2
1250	4	4	1350	3	3	1450	2	2
1260	4	4	1360	3	3	1460	2	2
1270	4	4	1370	3	3	1470	2	2
1280	4	4	1380	3	3	1480	2	2
1290	4	4	1390	3	3	1490	2	2

Appendix B
Graphical
Representation of
Selected Water
Budgets by
Continents

Sources for the eight plates of water budget graphs are J.R. Mather (ed.), "Average Climatic Water Balance Data of the Continents: Part I. Africa; Part II. Asia (excluding U.S.S.R.); Part III. U.S.S.R.; Part IV. Australia, New Zealand and Oceania; Part V. Europe; Part VI. North America (excluding United States); Part VII. United States; Part VIII. South America." *Publications in Climatology,* Laboratory of Climatology, vol. 15, no. 2; vol. 16, nos. 1, 2, 3; vol. 17, nos. 1, 2, 3; vol. 18, no. 2 (1962, 1963, 1964, 1965).

WATER BALANCES OF SELECTED STATIONS IN AFRICA

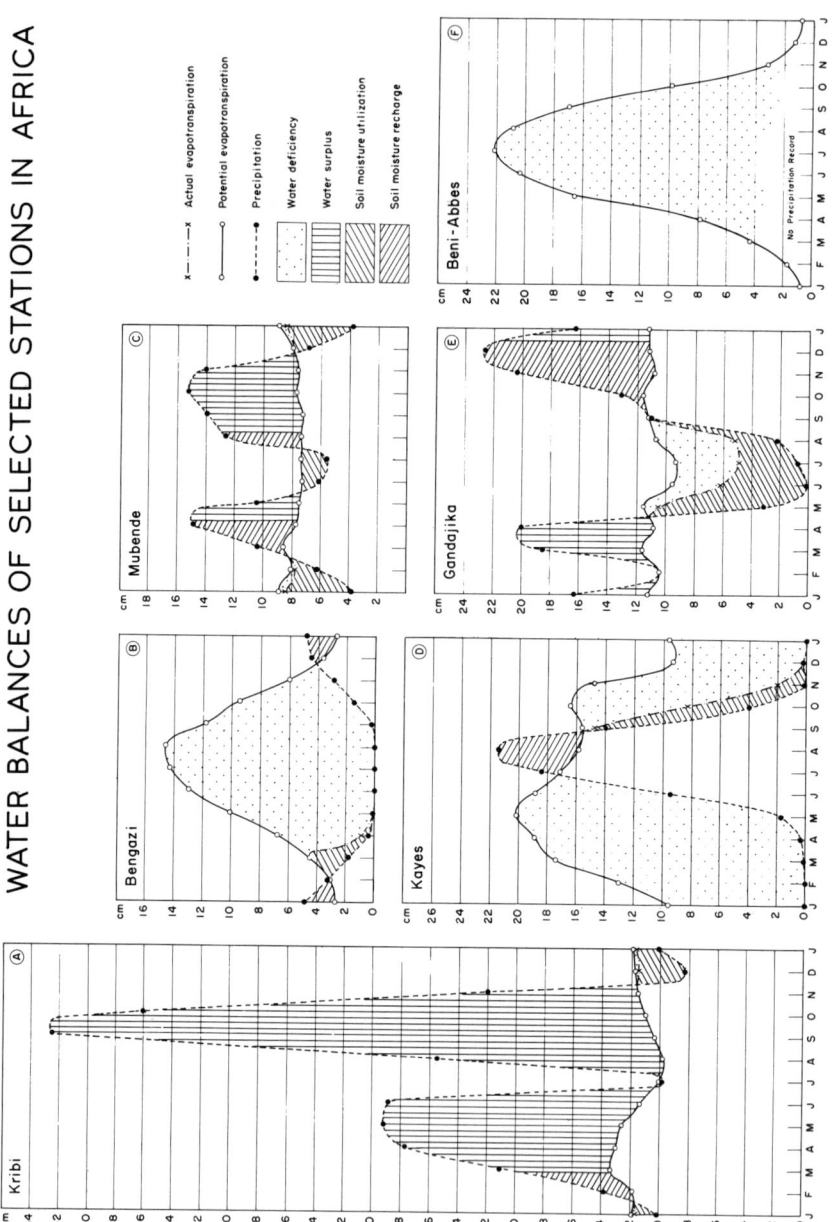

x———x Actual evapotranspiration

o———o Potential evapotranspiration

•———• Precipitation

Water deficiency

Water surplus

Soil moisture utilization

Soil moisture recharge

Figure B-1.

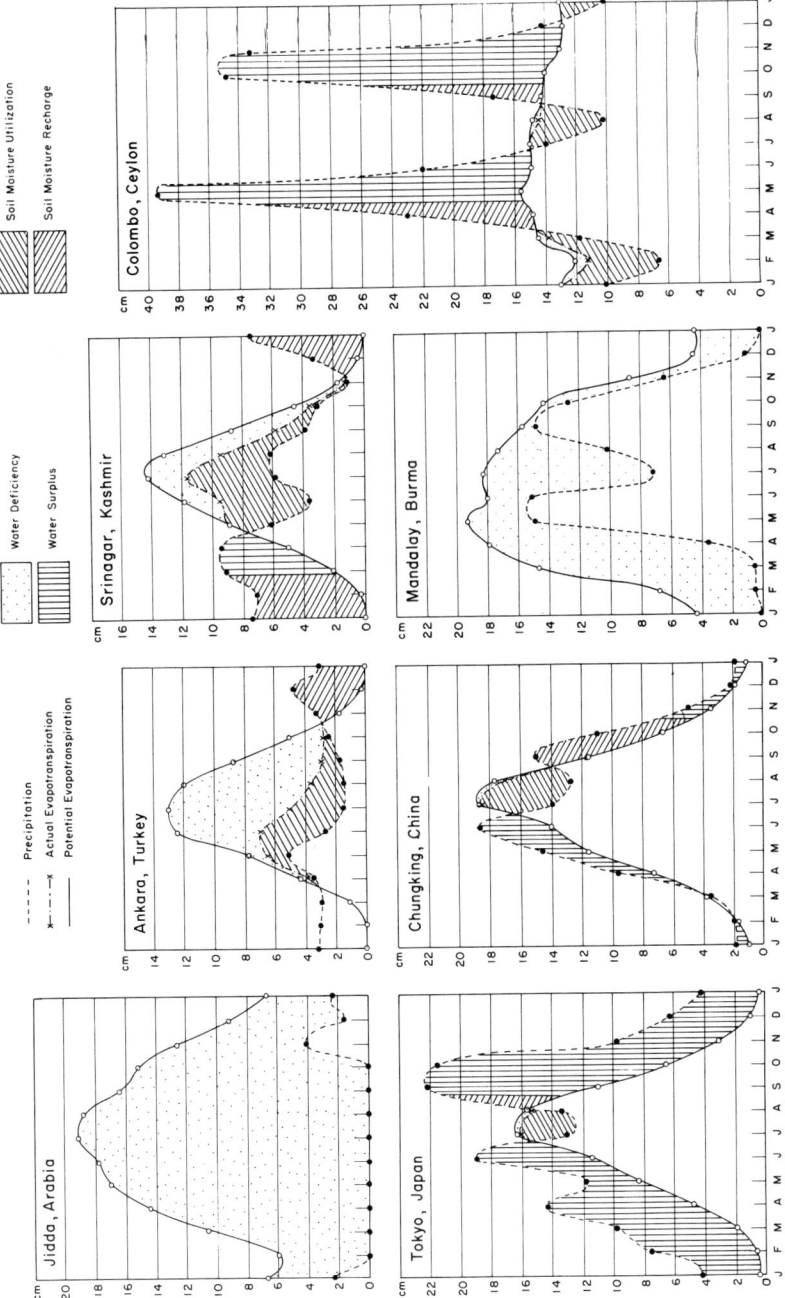

WATER BALANCES OF SELECTED STATIONS IN ASIA

Figure B-2.

198

WATER BALANCES OF SELECTED STATIONS IN AUSTRALIA AND OCEANIA

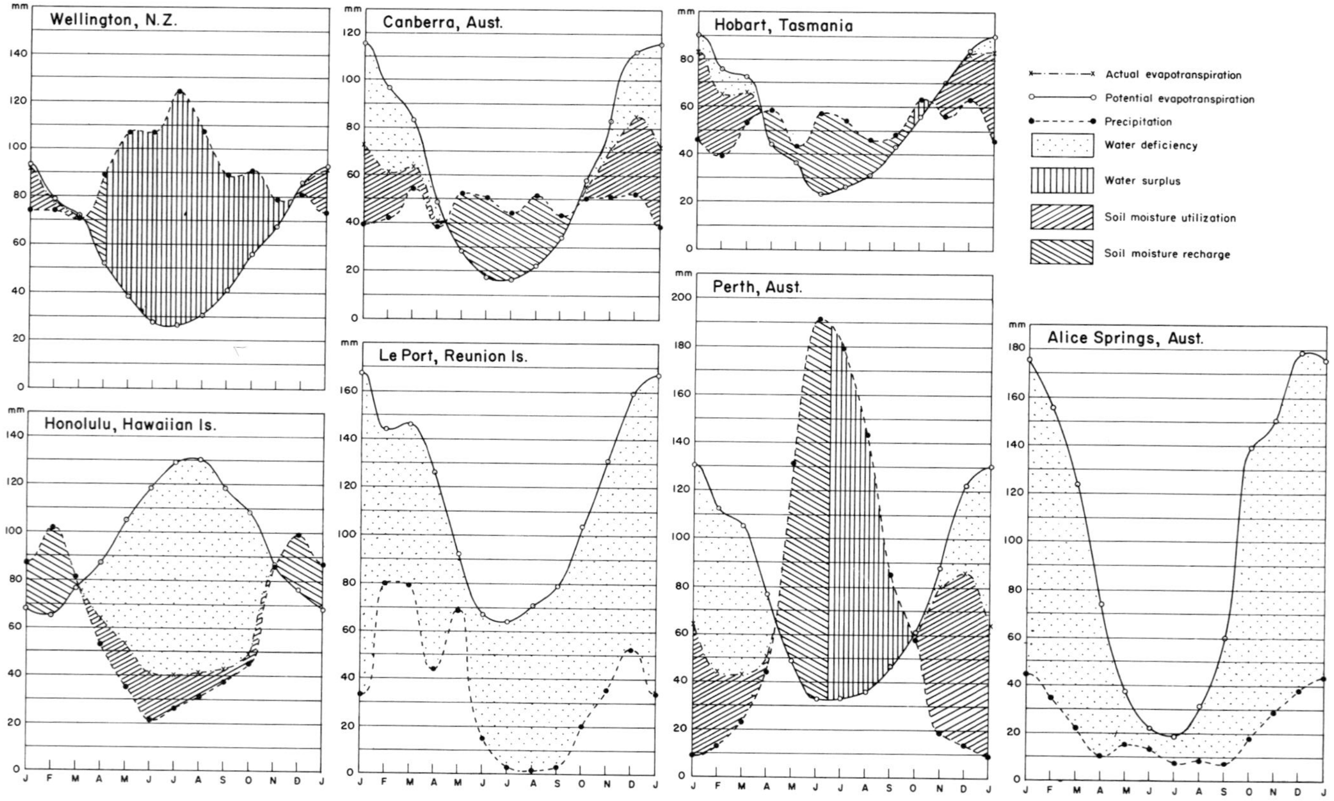

Figure B-3.

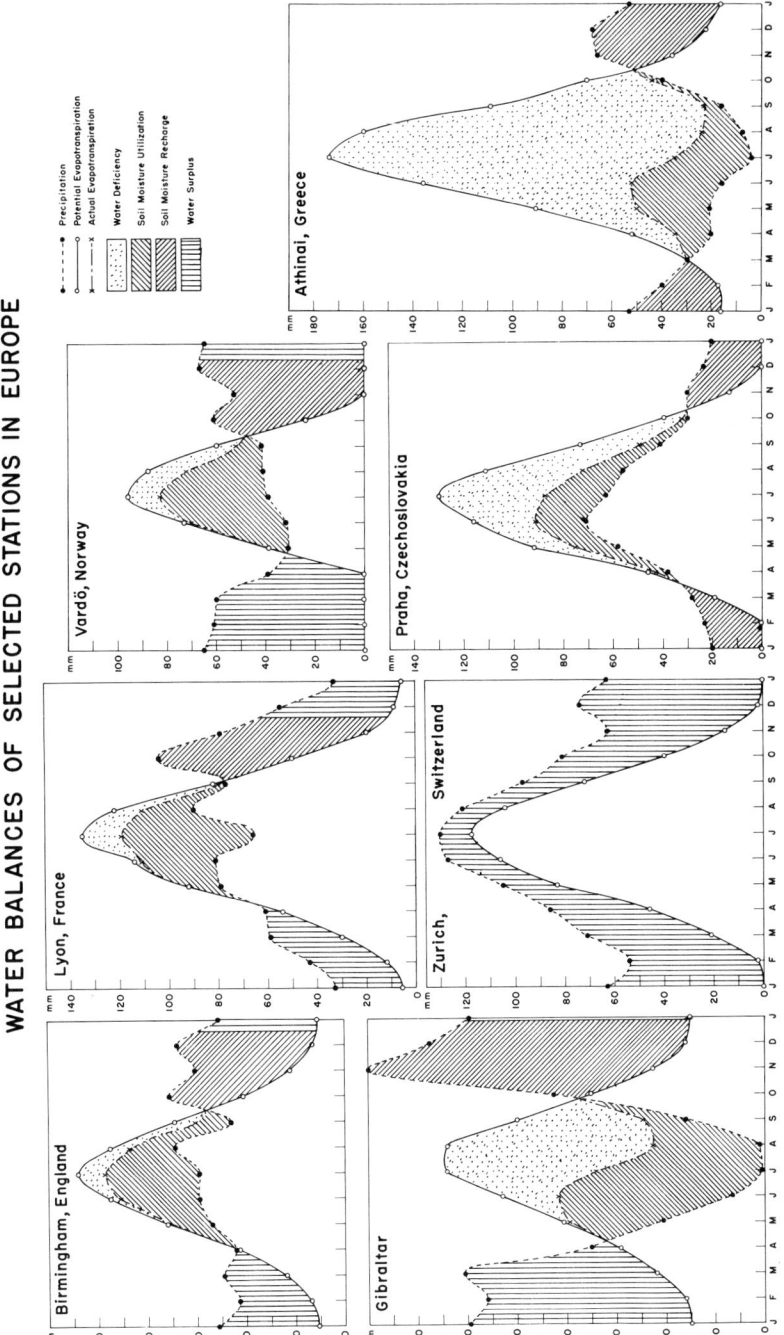

WATER BALANCES OF SELECTED STATIONS IN EUROPE

Figure B-4.

200

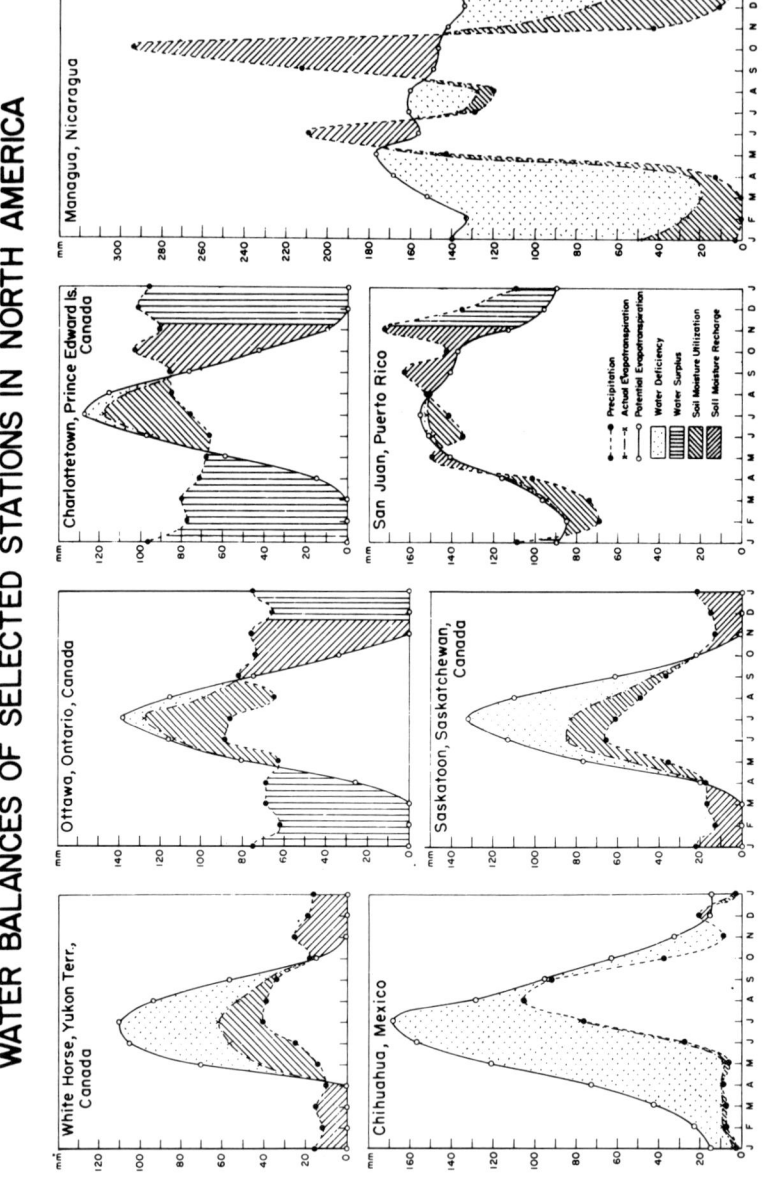

Figure B-5.

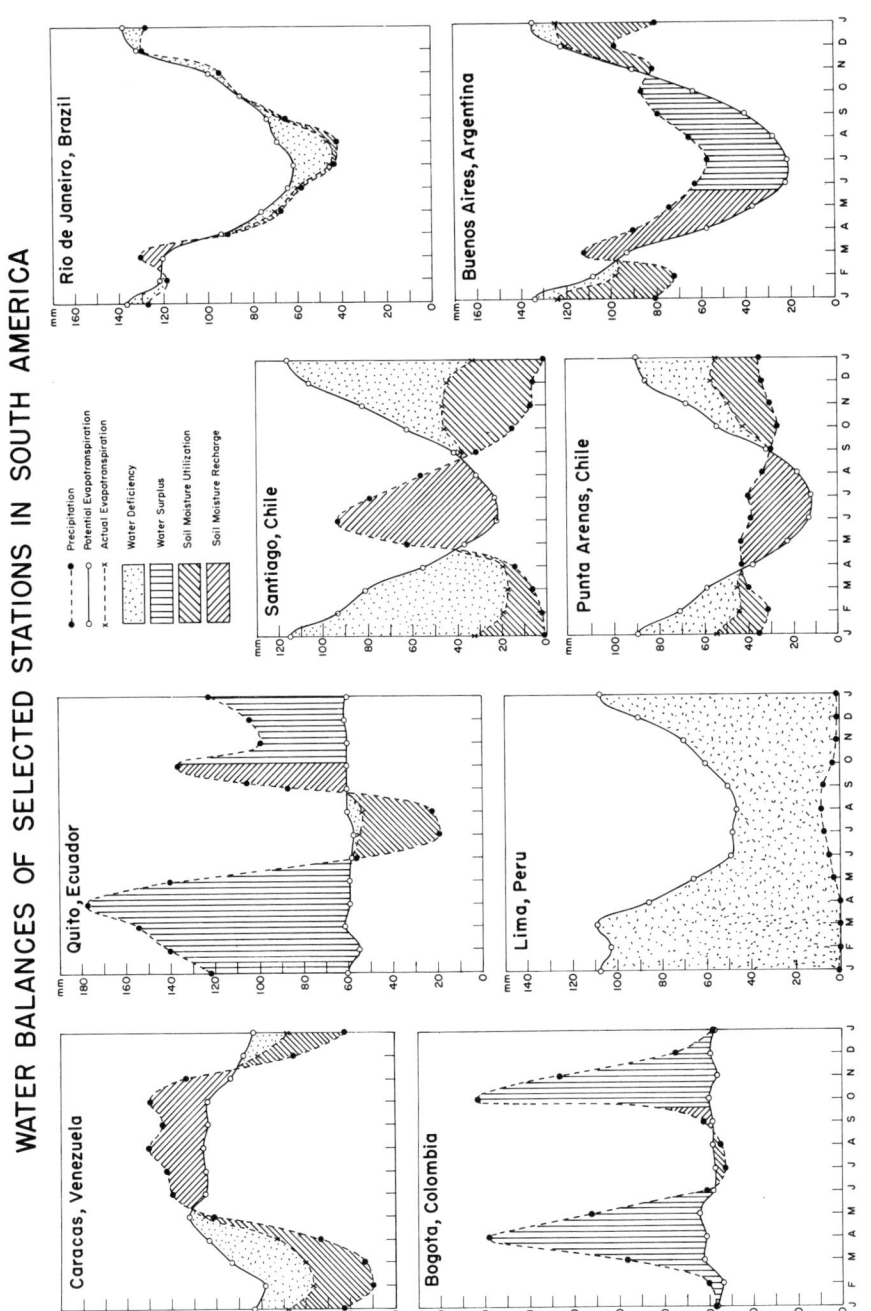

WATER BALANCES OF SELECTED STATIONS IN SOUTH AMERICA

Figure B-6.

WATER BALANCES OF SELECTED STATIONS IN THE UNITED STATES

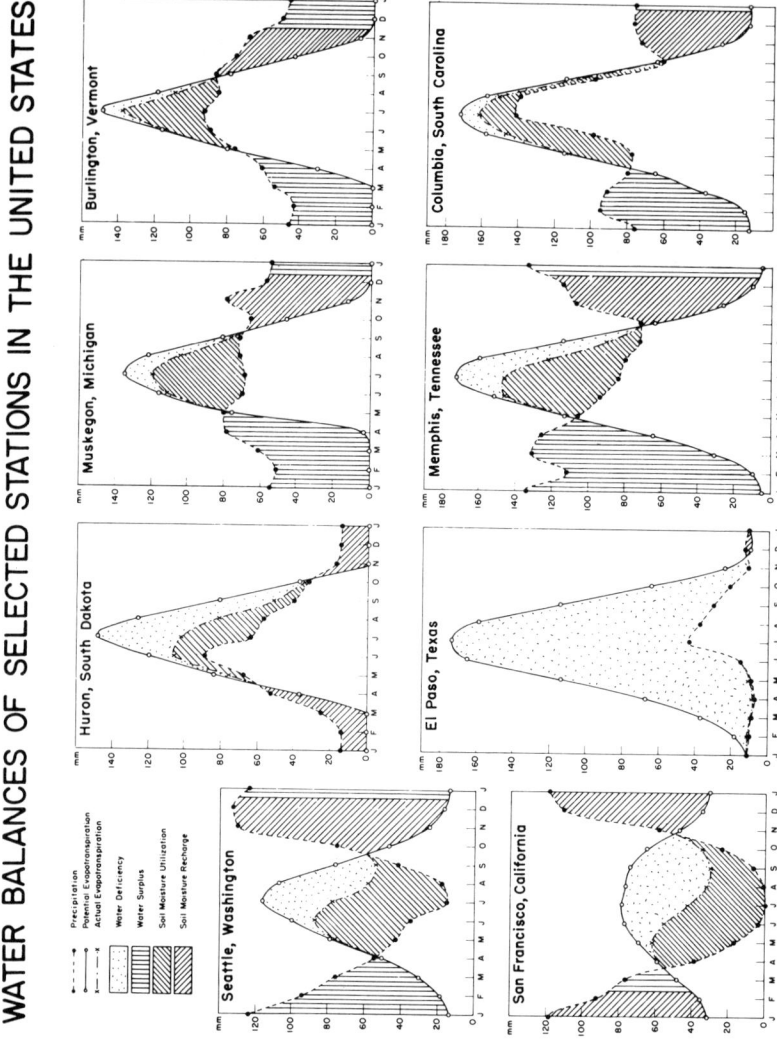

Figure B-7.

WATER BALANCES OF SELECTED STATIONS IN THE U.S.S.R.

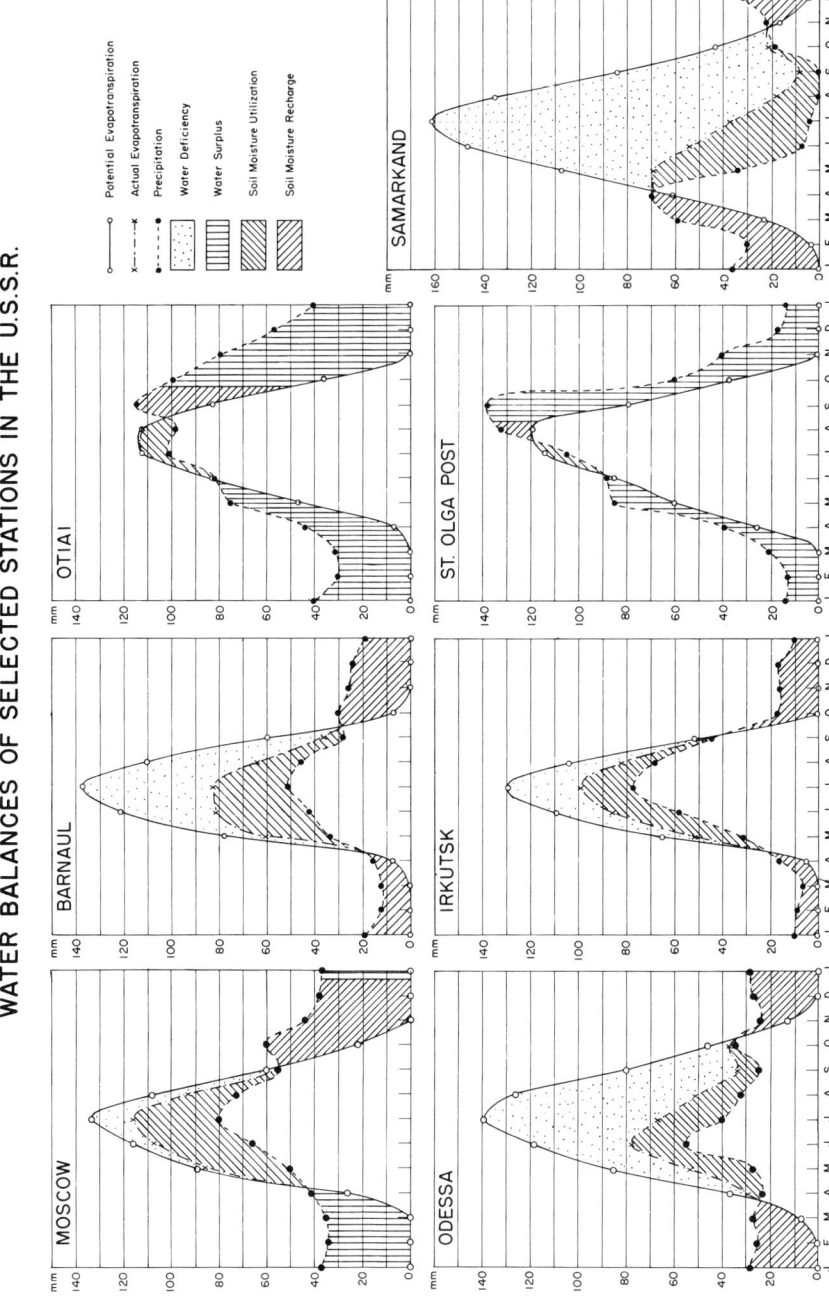

Figure B-8.

Notes

Chapter 2
Evaluation of the Climatic Water Budget

1. N.J. Rosenberg, H.E. Hart, and K.W. Brown, "Evapotranspiration: review of research," MP 20, University of Nebraska, College of Agriculture and Home Economics and Nebraska Water Resources Institute (1968):1-78.

2. J. Dalton, "Experimental essays on the constitution of mixed gases; on the force of steam or vapour from water and other liquids in different temperatures, both in a Torricellian vacuum and in air; on evaporation; and on the expansion of gases by heat," *Manchester Literary and Philosophical Society Memoirs*, vol. 5 (1802):535-602.

3. I.S. Bowen, "The ratio of heat losses by conduction and by evaporation from any water surface," *Physical Review*, vol. 27 (1926):779-89.

4. C.W. Thornthwaite and J.R. Mather, "The water balance," *Publications in Climatology*, Laboratory of Climatology, vol. 8, no. 1 (1955):1-84.

5. H.L. Penman, "Natural evaporation from open water, bare soil and grass," *Proceedings of the Royal Society, Series A*, vol. 193 (1948):120-45; also H.L. Penman, "Evaporation: an introductory survey," *Netherlands Journal of Agricultural Science*, vol. 4, no. 1, (1956):9-29.

6. C.W. Thornthwaite, "An approach toward a rational classification of climate," *Geographical Review*, vol. 38 (1948):55-94.

7. C.W. Thornthwaite and J.R. Mather, "Instructions and tables for computing potential evapotranspiration and the water balance," *Publications in Climatology*, Laboratory of Climatology, vol. 10, no. 3(1957):185-311.

8. H. Gaussen, "Les climats analogues a l'echelle du monde," *Compte Rendu Acad. Agr. France*, vol. 41 (1955).

9. H. Walter, "Die klimagramme als mittel zur deurteilung der klimaver-hältnisse für ökologische, vegetationskundliche und landwirtschafltiche zwecke," *Bericht Deutschen Botanischen Gesellschaft Jahrgang*, vol. 68, no. 8 (1955):331-34.

10. Penman, "Natural evaporation" (1948), and "Evaporation" (1956).

11. W. Baier and G.W. Robertson, "Estimation of latent evaporation from simple weather observation," *Canadian Journal of Plant Science*, vol. 45 (1965):276-84.

12. H.F. Blaney and W.D. Criddle, "Determining water requirements in irrigated areas from climatological and irrigation data," *Soil Conservation Service, Technical Paper 96* (Washington, D.C.: U.S. Department of Agriculture, 1950):1-48; also M.E. Jensen and H.R. Haise, "Estimating evapotranspiration from solar radiation," *Journal Irrigation Drainage Division*, American Society of Civil Engineers, vol. 89 (1963):15-41; also L. Turc, "Le bilan d'eau des sols.

Relations entre les precipitations, l'evaporation et l'ecoulement," *Annales Agronomie*, vol. 5 (1955):5-31.

13. C.W. Thornthwaite and J.R. Mather, "The water balance" (1955):20.

Chapter 3
Environmental Systems

1. D.B. Carter and J.R. Mather, "Climatic classification for environmental biology," *Publications in Climatology*, Laboratory of Climatology, vol. 19, no. 4 (1966):305-95.

2. H. Landsberg, "Trends in climatology," *Science*, vol. 128, no. 3327 (1958):749-58.

3. W.J. Maunder, "A human classification of climate," *Weather*, vol. 17 (1962):3-12; also W.H. Terjung, "Physiologic climates of the conterminous United States: a bioclimatic classification based on man," *Annals, Association of American Geographers*, vol. 56, no. 1 (1966):141-79.

4. Carter and Mather, "Climatic classification," p. 305.

5. W. Köppen, "Versuch einer klassifikation der klimate, vorzugsweise nach ihren beziehungen zur pflanzenwelt," *Geographische Zeitschrift*, vol. 6 (1900):593-611, 657-79.

6. C.W. Thornthwaite, "An approach toward a rational classification of climate," *Geographical Review*, vol. 38 (1948):55-94; also C.W. Thornthwaite and J.R. Mather, "The water budget," *Publications in Climatology*, Laboratory of Climatology, vol. 8, no. 1 (1955):1-104.

7. H.L. Shantz and R. Zon, "Natural vegetation," in *Atlas of American Agriculture* (Washington, D.C.: U.S. Department of Agriculture, 1924); also A.W. Küchler, *Potential Natural Vegetation of Conterminous United States* (New York: American Geographical Society, 1964).

8. J.R. Mather and G.A. Yoshioka, "The role of climate in the distribution of vegetation," *Annals, Association of American Geographers*, vol. 58, no. 1 (1968):29-41.

9. U.S. Geological Survey, *The National Atlas of the United States of America* (Washington, D.C.: U.S. Department of the Interior, 1970).

10. D. Steila, *The Geography of Soils: Formation, Distribution, Management* (Englewood Cliffs, N.J.: Prentice-Hall, 1976).

11. T.E.A. van Hylckama, "The water balance of the earth," *Publications in Climatology*, Laboratory of Climatology, vol. 9, no. 2 (1956):59-117.

Chapter 4
Hydrologic Studies

1. J.R. Mather, "Factors of the climatic water balance over the Delmarva peninsula," *Publications in Climatology*, Laboratory of Climatology, vol. 22, no. 3 (1969):1-129.

2. Ibid., p. 3.

3. U.S. Soil Conservation Service, *National Engineering Handbook, Hydrology, Section 4* (Washington, D.C.: U.S. Department of Agriculture, 1972).

4. M.L. Shelton, "Simulating uniform streamflow by water budget analysis," *Publications in Climatology*, Laboratory of Climatology, vol. 27, no. 2 (1974):1-61.

5. J.C.I. Dooge, "The routing of groundwater recharge through typical elements of linear storage," *International Association of Scientific Hydrology* 52 (1960):286-300.

6. Shelton, "Simulating uniform streamflow," p. 44.

7. H. Lettau and M.W. Baradas, "Evapotranspiration climatonomy II: refinement of parameterization, exemplified by application to the Mabacan River watershed," *Monthly Weather Review*, vol. 101, no. 8 (1973):636-49.

8. Ibid., pp. 637-38.

9. Ibid., p. 643.

10. C.T. Haan, "A water yield model for small watersheds," *Water Resources Research*, vol. 8, no. 1 (1972):58-69.

11. K.M. Kent, "A method for estimating volume and rate of runoff in small watersheds," *Soil Conservation Service* TP-149 (Washington, D.C.: U.S. Department of Agriculture, 1968).

12. U.S. Soil Conservation Service, *National Engineering Handbook Supplement A, Hydrology, Section 4* (Washington, D.C.: U.S. Department of Agriculture, 1957).

13. H.E. Hurst, "The Sudd region of the Nile," *Journal of the Royal Society of Arts*, vol. 81 (1933):721-36.

14. D.B. Carter, "The water balance of the Mediterranean and Black Seas," *Publications in Climatology*, Laboratory of Climatology, vol. 9, no. 3 (1956):125-74.

15. Ibid., p. 152.

16. Ibid., pp. 152-53.

17. Hurst, "The Sudd region," pp. 733-34.

18. G.S. Benton and R.T. Blackburn, "A Comparison of precipitation from maritime and continental air," *Bulletin American Meteorological Society*, vol. 31, no. 7 (1950):254-56; also M.I. Budyko, *The Heat Balance of the Earth's Surface* (Leningrad: Gidrometeoizdat, 1956; trans. N.A. Stepanova, Office of Climatology, U.S. Weather Bureau, Washington, 1958).

19. D.B. Carter, "The water balance of the Lake Maracaibo basin during 1946-53," *Publications in Climatology*, Laboratory of Climatology, vol. 8, no. 3 (1955):209-27.

20. M. Sanderson, "A climatic water balance of the Lake Erie basin," *Publications in Climatology*, Laboratory of Climatology, vol. 19, no. 1 (1966):1-87.

Chapter 5
Agriculture

1. C.W. Thornthwaite, "Report of the committee on transpiration and evaporation, 1943-1944," *Transactions, American Geophysical Union,* part 5 (1945):686-93; and also C.W. Thornthwaite, "Climate and moisture conservation," *Annals, Association of American Geographers,* vol. 37, no. 2 (1947):87-100.

2. J.C. Albrecht, "A climatic model of agricultural productivity in the Missouri River basin," *Publications in Climatology,* Laboratory of Climatology, vol. 24, no. 2 (1971):1-107.

3. J.R. Mather, *Climatology: Fundamentals and Applications* (New York: McGraw-Hill, 1974), pp. 134-35.

4. R. Zahner, "Refinement in empirical functions for realistic soil-moisture regimes under forest cover," in *Forest Hydrology,* ed. W.E. Sopper and H.W. Lull, Proceedings, National Science Foundation Advanced Science Seminar, Pennsylvania State University, August 29-September 10, 1965 (Oxford: Pergamon Press, 1967), pp. 261-74.

5. Zahner, *Forest Hydrology,* p. 269.

6. J.K. Aase, J.R. Wight, and F.H. Siddoway, "Estimating soil water content on native rangeland," *Agricultural Meteorology,* vol. 12 (1973):185-91.

7. R.L. McCown, "An evaluation of the influence of available soil water storage capacity on growing season length and yield of tropical pastures using simple water balance models," *Agricultural Meteorology,* vol. 11 (1973):53-63.

8. W. Baier and D.A. Russelo, *A Computer Program for Estimating Risks of Irrigation Requirements from Climatic Data,* Technical Bulletin 59, Agrometeorological Section, Plant Research Institute, Canadian Department of Agriculture, Ottawa (1968):1-48; also W. Baier, D.Z. Chaput, D.A. Russelo, and W.R. Sharp, *Soil Moisture Estimator Program System,* Technical Bulletin 78, Agrometeorological Section, Plant Research Institute, Canadian Department of Agriculture, Ottawa (1972):1-55.

9. W. Baier and G.W. Robertson, "Estimating supplemental irrigation water requirements for climatological data," *Canadian Agricultural Engineering,* vol. 9 (1967):46-50.

10. C.W. Thornthwaite, "Application of the mathematical model to the movement of calcium in an agricultural soil," in J.R. Mather and J.K. Nakamura, "The climatic and hydrologic factors affecting the redistribution of strontium in soils," *Publications in Climatology,* Laboratory of Climatology, vol. 15, no. 1 (1962):53-61.

11. Ibid., p. 54.

12. Ibid., p. 55.

13. T.L. Lyon and J.A. Bizzell, "Lysimeter experiment-IV records for tanks 17 to 20 during the years 1922 to 1933 and for tanks 13 to 16 during

the years 1913 to 1928," *Memoir 194, Cornell University Agricultural Experiment Station* (1936).

14. Ismail Bin Hj Ahmad, "A water budget approach to the prediction of caliche depths in soils of the western United States," Master of Arts thesis, Department of Geography, Ohio University, Athens, Ohio, 1976.

15. W.R. Rouse, "Moisture balance of Barbados and its influence on sugar cane yield," Master of Science thesis, Department of Geography, McGill University, Montreal, Canada, 1962.

16. J.R. Mather, "Irrigation agriculture in humid areas," in *Eclectic climatology*, ed. A. Court, Yearbook, Association of Pacific Coast Geographers, vol. 30 (1968):107-22.

17. Jen-Hu Chang, R.B. Campbell and F.E. Robinson, "On the relationship between water and sugar cane yield in Hawaii," *Agronomy Journal*, vol. 55, no. 5 (1963):450-53.

18. G.W. Hurst and L.P. Smith, "Grass-growing days," in *Weather and Agriculture*, ed. J.A. Taylor (London: Pergamon Press, Symposium Publishing Division, 1967), pp. 147-55.

19. L.P. Smith, "Meadow hay yields," *Outlook in Agriculture*, vol. 3, no. 5 (1956):219.

20. Hurst and Smith, "Grass-growing days."

21. C.W. Rose, J.E. Begg, G.F. Byrne, B.W.R. Torssell, and J.H. Goncz, "A simulation model of growth-field environment relationships for Townsville stylo (*Stylosanthes humilis* H.B.K.) pasture," *Agricultural Meteorology*, vol. 10 (1972):161-83.

22. Ibid., p. 167; also M.J. Fisher, "The effects of superphosphate on the growth and development of Townsville stylo (*Stylosanthes humilis*) in pure ungrazed swards at Katherine, N.T.," *Australian Journal of Experimental Agriculture and Animal Husbandry*, vol. 10 (1970):716-24.

23. J. Lewin, "A simple soil water simulation model for assessing the irrigation requirements of wheat," *Israel Journal of Agricultural Research*, vol. 22, no. 4 (1972):201-13.

24. Ibid., p. 209.

25. A.R. Mack and W.S. Ferguson, "A moisture stress index for wheat by means of a modulated soil moisture budget," *Canadian Journal of Plant Science*, vol. 48 (1968):535-43.

26. R.M. Holmes and G.W. Robertson, "A modulated soil moisture budget," *Monthly Weather Review*, vol. 87 (1959):101-106.

27. Mack and Ferguson, "A moisture stress index," p. 543.

28. H.A. Nix and E.A. Fitzpatrick, "An index of crop water stress related to wheat and grain sorghum yields," *Agricultural Meteorology*, vol. 6 (1969):321-37.

29. G.W. Smith, "The relation between rainfall, soil water and yield of copra on a coconut estate in Trinidad," *Journal of Applied Ecology*, vol. 3 (1966):117-25.

30. A.Y.M. Yao, "Evaluating climatic limitations for a specific agricultural enterprise," *Agricultural Meteorology*, vol. 12 (1973):65-73.

31. Ibid., p. 70.

32. Ibid., pp. 71-72.

Chapter 6
Forest Ecosystems

1. J. Major, "A climatic index to vascular plant activity," *Ecology,* vol. 44, no. 3 (1963):485-98; also M.L. Rosenzweig, "Net primary productivity of terrestrial communities: prediction from climatological data," *The American Naturalist,* vol. 102, no. 923 (1968):67-74.

2. Rosenzweig, "Net primary productivity," p. 71.

3. W.D. Sellers, *Physical Climatology* (Chicago: University of Chicago Press, 1965).

4. H. Lieth and E. Box, "Evapotranspiration and primary productivity: C.W. Thornthwaite Memorial model," *Publications in Climatology,* Laboratory of Climatology, vol. 25, no. 3 (1972):37-46.

5. H. Lieth, "Modeling the primary productivity of the world," in *Primary Productivity of the Biosphere,* ed. H. Lieth and R.H. Whittaker, (New York: Springer-Verlag, 1975), pp. 237-63.

6. Lieth and Box, "Evapotranspiration," p. 43.

7. R. Geiger, *The Atmosphere of the Earth* (Darmstadt, Germany: Justus Perthes, 1965).

8. Lieth and Box, "Evapotranspiration," p. 44.

9. H.C. Fritts, "Growth-rings of trees: their correlation with climate," *Science*, vol. 154, no. 3752 (1966):973-79.

10. C. Manogaran, "Economic feasibility of irrigating southern pines," *Water Resources Research,* vol. 9, no. 6 (1973):1485-96.

11. Ibid., p. 1487.

12. Ibid., p. 1489.

13. F.M. Buckingham and F.W. Woods, "Loblolly pine (*Pinus taeda* L) as influenced by soil moisture and other environmental factors," *Journal of Applied Ecology,* vol. 6 (1969):47-59.

14. Ibid., p. 52.

15. Ibid., p. 54.

16. D.F. Fourt and W.H. Hinson, "Water relations of tree crops: a comparison between Corsican pine and Douglas fir in South-East England," *Journal of Applied Ecology,* vol. 7 (1970):295-309.

17. Ibid., pp. 305-307.

18. J.E. Deeming, J.W. Lancaster, M.A. Fosberg, R.W. Furman, and M.J. Schroeder, *National Fire-Danger Rating System* (Fort Collins, Col.: U.S. Depart-

ment of Agriculture, Rocky Mountain Forest and Range Experiment Station, 1974).

19. D.A. Haines and R.W. Sando, "Climatic conditions preceding historically great fires in the North Central Region," *Forest Service Research Paper NC-34* (St. Paul, Minn.: U.S. Department of Agriculture, North Central Forest Experiment Station, 1969).

20. Ibid., pp. 14-15.

21. V. Meentemeyer, "Climatic water budget approach to forest problems. I. The prediction of forest fire hazard through moisture budgeting," *Publications in Climatology,* Laboratory of Climatology, vol. 27, no. 1 (1974):1-34.

22. J. Kittredge, "Some characteristics of forest floors in California," *Journal of Forestry,* vol. 53 (1955):645-47.

23. Meentemeyer, "Climatic water budget approach to forest problems," p. 19.

24. Ibid., p. 21.

25. Ibid., p. 27.

26. P. Mikola, "Comparative experiments on decomposition rates of forest litter in southern and northern Finland," *Oikos,* vol. 11 (1960):161-66; also J. Van der Drift, "The disappearance of litter in mull and mor in connection with weather conditions and the activity of the macrofauna," in *Soil Organisms,* ed. J. Doeksen and J. Van der Drift (Amsterdam: North Holland Publishing Company, 1963), pp. 124-32; also J. Van der Drift, "The effects of animal activity in the litter layer," in *Experimental Pedology,* ed. E.G. Hallsworth and D.V. Crawford (London: Butterworths, 1965).

27. V. Meentemeyer, "Climatic water budget approach to forest problems. II. The prediction of regional differences in decomposition rate of organic debris," *Publications in Climatology,* Laboratory of Climatology, vol. 27, no. 1 (1974):35-74.

28. Ibid., pp. 63-64.

29. L.S. Kalkstein, "The effect of climate upon outbreaks of the southern pine beetle," *Publications in Climatology,* Laboratory of Climatology, vol. 27, no. 3 (1974):1-65.

30. Southern Pine Beetle Action Council, "Action plans to control the southern pine beetle" (Atlanta, Ga.: Southern Pine Beetle Action Council, 1974).

31. J.P. Vite, "The influence of water supply on oleoresin exudation pressure and resistance to bark beetle attack in *Pinus Ponderosa,*" *Contribution of the Boyce Thompson Institute,* vol. 21 (1961):37-66.

32. Kalkstein, "The effect of climate," pp. 4-5.

33. E.W. King, "Rainfall and epidemics of the southern pine beetle," *Environmental Entomology,* vol. 1 (1971):279-85.

34. Kalkstein, "The effect of climate," pp. 30-45.

35. Ibid., p. 47.

Chapter 7
Urban Planning

1. L.B. Leopold, "Hydrology for urban land planning–a guidebook on the hydrologic effects of urban land use," *Geological Survey Circular 554* (Washington, D.C.: U.S. Department of the Interior, 1968), p. 1.

2. Ibid., p. 2.

3. B.J. Hartmann, "The effect of urbanization on annual water yield," in J.R. Mather, F.J. Swaye and B.J. Hartmann, "The influence of the climatic water balance on conditions in the estuarine environment," *Publications in Climatology*, Laboratory of Climatology, vol. 25, no. 1 (1972):53-55.

4. J.C. Albrecht, "Alterations in the hydrologic cycle induced by urbanization in Northern New Castle County, Delaware: magnitudes and projections" (Newark, Del.: Technical Completion Report, O.W.R.R. Project No. A-017-DEL, University of Delaware, 1974).

5. R.A. Muller, "A water balance evaluation of the effects of urbanization on water yield in Metropolitan Northeastern New Jersey," Appendix H. in *Benefits from Integrated Water Management in Urban Areas–The Case of the New York Metropolitan Region,* by L. Zobler and G.W. Cary, Report submitted to the Office of Water Resources and Research (Washington, D.C.: U.S. Department of the Interior, 1969).

6. Leopold, "Hydrology for urban land planning," p. 3.

7. J.R. Sheaffer, "Flood-to-peak interval," in *Papers on Flood Problems,* ed. G.F. White (Chicago: Research Paper No. 70, Department of Geography, University of Chicago, 1961), pp. 95-113.

8. Leopold, "Hydrology for urban land planning," p. 5.

9. Ibid., p. 9.

10. Ibid., p. 14.

11. W.L. Graf, "The impact of suburbanization on fluvial geomorphology," *Water Resources Research*, vol. 11, no. 5 (1975):690-92.

12. Ibid., p. 692.

13. E.J. Pluhowski, "Urbanization and its effect on the temperature of the streams on Long Island, New York," *Geological Survey Professional Paper 627-D* (Washington, D.C.: U.S. Department of Interior, 1970).

14. Hartmann, "The effects of urbanization on annual water yield," pp. 53-55.

15. Muller, "A water balance evaluation of the effects of urbanization"; also H.W. Lull and W.E. Sopper, "Hydrologic effects from urbanization of forested watersheds in the Northeast," *Research Paper NE-146* (Washington, D.C.: Forest Service, U.S. Department of Agriculture, 1969).

16. L.H. Antoine, "Drainage and best use of urban land," *Public Works,* vol. 95 (1964):88-90.

17. R.A. Muller, "Water balance evaluation of effects of subdivisions on

water yield in Middlesex County, New Jersey," *Proceedings of the Association of American Geographers,* vol. 1 (1969):122.

18. D.G. Fenn, K.J. Hanley, and T.V. DeGeare, "Use of the water balance method for predicting leachate generation from solid waste disposal sites," *Solid Waste Information (SW-168)* (Cincinnati, Ohio: U.S. Environmental Protection Agency, 1975).

19. Ibid., pp. 19-22.

20. O.L. Franke and N.E. McClymonds, "Summary of the hydrologic situation on Long Island, New York, as a guide to water management alternatives," in *Hydrology and Some Effects of Urbanization on Long Island, New York* (Washington, D.C.: Geological Survey Professional Paper 627F, U.S. Department of Interior, 1972).

21. Ibid., p. 37.

22. Ibid., p. 39.

23. Ibid., p. 48.

24. Ibid., pp. 52-55.

Chapter 8
Society's Impact on the Water Budget

1. H. Landsberg, "The definition and determination of climatic changes, fluctuations and outlooks," in *Atmospheric Quality and Climatic Change,* ed. R.J. Kopec (Chapel Hill: Papers of the Second Carolina Geographical Symposium, Studies in Geography, No. 9, University of North Carolina, 1976), p. 59.

2. Massachusetts Institute of Technology, *Inadvertent Climatic Modification* (Cambridge, Mass.: Report of the Study of Man's Impact on Climate [SMIC], MIT Press, 1971).

3. B. Seddon, "Prehistoric climate and agriculture: review of recent paleoecological investigations," in *Weather and Agriculture,* ed. J.S. Taylor (Oxford: Pergamon Press, 1967), pp. 173-85.

4. E. Eckholm and L.R. Brown, "Spreading deserts—the hand of man," *Worldwatch Paper* 13 (Washington, D.C.: Worldwatch Institute, 1977).

5. Massachusetts Institute of Technology, *Inadvertent Climatic Modification,* p. 63.

6. R.A. Muller, "The effect of reforestation on water yield: a case study using energy and water balance models for the Allegheny plateau, New York," *Publications in Climatology,* Laboratory of Climatology, vol. 10, no. 3 (1966):251-62.

7. A.R. Hibbert, "Forest treatment effects on water yield," in *Forest Hydrology,* ed. W.E. Sopper and H.W. Lull, Proceedings of a N.S.F. Advanced Science Seminar held at Penn State University, University Park, PA, August 29-September 10, 1965 (Oxford: Pergamon Press, 1967), pp. 536-38.

214

8. Ibid., pp. 527-43.

9. H.C. Pereira, *Land Use and Water Resources* (Cambridge: At the University Press, 1973), p. 89.

10. Muller, "The effect of reforestation on water yield," pp. 251-304.

11. Ibid., pp. 295-97.

12. P.E. Waggoner, P.M. Miller, and H.C. DeRoo, "Plastic mulching: principles and benefits," *Bulletin* 634 (New Haven: The Connecticut Agricultural Experiment Station, 1960).

13. D.C. Davenport, R.M. Hagan, and P.E. Martin, "Antitranspirants—uses and effects on plant life," *California Agriculture,* vol. 23, no. 5 (1969):14-16.

14. H.E. Landsberg, "The climate of towns," in *Man's Role in Changing the Face of the Earth,* ed. W.L. Thomas (Chicago: University of Chicago Press, 1956), pp. 592-96.

15. J.T. Peterson, "The climate of cities: a survey of recent literature," *National Air Pollution Control Administration* AP-59 (1969); also S.A. Changnon, Jr., "Recent studies of urban effects on precipitation in the United States," *Bulletin American Meteorological Society,* vol. 50 (1969):411-21; also W. Terjung, "Climatic modification," in *Perspectives on Environment,* ed. J.R. Manners and M.W. Mikesell (Washington, D.C.: Association of American Geographers Publication 13, Commission on College Geography, 1974), pp. 105-51.

16. S.A. Changnon, Jr., "The LaPorte weather anomaly—fact or fiction?" *Bulletin American Meteorological Society*, vol. 49, no. 1 (1968):4-11.

17. S.A. Changnon, Jr., F.A. Huff, and R.G. Semonin, "METROMEX: An investigation of inadvertent weather modification," *Bulletin American Meteorological Society,* vol. 52, no. 10 (1971):958-67.

18. E. Fels and R. Keller, "World register on manmade lakes," Paper presented at COWAR Symposium on Man-Made Lakes, Knoxville, Tennessee, 1971.

19. U.S. National Academy of Sciences, *Weather and Climate: Modification Problems and Prospects* (Washington, D.C.: National Academy of Sciences-National Research Council Publication 1350, 1966).

20. J. Warner and S. Twomey, "The production of cloud nuclei by cane fires and their effect on cloud droplet concentration," *Journal of Atmospheric Science,* vol. 25 (1967):704-706.

21. D.R. Satterlund, "Combined weather and vegetation modification promises synergistic streamflow response," *Journal of Hydrology,* vol. 9 (1969):155-66.

22. N.H. Crawford, "Hydrologic consequences of weather modification: case studies," in *Human Dimensions of Weather Modification,* ed. W.R. Derrick Sewell (Chicago: Department of Geography Research Paper 105, University of Chicago Press, 1966), pp. 41-57.

23. Satterlund, "Combined weather and vegetation modification," pp. 160-64.

Glossary

Absorption blocks Blocks of gypsum or other similar material usually containing electrodes, placed in direct contact with the soil to measure changing soil moisture content by means of changing electrical resistance or conductance.

Actual evapotranspiration The actual loss of water from combined plant and soil surfaces under varying conditions of soil moisture content and vegetation cover.

Advection Horizontal flow of the air either at the surface or aloft.

Air mass A large body of air with fairly uniform temperature and moisture characteristics in a horizontal direction.

Albedo Percentage of the incoming solar radiation that is reflected from a surface.

Ambient temperature The temperature in the immediate surrounding atmosphere.

Antecedent moisture condition A value indicating the degree of wetness at a place or in a basin at the beginning of a storm.

Antitranspirant A substance applied to either the surface or subsurface portions of plants (external or internal) to reduce transpiration water losses.

Artesian aquifer A water-bearing strata (surrounded by impervious layers) in which the water is under sufficient pressure so that it will rise above the zone of saturation if tapped.

Atmometer An instrument involving a porous, ceramic bulb filled with water used to estimate the rate of evaporation into the atmosphere or the evaporation power of the air.

Basin lag The time between the occurrence of the center of mass of the precipitation and the center of mass of the discharge hydrograph.

Cambium The single soft row of living cells between the bark and living wood of a tree.

Cation exchange capacity A measure of the total exchangeable cations that can be held by the soil (cations are ions having a positive charge).

Climatonomy The term implies a more physical-mathematical approach to the problems of climate as opposed to the more empirical and statistical approach of the traditional climatology.

Condensation The change of state of water vapor to a liquid or solid.

Coniferous forest A forest of evergreen, cone-bearing trees with needle-shaped leaves.

Control basin A watershed managed under the initial conditions of vegetation cover that is used as a standard in comparison with a second basin that has been modified in some manner.

Convection Transfer of heat by vertical movement of heated particles.

Deciduous forest A forest of trees that drop their leaves at some regular season each year.

Delayed evaporivity That portion of the evapotranspiration derived from stored soil moisture.

Dewpoint temperature The temperature at which a sample of air being cooled reaches saturation; further cooling results in condensation of water vapor.

Duff (forest) The organic material on the forest floor in the process of decomposition.

Eddy kinetic energy The total kinetic energy of a fluid less that energy attributable to the mean motion of the fluid.

Effective precipitation The precipitation that actually enters the soil and is available for plant use, storage, or recharge to the water table; precipitation minus the direct overland runoff.

Effluent stream Surface stream fed by water from the soil, from groundwater storage, and from overland flow.

Evaporation Process involving the change of state of water from liquid to vapor.

Evapotranspiration The combined evaporation from the surface of the ground and the transpiration from the vegetation covering the ground.

Evapotranspirometer A soil-filled, vegetation-covered field tank used to estimate the rate of water loss by evapotranspiration from observations of water added, percolation from the soil mass, and changes in storage in the tank.

Field capacity The quantity of water remaining in the capillaries of an originally saturated soil after several days of drainage.

Flood-to-peak interval The period of time from the initial occurrence of a storm-induced flood stage in a stream discharge to the peak discharge resulting from that particular storm.

Gravimetric plug A porous ceramic block placed in direct contact with the soil, used to measure changing soil moisture content by means of its change in weight.

Gravitational water The water in the pore spaces in soil that will drain downward under the force of gravity.

Groundwater table The upper limit of the zone of saturation, the zone where water completely fills the pore spaces of the soil or rock material.

Hydrograph (stream) A graphical relation of the changing rate of streamflow over time.

Hydrologic cycle The unending flow of water in all its various states from ocean to atmosphere, to land, and back to the ocean again.

Hydrologic soil group Those soils with similar runoff characteristics under similar vegetation covers and storm conditions.

Hygroscopic particles Particles such as dust or salt that attract and absorb moisture.

Ice Nuclei Any atmospheric particle about which ice crystals form by freezing.

Immediate evaporivity That portion of the precipitation which is lost immediately by evapotranspiration and does not enter into a change in soil moisture storage or runoff.

Index of thermal efficiency Potential evapotranspiration in the Thornthwaite system is an index of thermal efficiency expressing plant development in terms of the water needed.

Infiltration The passage of water from the soil surface into the pore spaces in the soil.

Influent stream Surface stream fed only by water from melting snow or excessive precipitation, with streamwater being lost to the water table.

Insolation The short-wave radiant energy received from the sun.

Interception The process by which vegetation leaves and branches prevent a portion of each fall of precipitation from reaching the soil.

Isohyet A line on a map connecting places having the same depth of precipitation.

Latent heat The heat absorbed without change in temperature by a substance while changing state from a liquid to a vapor or from a solid to a liquid; this heat is released as the change of state is reversed.

Leaching The process of washing material (organic matter or mineral salts) from one layer of soil to a lower layer by percolating water.

Lysimeter A field tank used to measure the quality, quantity, or rate of downward water movement through a block of soil.

Mesothermal Moderate heat or temperature; usually refers to a type of climate marked by moderate temperature with ample sunshine.

Moisture deficit See water deficit.

Moisture detention The total amount of moisture that is held temporarily on or within the soil.

Moisture index An expression of the relative moistness or aridity of a climate, derived from a comparison of the climatic supply of water (precipitation) with the climatic need for water (potential evapotranspiration) $Im = 100$ $(\frac{P}{PE} - 1)$ in the Thornthwaite relation.

Moisture surplus See water surplus.

Mulch A protective layer of natural or artificial material (such as straw, wood chips, plastic sheets, paper) applied to the soil surface.

Net basin supply The water contributed to a whole lake system by the individual lake basin; NBS = Runoff + Precipitation − Evaporation for the individual basin.

Net radiometer An instrument to measure the difference between all incoming long- and short-wave radiation and all outgoing long- and short-wave radiation at a point.

Neutron logger A device to estimate the moisture content in a soil layer by measuring the return flow of scattered neutron radiation from a nearby point source.

Oleoresin exudation pressure The pressure at which resin is being transported through the phloem of the tree.

Perched water table The upper surface of a relatively limited groundwater body supported above the general groundwater, usually by an impervious layer of soil or rock.

Percolation The slow movement of water through the pore spaces of rock or soil.

Phreatophyte A plant that generally extracts its water directly from the water table or from the soil layer just above it.

Plant biomass The portion of a particular habitat that consists of living matter from plants.

Potable water Water that is suitable for human consumption.

Potential evapotranspiration Water loss from a homogeneous, closed, vigorously growing vegetation cover that never suffers from a lack of water.

Potential water recharge A period in which the precipitation supply exceeds the climatic demands for water (P is greater than PE) so that water is available to increase the storage in the root zone of the soil.

Precipitation General term covering all forms of falling moisture whether liquid or solid.

Pumping galleries (infiltration galleries) Generally horizontal conduits that intercept the groundwater table, providing a constant supply of water to the gallery (or conduit) for pumping. Often run parallel to a river course.

Relative humidity The ratio of the actual amount of moisture in the air to the maximum amount of moisture in saturated air at that temperature.

Runoff Flow of water from a basin or drainage area overland or as water in stream channels.

Saturation deficit The difference between the saturation vapor pressure at a surface and the actual vapor pressure of the surroundings.

Saturation vapor pressure The partial pressure exerted by the water vapor in the atmosphere when the air is saturated (100 percent humidity).

Skimming well A shallow well permitting the withdrawal of fresh groundwater existing as a thin lens above salt water; a shallow well filled by overflow from a stream or from a water table to avoid contamination by sand, silt, debris, or salt water.

Soil moisture recharge Moisture added to storage in the root zone of the soil during periods when potential evapotranspiration is less than precipitation.

Soil moisture storage Moisture (usually expressed as a depth) stored in the capillaries of the root zone of a soil against the pull of gravity.

Soil moisture tension The force by which water is held in the pore spaces of the soil against the pull of gravity.

Soil moisture utilization Moisture removed from the soil by vegetation during periods when potential evapotranspiration is greater than actual evapotranspiration.

Synergistic Action Any action in which the combined effect of two distinct components is greater than the sum of their individual effects.

Tensiometer A device consisting of a porous cup and a vacuum gage for measuring the tension with which water is held in the capillaries of the soil.

Throughflow Water that moves downslope through the upper soil layers ultimately reaching surface water courses.

Tile drains A network of buried porous pipes used to speed the flow of water through the soil and hence improve drainage.

Transpiration The loss of water in vapor form from a living plant (principally through the leaves).

Tree crown The upper portion of a tree, including both branches and foliage.

Tree growth ring The formation of two concentric layers of new wood growth each year of varying thickness used as a basis for determining tree age and possible climatic conditions during formation.

Urban heat island The urban-centered region of higher than normal temperatures (compared to rural areas nearby) caused by changes in the heat and moisture budgets within the built-up area.

Vapor pressure gradient The difference in vapor pressure between an evaporating surface and the air at a given distance from the surface.

Vascular plants Plants with veins, ducts, or other vessels aiding in the flow of liquids within them.

Water budget Daily, monthly, or annual accounting of the total moisture gains and losses at a given place or over a given area.

Water deficit The amount by which available moisture (either from precipitation or stored soil moisture) fails to satisfy the climatic demands for water.

Watershed The total surface area above a particular point on a stream that contributes water to streamflow at that point; also called drainage basin or catchment basin.

Water surplus Soil moisture over and above that needed for evapotranspiration or soil moisture recharge which is lost from the soil by subsurface flow; gravitational water that moves out of the root zone of the soil.

Wilting point The amount of moisture in a soil when plant roots can no longer extract water for growth.

Bibliography

Aase, J.K., J.R. Wight, and F.H. Siddoway. "Estimating Soil Water Content on Native Rangeland." *Agricultural Meteorology,* vol. 12 (1973).

Ahmad, Ismail bin Hj. "A Water Budget Approach to the Prediction of Caliche Depths in Soils of the Western United States." Master of Arts thesis, Department of Geography, Ohio University, Athens, Ohio, 1976.

Albrecht, J.C. "A Climatic Model of Agricultural Productivity in the Missouri River Basin." *Publications in Climatology,* Laboratory of Climatology, vol. 24, no. 2 (1971).

Albrecht, J.C. "Alterations in the Hydrologic Cycle Induced by Urbanization in Northern New Castle County, Delaware: Magnitudes and Projections." *Technical Completion Report, O.W.R.R. Project No. A-017-Del.* Newark, Del.: University of Delaware, 1974.

Antoine, L.H. "Drainage and Best Use of Urban Land." *Public Works,* vol. 95 (1964).

Baier, W. "Recent Advancements in the Use of Standard Climatic Data for Estimating Soil Moisture." *Annals of Arid Zones,* vol. 6, no. 1 (1967).

Baier, W., and G.W. Robertson. "Estimation of Latent Evaporation from Simple Weather Observations." *Canadian Journal of Plant Science,* vol. 45 (1965).

Baier, W., and G.W. Robertson. "A New Versatile Soil Moisture Budget." *Canadian Journal of Plant Science,* vol. 46 (1966).

Baier, W., and G.W. Robertson. "Estimating Supplemental Irrigation Water Requirements for Climatological Data." *Canadian Agricultural Engineering,* vol. 9 (1967).

Baier, W., and D.A. Russelo. "A Computer Program for Estimating Risks of Irrigation Requirements from Climatic Data." *Technical Bulletin 59.* Ottawa: Agrometeorological Section, Plant Research Institute, Canadian Department of Agriculture, 1968.

Baier, W., D.Z. Chaput, D.A. Russelo, and W.R. Sharp. "Soil Moisture Estimator Program System." *Technical Bulletin 78.* Ottawa: Agrometeorological Section, Plant Research Institute, Canadian Department of Agriculture, 1972.

Bates, C.G., and A.J. Henry. "Forest and Streamflow Experiment at Wagon Wheel Gap, Colorado." *Monthly Weather Review, Supplement 30.* Washington, D.C.: U.S. Government Printing Office, 1928.

Benton, G.S., and R.T. Blackburn. "A Comparison of Precipitation from Maritime and Continental Air." *Bulletin, American Meteorological Society,* vol. 31, no. 7 (1950).

Benton, G.S., R.T. Blackburn, and V.O. Snead. "The Role of the Atmosphere in the Hydrologic Cycle." *Transactions American Geophysical Union,* vol. 31, no. 1 (1950).

Blaney, H.F., and W.D. Criddle. "Determining Water Requirements in Irrigated

Areas from Climatological and Irrigation Data." *Soil Conservation Service Technical Paper 96*. Washington, D.C.: U.S. Department of Agriculture, 1950.

Blumenstock, D.I., and C.W. Thornthwaite. "Climate and the World Pattern," in *Climate and Man*, Yearbook of Agriculture. Washington D.C.: U.S. Department of Agriculture, 1941.

Bowen, I.S. "The Ratio of Heat Losses by Conduction and by Evaporation from Any Water Surface." *Physical Review*, vol. 27 (1926).

Buckingham, F.M., and F.W. Woods. "Loblolly Pine (*Pinus taeda* L.) as Influenced by Soil Moisture and Other Environmental Factors." *Journal of Applied Ecology*, vol. 6 (1969).

Budyko, M.I. *The Heat Balance of the Earth's Surface*. Leningrad: Gidrometeoizdat (trans. N.A. Stepanova, Office of Climatology, U.S. Weather Bureau, 1958), 1956.

Budyko, M.I. *Climate and Life*. Leningrad: Hydrological Publishing House, 1971.

Carter, D.B. "The Water Balance of the Lake Maracaibo Basin During 1946-53." *Publications in Climatology*, Laboratory of Climatology, vol. 8, no. 3 (1955).

Carter, D.B. "The Water Balance of the Mediterranean and Black Seas." *Publications in Climatology*, Laboratory of Climatology, vol. 9, no. 3 (1956).

Carter, D.B., and J.R. Mather. "Climatic Classification for Environmental Biology." *Publications in Climatology*, Laboratory of Climatology, vol. 19, no. 4 (1966).

Chang, Jen-Hu, R.B. Campbell, and F.E. Robinson. "On the Relationship between Water and Sugar Cane Yield in Hawaii." *Agronomy Journal*, vol. 55, no. 5 (1963).

Changnon, S.A., Jr. "The LaPorte Weather Anomaly—Fact or Fiction?" *Bulletin, American Meteorological Society*, vol. 49, no. 1 (1968).

Changnon, S.A., Jr. "Recent Studies of Urban Effects on Precipitation in the United States." *Bulletin, American Meteorological Society*, vol. 50 (1969).

Changnon, S.A. Jr. F.A. Huff, and R.G. Semonin. "METROMEX: An Investigation of Inadvertent Weather Modification." *Bulletin, American Meteorological Society*, vol. 52, no. 10 (1971).

Cooper, C.F., and W.C. Jolly. "Ecological Effects of Weather Modification: A Problem Analysis." *Report on Contract 14-06-D-6576*, University of Michigan, School of Natural Resources. Washington, D.C.: U.S. Department of the Interior, Bureau of Reclamation, Office of Atmospheric Water Research, 1969.

Crawford, N.H. "Hydrologic Consequences of Weather Modification: Case Studies," in *Human Dimensions of Weather Modification*, ed. W.R. Derrick Sewell, Department of Geography Research Paper 105. Chicago, Ill.: University of Chicago, 1966.

Dalton, J. "Experimental Essays on the Constitution of Mixed Gases; On the Force of Steam or Vapour from Water and Other Liquids in Different Temperatures, both in a Torricellian Vacuum and in Air; On Evaporation; and on the Expansion of Gases by Heat." *Manchester Literary and Philosophical Society Memoirs,* vol. 5 (1802).

Davenport, D.C., R.M. Hagan, and P.E. Martin. "Antitranspirants . . . Uses and Effects on Plant Life." *California Agriculture,* vol. 23, no. 5 (1969).

Deeming, J.E., J.W. Lancaster, M.A. Fosberg, R.W. Furman, and M.J. Schroeder. *National Fire-Danger Rating System.* Fort Collins, Col.: Rocky Mountain Forest and Range Experiment Station, U.S. Department of Agriculture, 1974.

Dooge, J.C.I. "The Routing of Groundwater Recharge through Typical Elements of Linear Storage." *International Association of Scientific Hydrology, Publication 52* (1960).

Eckholm, E., and L.R. Brown. "Spreading Deserts—The Hand of Man." *Worldwatch Paper 13.* Washington, D.C.: Worldwatch Institute, 1977.

Fels, E., and R. Keller. "World Register on Man-Made Lakes." Presented at COWAR Symposium on Man-Made Lakes, Knoxville, Tenn., 1971.

Fenn, D.G., K.J. Hanley, and T.V. DeGeare. "Use of the Water Balance Method for Predicting Leachate Generation from Solid Waste Disposal Sites." *Solid Waste Information (SW-168).* Cincinnati, Ohio: U.S. Environmental Protection Agency, 1975.

Fisher, M.J. "The Effects of Superphosphate on the Growth and Development of Townsville Stylo (*Stylosanthes humilis*) in Pure Ungrazed Swards at Katherine, N.T." *Australian Journal Experimental Agriculture and Animal Husbandry,* vol. 10 (1970).

Fourt, D.F., and W.H. Hinson. "Water Relations of Tree Crops: A Comparison between Corsican Pine and Douglas Fir in South-East England." *Journal of Applied Ecology,* vol. 7 (1970).

Franke, O.L., and N.E. McClymonds. "Summary of the Hydrologic Situation on Long Island, New York, as a Guide to Water-Management Alternatives," in *Hydrology and Some Effects of Urbanization on Long Island, New York.* Geological Survey Professional Paper 627F. Washington, D.C.: U.S. Department of the Interior, 1972.

Fritts, H.C. "Growth-Rings of Trees: Their Correlation with Climate." *Science,* vol. 154, no. 3752 (1966).

Gaussen, H. "Les Climats Analogues a l'Echelle du Monde." *Compte Rendu Acad. Agr. France*, vol. 41 (1955).

Geiger, R. *The Atmosphere of the Earth.* Darmstadt, Germany: Justus Perthes, 1965. 12 wall maps and text.

Graf, W.L. "The Impact of Suburbanization on Fluvial Geomorphology." *Water Resources Research,* vol. 11, no. 5 (1975).

Haan, C.T. "A Water Yield Model for Small Watersheds." *Water Resources Research*, vol. 8, no. 1 (1972).

Haines, D.A., and R.W. Sando. "Climatic Conditions Preceding Historically Great Fires in the North Central Region." *Forest Service Research Paper NC-34.* St. Paul, Minn.: North Central Forest Experiment Station, U.S. Department of Agriculture, 1969.

Heath, R.C., B.L. Foxworthy, and P. Cohen. "The Changing Pattern of Ground-Water Development on Long Island, New York." *Geological Survey Circular 524.* Washington, D.C.: U.S. Department of the Interior, 1966.

Hewlett, J.D., and W.L. Nutter. *An Outline of Forest Hydrology.* Athens: University of Georgia Press, 1969.

Hibbert, A.R. "Forest Treatment Effects on Water Yield," in *Forest Hydrology,* ed. W.E. Sopper and H.W. Lull. Proceedings National Science Foundation Advanced Science Seminar, Pennsylvania State University, August 29-September 10, 1965. Oxford: Pergamon Press, 1967.

Hidore, J.J. "The Effects of Accidental Weather Modification on the Flow of the Kankakee River." *Bulletin, American Meteorological Society,* vol. 53 (1971).

Holmes, R.M., and G.W. Robertson. "A Modulated Soil Moisture Budget." *Monthly Weather Review,* vol. 87 (1959).

Holzman, B., and H.C.S. Thom. "The La Porte Precipitation Anomaly." *Bulletin, American Meteorological Society,* vol. 51 (1970).

Hurst, H.E. "The Sudd Region of the Nile." *Journal Royal Society of Arts,* vol. 81 (1933).

Hurst, G.W., and L.P. Smith. "Grass Growing Days," in *Weather and Agriculture,* ed. J.A. Taylor. London: Pergamon Press, Symposium Publishing Division, 1967.

Jensen, M.E., and H.R. Haise. "Estimating Evapotranspiration from Solar Radiation." *Journal of the Irrigation Drainage Division,* American Society of Civil Engineers, vol. 89 (1963).

Kalkstein, L.S. "The Effect of Climate upon Outbreaks of the Southern Pine Beetle." *Publications in Climatology,* Laboratory of Climatology, vol. 27, no. 3 (1974).

Kazmann, R.G. *Modern Hydrology.* New York: Harper & Row, 1972.

Kent, K.M. "A Method for Estimating Volume and Rate of Runoff in Small Watersheds." *Soil Conservation Service-TP-149.* Washington, D.C.: U.S. Department of Agriculture, 1968.

King, E.W. "Rainfall and Epidemics of the Southern Pine Beetle." *Environmental Entomology* vol. 1 (1971).

Köppen, W. "Versuch einer Klassifikation der Klimate, Vorzugsweise nach ihren Beziehungen zur Pflanzenwelt." *Geographische Zeitschrift,* vol. 6 (1900).

Kittredge, J. "Some Characteristics of Forest Floors in California." *Journal of Forestry,* vol. 53 (1955).

Krimgold, D.B. "Estimating Soil Tractionability from Climatic Data." *Progress Report No. 2, Contract No. AF 19(604)-193.* Seabrook, N.J.: The Johns Hopkins University, Laboratory of Climatology, 1952.

225

Küchler, A.W. *Potential Natural Vegetation of Conterminous United States.* New York: American Geographical Society, 1964.

Landsberg, H.E. "The Climate of Towns," in *Man's Role in Changing the Face of the Earth,* ed. W.L. Thomas. Wenner-Gren Foundation and the National Science Foundation. Chicago: University of Chicago Press, 1956.

Landsberg, H.E. "Trends in Climatology." *Science,* vol. 128, no. 3327 (1958).

Landsberg, H.E. "The Definition and Determination of Climatic Changes, Fluctuations and Outlooks," in *Atmospheric Quality and Climatic Change,* ed. R.J. Kopec. Papers of the Second Carolina Geographical Symposium, Studies in Geography no. 9. Chapel Hill: University of North Carolina, 1976.

Leopold, L.B. "Hydrology for Urban Land Planning—A Guidebook on the Hydrologic Effects of Urban Land Use." *Geological Survey Circular 554.* Washington, D.C.: U.S. Department of the Interior, 1968.

Lettau, H. "Evapotranspiration Climatonomy I: A New Approach to Numerical Prediction of Monthly Evapotranspiration, Runoff, and Soil Moisture Storage." *Monthly Weather Review,* vol. 97, no. 10 (1969).

Lettau, H., and M.W. Baradas. "Evapotranspiration Climatonomy II: Refinement of Parameterization, Exemplified by Application to the Mabacan River Watershed." *Monthly Weather Review,* vol. 101, no. 8 (1973).

Lewin, J. "A Simple Soil Water Simulation Model for Assessing the Irrigation Requirements of Wheat." *Israel Journal of Agricultural Research,* vol. 22, no. 4 (1972).

Lieth, H. "Uber die Primarproduktion der Pflanzendecke der Erde." *Angewandte Botanik,* vol. 46 (1972).

Lieth, H. "Primary Productivity: Terrestrial Ecosystems." *Human Ecology,* vol. 1, no. 4 (1973).

Lieth, H. "Modeling the Primary Productivity of the World," in *Primary Productivity of the Biosphere,* ed. H. Lieth and R.H. Whittaker. New York: Springer-Verlag, 1975.

Lieth, H. and E. Box. "Evapotranspiration and Primary Productivity: C.W. Thornthwaite Memorial Model." *Publications in Climatology,* Laboratory of Climatology, vol. 25, no. 3 (1972).

Lull, H.W., and J.H. Axley. "Forest Soil-Moisture Relations in the Coastal Plain Sands of Southern New Jersey." *Forest Science,* vol. 4 (1958).

Lull, H.W. and K.G. Reinhart. "Forests and Floods in the Eastern United States." *Forest Service Research Paper NE-226.* Upper Darby, Pa.: U.S. Department of Agriculture, 1972.

Lull, H.W., and W.E. Sopper. "Hydrologic Effects from Urbanization of Forested Watersheds in the Northeast." *Forest Service Research Paper NE-146.* Upper Darby, Pa.: U.S. Department of Agriculture, 1969.

L'vovich, M.I. *Vednie Resoursi Budushevo* (Water Resources of the Future). Moscow: Prosveschenie, 1969.

L'vovich, M.I. "The Water Balance of the World's Continents and a Balance

Estimate of the World's Freshwater Resources." *Soviet Geography: Review and Translation*, vol. 14, no. 3 (1973). (Trans. from *Izvestiya Akademii Nauk SSSR, Seriya Geograficheskaya*, vol. 5.)

Lyon, T.L., and J.A. Bizzell. "Lysimeter Experiment-IV Records for Tanks 17 to 20 During the Years 1922 to 1933 and for Tanks 13 to 16 During the Years 1913 to 1928." *Agricultural Experiment Station Memoir 194*. Ithaca, N.Y.: Cornell University, 1936.

McCown, R.L. "An Evaluation of the Influence of Available Soil Water Storage Capacity on Growing Season Length and Yield of Tropical Pastures Using Simple Water Balance Models." *Agricultural Meteorology*, vol. 11 (1973).

Mack, A.R., and W.S. Ferguson. "A Moisture Stress Index for Wheat by Means of a Modulated Soil Moisture Budget." *Canadian Journal of Plant Science*, vol. 48 (1968).

Major, J. "A Climatic Index to Vascular Plant Activity." *Ecology*, vol. 44, no. 3 (1963).

Manogaran, C. "Economic Feasibility of Irrigating Southern Pines." *Water Resources Research*, vol. 9, no. 6 (1973).

Marbut, E. "Soils of the United States, Part III," in *Atlas of American Agriculture*. Washington, D.C.: U.S. Department of Agriculture, 1936.

Massachusetts Institute of Technology. *Inadvertent Climate Modification*. Report of the Study of Man's Impact on Climate (SMIC). Cambridge, Mass.: MIT Press, 1971.

Mather, J.R. "The Determination of Soil Moisture from Climatic Data." *Bulletin, American Meteorological Society*, vol. 35, no. 2 (1954).

Mather, J.R. "The Measurement of Potential Evapotranspiration." *Publications in Climatology*, Laboratory of Climatology, vol. 7, no. 1 (1954).

Mather, J.R., ed. "Average Climatic Water Balance Data of the Continents, Part I. Africa; Part II. Asia (excluding U.S.S.R.); Part III. U.S.S.R.; Part IV. Australia, New Zealand and Oceania; Part V. Europe; Part VI. North America (excluding United States); Part VII. United States; Part VIII. South America." *Publications in Climatology*, Laboratory of Climatology, vol. 15, no. 2; vol. 16, nos. 1, 2, 3; vol. 17, nos. 1, 2, 3; vol. 18, no. 2 (1962, 1963, 1964, 1965).

Mather, J.R. "Irrigation Agriculture in Humid Areas," in *Eclectic Climatology*, ed. A. Court. Yearbook, Association of Pacific Coast Geographers, vol. 30. Corvallis: Oregon State University Press, 1968,

Mather, J.R. "The Average Annual Water Balance of the World." *Proceeding of the Symposium on the Water Balance in North America*. American Water Resources Association, Proceedings, series 7 (1969).

Mather, J.R. "Factors of the Climatic Water Balance over the Delmarva Peninsula." *Publications in Climatology*, Laboratory of Climatology, vol. 22, no. 3 (1969).

Mather, J.R. *Climatology: Fundamentals and Applications*. New York: McGraw-Hill, 1974.

Mather, J.R. "Estimation of Areal Average Precipitation Using Different Network Densities and Averaging Techniques." *Publications in Climatology,* Laboratory of Climatology, vol. 28, no. 2 (1975).

Mather, J.R., and J.K. Nakamura. "The Climatic and Hydrologic Factors Affecting the Redistribution of Strontium in Soils." *Publications in Climatology,* Laboratory of Climatology, vol. 15, no. 1 (1962).

Mather, J.R., and G.A. Yoshioka. "The Role of Climate in the Distribution of Vegetation." *Annals Association American Geographers,* vol. 58, no. 1 (1968).

Mather, J.R., F.J. Swaye, Jr., and B.J. Hartmann. "The Influence of the Climatic Water Balance on Conditions in the Estuarine Environment." *Publications in Climatology,* Laboratory of Climatology, vol. 25, no. 1 (1972).

Maunder, W.J. "A Human Classification of Climate." *Weather,* vol. 17 (1962).

Meentemeyer, V. "Climatic Water Budget Approach to Forest Problems. I. The Prediction of Forest Fire Hazard Through Moisture Budgeting." *Publications in Climatology,* Laboratory of Climatology, vol. 27, no. 1 (1974).

Meentemeyer, V. "Climatic Water Budget Approach to Forest Problems. II. The Prediction of Regional Differences in Decomposition Rate of Organic Debris." *Publications in Climatology,* Laboratory of Climatology, vol. 27, no. 1 (1974).

Metz, L.J., and J.E. Douglass. "Soil Moisture Depletion under Several Piedmont Cover Types." *Forest Service Tech. Bulletin 1207.* Washington, D.C.: U.S. Department of Agriculture, 1959.

Mikola, Peitsa. "Comparative Experiments on Decomposition Rates of Forest Litter in Southern and Northern Finland." *Oikos,* vol. 11 (1960).

Muller, R.A. "The Effects of Reforestation on Water Yield: A Case Study Using Energy and Water Balance Models for the Allegheny Plateau, New York." *Publications in Climatology,* Laboratory of Climatology, vol. 10, no. 3 (1966).

Muller, R.A. "A Water Balance Evaluation of the Effects of Urbanization on Water Yield in Metropolitan Northeastern New Jersey." Appendix H, in *Benefits from Integrated Water Management in Urban Areas–the Case of the New York Metropolitan Region* by L. Zobler and G.W. Cary. Report to the Office of Water Resources Research. Washington, D.C.: U.S. Department of the Interior, 1969.

Muller, R.A. "Water Balance Evaluation of Effects of Subdivisions on Water Yield in Middlesex County, New Jersey." *Proceedings of the Association of American Geographers,* vol. 1 (1969).

Nix, H.A., and E.A. Fitzpatrick. "An Index of Crop Water Stress Related to Wheat and Grain Sorghum Yields." *Agricultural Meteorology,* vol. 6 (1969).

Penman, H.L. "Natural Evaporation from Open Water, Bare Soil and Grass." *Proceedings of the Royal Society,* Series A, vol. 193 (1948).

Penman, H.L. "Evaporation: An Introductory Survey." *Netherlands Journal of Agricultural Science,* vol. 4. no. 1 (1956).

Penman, H.L. *Vegetation and Hydrology.* Technical Communication no. 53. Commonwealth Bureau of Soils, Farnham Royal, Bucks, England: Commonwealth Agricultural Bureaux, 1963.

Pereira, H.C. *Land Use and Water Resources.* Cambridge, England: At the University Press, 1973.

Peterson, J.T. *The Climate of Cities: A Survey of Recent Literature.* Publication AP-59. Washington, D.C.: National Air Pollution Control Administration, 1969.

Pluhowski, E.J. "Urbanization and Its Effects on the Temperature of the Streams on Long Island, New York." *Geological Survey Professional Paper 627-D.* Washington, D.C.: Department of the Interior, 1970.

Reinhart, K.G., A.R. Eschner, and G.R. Trimble, Jr. "Effect on Streamflow of Four Forest Practices in the Mountains of West Virginia." *Forest Service Research Paper NE-1.* Upper Darby, Pa.: U.S. Department of Agriculture, 1963.

Rochester, E.W., and C.D. Busch. "An Irrigation Scheduling Model Which Incorporates Rainfall Predictions." *Water Resources Bulletin,* vol. 8, no. 3 (1972).

Rose, C.W., J.E. Begg, G.F. Byrne, B.W.R. Torssell, and J.H. Goncz. "A Simulation Model of Growth-Field Environment Relationships for Townsville Stylo (*Stylosanthes humilis* H.B.K.) Pasture." *Agricultural Meteorology,* vol. 10 (1972).

Rosenberg, N.J., H.E. Hart, and K.W. Brown. *Evapotranspiration: Review of Research.* Publication 20. Lincoln: University of Nebraska, College of Agriculture and Home Economics and Nebraska Water Resources Research Institute, 1968.

Rosenzweig, M.L. "Net Primary Productivity of Terrestrial Communities: Prediction from Climatological Data." *The American Naturalist,* vol. 102, no. 923 (1968).

Rouse, W.R. "Moisture Balance of Barbados and Its Influence on Sugar Cane Yield." Master of Science thesis, McGill University, Department of Geography, 1962.

Sanderson, M. "A Climatic Water Balance of the Lake Erie Basin." *Publications in Climatology,* Laboratory of Climatology, vol. 19, no. 1 (1966).

Satterlund, D.R. "Combined Weather and Vegetation Modification Promises Synergistic Streamflow Response." *Journal of Hydrology,* vol. 9 (1969).

Seddon, B. "Prehistoric Climate and Agriculture: Review of Recent Paleoecological Investigations," in *Weather and Agriculture,* ed. J.A. Taylor. Oxford: Pergamon Press, 1967.

Sellers, W.D. *Physical Climatology.* Chicago: University of Chicago Press, 1965.

Shantz, H.L., and R. Zon. "Natural Vegetation," in *Atlas of American Agriculture.* Washington, D.C.: U.S. Department of Agriculture, 1924.

Sheaffer, J.R. "Flood-to-Peak Interval," in *Papers on Flood Problems,* ed. G.F.

White, Research Paper No. 70, Department of Geography. Chicago: University of Chicago Press, 1961.

Shelton, M.L. "Simulating Uniform Streamflow by Water Budget Analysis." *Publications in Climatology*, Laboratory of Climatology, vol. 27, no. 2 (1974).

Smith, G.W. "The Relation Between Rainfall, Soil Water and Yield of Copra on a Coconut Estate in Trinidad." *Journal of Applied Ecology*, vol. 3 (1966).

Smith, L.P. "Meadow Hay Yields." *Outlook in Agriculture*, vol. 3, no. 5 (1956).

Southern Pine Beetle Action Council. "Action Plans to Control the Southern Pine Beetle." Atlanta, Ga.: Southern Pine Beetle Action Council, 1974.

Steila, D. *The Geography of Soils: Formation, Distribution, Management.* Englewood Cliffs, N.J.: Prentice-Hall, 1976.

Terjung, W.H. "Physiologic Climates of the Conterminous United States: A Bioclimatic Classification Based on Man." *Annals Association American Geographers*, vol. 56, no. 1 (1966).

Terjung, W.H. "Climatic Modification," in *Perspectives on Environment*, ed. J.R. Manners and M.W. Mikesell, Publication 13. Washington, D.C.: Commission on College Geography, Association of American Geographers, 1974.

Thornthwaite, C.W. "Report of the Committee on Transpiration and Evaporation, 1943-1944." *Transactions American Geophysical Union*, Part 5 (1945).

Thornthwaite, C.W. "Climate and Moisture Conservation." *Annals Association American Geographers*, vol. 37, no. 2 (1947).

Thornthwaite, C.W. "An Approach Toward a Rational Classification of Climate." *Geographical Review*, vol. 38 (1948).

Thornthwaite, C.W. "Estimating Soil Tractionability from Climatic Data." *Publications in Climatology*, Laboratory of Climatology, vol. 7, no. 3 (1954).

Thornthwaite, C.W., and J.R. Mather. "Climatology and Irrigation Scheduling." *Weekly Weather and Crop Bulletin*, National Summary of June 27, U.S. Weather Bureau (1955).

Thornthwaite, C.W., and J.R. Mather. "The Water Balance." *Publications in Climatology*, Laboratory of Climatology, vol. 8, no. 1 (1955).

Thornthwaite, C.W., and J.R. Mather. "Instructions and Tables for Computing Potential Evapotranspiration and the Water Balance." *Publications in Climatology*, Laboratory of Climatology, vol. 10, no. 3 (1957).

Toumey, J.A. "The Relations of Forests to Streamflow." *Yearbook of Agriculture.* Washington, D.C.: U.S. Department of Agriculture, 1903.

Turc, L. "Le Bilan d'Eau des Sols. Relations entre les Precipitations, l'Evaporation et l'Ecoulement." *Annales Agronomie*, vol. 5 (1955).

U.S. Army Corps of Engineers. *Snow Hydrology.* Portland, Oregon: North Pacific Division, U.S. Army Corps of Engineers, June 30, 1956.

U.S. Environmental Science Services Administration. *Climatic Atlas of the*

United States. Washington, D.C.: Environmental Data Service, U.S. Department of Commerce, 1968.

U.S. Geological Survey. *The National Atlas of the United States of America*. Washington, D.C.: U.S. Department of the Interior, 1970.

U.S. National Academy of Sciences-National Research Council. *Weather and Climate: Modification Problems and Prospects*. Publication 1350. Washington, D.C.: National Academy of Sciences/National Research Council, 1966.

U.S. Soil Conservation Service. *National Engineering Handbook. Supplement A, Hydrology, Section 4*. Washington, D.C.: U.S. Department of Agriculture, 1957.

U.S. Soil Conservation Service. *National Engineering Handbook. Hydrology, Section 4*. Washington, D.C.: U.S. Department of Agriculture, 1972.

Van der Drift, J. "The Disappearance of Litter in Mull and Mor in Connection with Weather Conditions and the Activity of the Macrofauna," in *Soil Organisms*, ed. J. Doeksen, and J. Van der Drift. Amsterdam: North Holland Publishing Company, 1963.

Van der Drift, J. "The Effects of Animal Activity in the Litter Layer," in *Experimental Pedology*, ed. E.G. Hallsworth and D.V. Crawford. London: Butterworths, 1965.

Van Hylckama, T.E.A. "The Water Balance of the Earth." *Publications in Climatology*, Laboratory of Climatology, vol. 9, no. 2 (1956).

Veihmeyer, F.J., and A.H. Hendrickson. "Does Transpiration Decrease as the Soil Moisture Decreases?" *Transactions American Geophysical Union,* vol. 36, no. 3 (1955).

Vite, J.P. "The Influence of Water Supply on Oleoresin Exudation Pressure and Resistance to Bark Beetle Attack in *Pinus Ponderosa*." Contribution Boyce Thompson Institute, vol. 21, 1961.

Waggoner, P.E., P.M. Miller, and H.C. DeRoo. "Plastic Mulching: Principles and Benefits." *Bulletin 634*. New Haven, Conn.: The Connecticut Agricultural Experiment Station, 1960.

Walter, H. "Die Klimagramme als Mittel zur Deurteilung der Klimäverhaltnisse für Ökologische, Vegetationskundliche und Landwirtschafltiche zwecke." *Bericht Deutschen Botanischen Gesellschaft Jahrgang*, vol. 68, no. 8 (1955).

Warner, J., and S. Twomey. "The Production of Cloud Nuclei by Cane Fires and Their Effect on Cloud Droplet Concentration." *Journal of Atmospheric Science*, vol. 25 (1967).

Yao, A.Y.M. "Evaluating Climatic Limitations for a Specific Agricultural Enterprise." *Agricultural Meteorology*, vol. 12 (1973).

Zahner, Robert. "Refinement in Empirical Functions for Realistic Soil-Moisture Régimes under Forest Cover," in *Forest Hydrology*, ed. W.E. Sopper, and H.W. Lull. Proceedings National Science Foundation Advanced Science Seminar, Pennsylvania State University, August 29-September 10, 1965. Oxford: Pergamon Press, 1967.

Index

Index

About the Author

John R. Mather is professor of geography, chair of the Department of Geography, and director of the Center for Climatic Research at the University of Delaware. His teaching and research interests focus on the moisture factors in climate, on applied climatology, and especially on the water budget. From 1948 to 1972, he was associated with the C.W. Thornthwaite Laboratory of Climatology, Centerton, New Jersey, the last ten years as its president. He is the author of a book on applied climatology as well as over eighty articles and reports on different applied aspects of climatology. He is the editor of the *Publications in Climatology* series of the Laboratory of Climatology and State Climatologist for Delaware. Dr. Mather received the Ph.D. degree in geography-climatology from the Johns Hopkins University, the M.S. and B.S. degrees in meteorology from the Massachusetts Institute of Technology, and the B.A. degree from Williams College.